Winemaking in California

Both authors are San Francisco residents and trace their interest in their subject to the mid-sixties, when both started working for the Regional Oral History Office of the Bancroft Library at the University of California, Berkeley, conducting and editing oral history interviews on California winemaking since the beginning of this century.

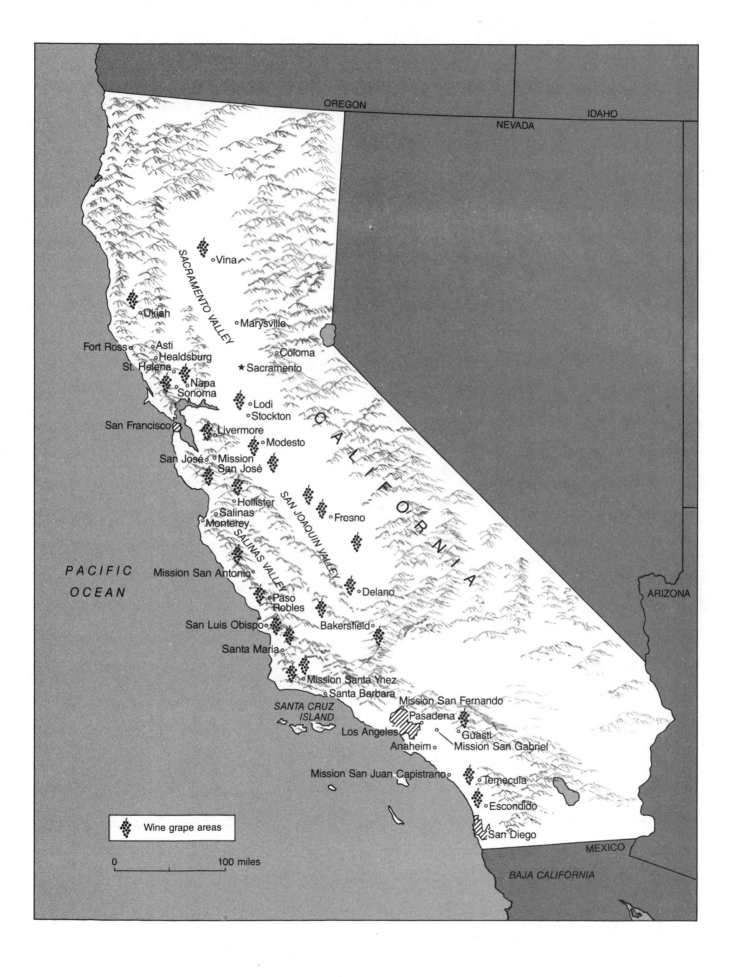

OREGON

IDAHO

NEVADA

*Vina

SACRAMENTO VALLEY

*Ukiah

*Marysville

Fort Ross
*Asti
*Healdsburg
*Coloma
St. Helena
★ Sacramento
*Napa
Sonoma
*Lodi
*Stockton
San Francisco
Livermore

CALIFORNIA

*Modesto
San José *Mission
San José

*Hollister
*Salinas
Monterey

SAN JOAQUIN VALLEY

*Fresno

PACIFIC
OCEAN

SALINAS VALLEY

Mission San Antonio

*Paso
Robles

*Delano

San Luis Obispo

*Bakersfield

ARIZONA

Santa Maria

Mission Santa Ynez
*Santa Barbara

Mission San Fernando
*Pasadena

SANTA CRUZ
ISLAND

Los Angeles
*Guasti
Anaheim
Mission San Gabriel

Mission San Juan Capistrano
*Temecula

*Escondido

Wine grape areas

*San Diego

MEXICO

0   100 miles

BAJA CALIFORNIA

Ruth Teiser
Catherine Harroun

*The account in words and pictures of the Golden
State's two-century-long adventure with wine*

WINEMAKING in California

McGRAW-HILL BOOK COMPANY
NEW YORK   ST. LOUIS   SAN FRANCISCO
TORONTO   HAMBURG   MEXICO

We acknowledge with thanks the following:

*From Warren R. Howell, permission to reprint
passages concerning Jean Louis Vignes from* Seventy-Five
Years in California *by William Heath Davis, John Howell-Books,
1967.*

*From Louis P. Martini and the American Chemical
Society, permission to reprint a passage from a paper by
Mr. Martini that appears in* Wine Production Technology in
the United States, *Maynard A. Amerine, Editor,* ACS
SYMPOSIUM SERIES *No. 145, p. 83. Copyright 1981 American
Chemical Society.*

*From James D. Hart, Director of the Bancroft
Library, permission to quote from manuscript papers in the
Eugene W. Hilgard collection; and from Professor Hart and
Willa Baum, Head of the Regional Oral History Office of the
Bancroft Library, permission to quote passages from oral
history interviews in the California Wine Industry series.*

R. T.
C. H.

1 2 3 4 5 6 7 8 9 BKPBKP 8 7 6 5 4 3 2

ISBN 0-07-063401-7

Library of Congress Cataloging in Publication Data

*Teiser, Ruth.
Winemaking in California.*

1. Wine and wine making—California.   I. Harroun, Catherine.   II. Title.
TP557.T44   641.2'22'09794   82–144
ISBN 0-07-063401-7   AACR2

Book design by Roberta Rezk.

to William F. Luttgens, M.D.

Contents

Foreword

Winemaking in California is the fascinating, long-needed, first comprehensive history of wine in this nation's principal winegrowing state. It augments earlier California wine histories with many important, previously unpublished facts. It traces the dramatic story from its eighteenth-century beginnings at the Franciscan missions through generations of successes and failures to the current nationwide table-wine revolution, which has begun at last to civilize drinking in America. Its hundreds of historic photographs, which document the written narrative, would even by themselves make this book an indispensable part of every serious wine student's collection of *viniana*.

Three years ago, when Ruth Teiser and Catherine Harroun, both experienced historical researchers, had completed some two dozen tape-recorded interviews with California wine industry leaders for the Bancroft Library Regional Oral History project, they mentioned to me the idea of their undertaking this major new project. I encouraged them to do it, and I offered to help. They since have devoted the years to intensive, meticulous research in many libraries, identifying and evaluating the documentary evidence for each historic development of winegrowing in the state. They have revisited scores of historic vineyards, conducted still more interviews, and have identified much of the physical evidence that remains from the state's vinicultural past.

This is the book I had long hoped to write myself someday. I am glad that these authors have utilized some of the historical material and photographs that I began collecting at the Wine Institute in the 1930s to help other writers disseminate the cultural lore of grapes and wine.

Their book is necessarily interpretive and selective, weighing the relative significance of each historic development and the contributions of individuals and institutions to the progress of the wine industry. I cannot agree with all of their interpretations because I was a participant in many events, working with such vinicultural industry leaders as Sophus Federspiel, Herman L. Wente, Lawrence K. Marshall, and Walter Sink, who did not live to be interviewed in the Oral History project. This may be why this new history omits mention of the contributions to progress by the Grape Growers League of California, which these men and I formed in 1931, and which led to the incorporation of the Wine Institute in 1934 and to the formation of the Wine Advisory Board in 1938.

Winemaking in California is nonetheless a major contribution to the understanding of wine's tremendous progress in California, including the technological advances that began in this state after the Second World War and which since have spread to winegrowing countries around the world. Moreover, this book is pleasurable popular reading, for while the authors identify their sources, they omit the customary clutter of annotated footnotes from their text. They capture the dramatic quality of the story, the setbacks, such as the death of the vines at Anaheim from Pierce's Disease, and the phylloxera epidemic that destroyed many northern vineyards between 1870 and 1900; such successes as the early triumphs of California wines in international competitions, soon followed by the tragedy of national Prohibition. The authors bring to life scores of colorful historic characters, describing their origins and human foibles.

They amplify the principal earlier sources of the state's wine history by Herbert B. Leggett and by Professors Irving McKee and Vincent Carosso, but *Winemaking in California* brings the entire story up to the present. Their book is a veritable treasure trove of historical gems. One that is new to me is that Los Angeles a century ago was popularly known as "the city of vineyards," which it literally was. Another is evidence these authors have found that the early California Indians made and imbibed an intoxicating drink from fermented wild cherries and wild tobacco. This contradicts the long-held opinion that no northern Native Americans have ever produced any fermented alcoholic beverage, while there is ample evidence that the Aztecs of Mexico made wine from the juice of cactus and that the Incas of Peru regularly fermented beer from grain.

Although this new book adds greatly to the understanding of wine history in California, the field remains rich for further exploration. My hope is that Misses Teiser and Harroun will continue their research and that they will undertake an even more urgently needed project: an equally well-researched history of wine in North America from colonial times to the present.

LEON D. ADAMS,
author of
The Wines of America

Winemaking in California

1. Wine of New California

EUROPEAN wine grapes take to California as if it were their native land. Which is fortunate, since the grapes that are actually natives, *Vitis californica* and *Vitis girdiana*, make miserable wine. The Indians who were the state's first inhabitants ate the grapes, but for their fermented beverage they used wild cherries, which they mixed with wild tobacco, powdered shells, and water. *Pispibata* they called it, and, according to one incredulous missionary, they insisted that it gave them comfort. But it could hardly have been in a class with Bordeaux, or even the crude California wine made from the first imported European grapes.

These were the Mission variety of *Vitis vinifera,* brought north from Baja California by the Franciscan fathers who also brought other aspects of European civilization to this land of heathen *pispibata* drinkers. Wine was important to the padres, requisite for the mass, customary for the table, and they immediately noticed the wild grapes.

"There are many fine wild vines, in some places heavily laden," wrote Father Junipero Serra on July 3, 1769, only two days after arriving in California. He was describing for his superior in Mexico the area where a few days later he would, as father-president, establish Mission San Diego de Alcalá, the first and southernmost of California's chain of twenty-one religious communities.

From time to time thereafter, the padres tried to make palatable wine from the fruit of these temptingly prolific vines, but always they found the effort unrewarding and turned their attention back to their variety of *vinifera.* Although it is far from the best variety of the European species, the Mission grape was to thrive and dominate California winemaking until the late nineteenth century.

The date this grape first set down its roots in California soil is a matter of fervid interest in some small circles. That the year was 1769 is backed by longstanding tradition, based principally upon a statement by General Mariano Guadalupe Vallejo, the famous Hispanic Californian, a gentleman with a profound interest in the history of his native land. In 1874, when he was sixty-six years old and of sound mind (as he remained to his dying day), he stated unequivocally that early California pioneers—including his own father, who had worked with Junipero Serra—had been told by Father Serra that he had brought grape vines with him when he first came to

1

Alta California in July of 1769. It is unlikely, however (although not impossible), that vine cuttings could have survived the Serra party's hot, dry overland trek from Baja California.

On the other hand, a meticulous twentieth-century scholar, Dr. Jacob N. Bowman, who after one career as a college professor created a second one combing through the state's early archives, came up with a "probable" date that is twelve years later than Vallejo's. He based his conclusions upon *not* finding earlier references to grape plantings than a letter of December 8, 1781, written by that same hard-working Father Serra. From Mission San Carlos in northern California, Serra wrote to a colleague at San Diego, "I hope that . . . the corn prospers and that the grape vines are living and thriving, for this lack of altar wine is becoming unbearable." (His Spanish word translated as "grape vines" is *sarmientos,* meaning "cuttings" or "recently rooted vines.") Dr. Bowman believed that the letter implied that no vines had ever been planted previously and that those referred to had been planted earlier that same year.

For all his searching, Professor Bowman failed to find, however, another pertinent letter that set the date back two years. It was dug out later by a similarly impassioned researcher, Edith Buckland Webb, who devoted years of her life to assembling a vast quantity of material for an authoritative book on Indian life in California in mission times. Father Pablo José de Mugártegui wrote this letter to Father Serra from Mission San Juan Capistrano on March 15, 1779. "Snow is plentiful," he reported, "wherefore, until the severe cold moderates and the floods subside, the vine cuttings [*sarmientos*] which at your request were sent from the lower country have been buried." They would have been actually planted, Mrs. Webb surmised, later that same spring. She also concluded that those cuttings, shared with Mission San Diego, were the ones Father Serra pinned his hopes on in December 1781.

Still later Roy Brady, a writer and editor long acquainted with wine in all its aspects, set the date back another year, to 1778. He re-examined Mrs. Webb's evidence, added to it some further historical research and practical knowledge of viticulture, and concluded that the first grape cuttings in California must have been brought from "the lower country," Baja California, on the packetboat *San Antonio* on May 16, 1778, and planted almost immediately. He accepted the translation of Father Mugártegui's word *sarmientos* as "young vines" rather than "cuttings," and assumed that his word for "buried," *plantaron,* can also mean "planted."

For those who wish to straddle the point, however, there is another recorded fact: Crops were planted at Mission San Diego de Alcalá in the summer of 1769 but were washed away by the next spring's rains. Father Serra could have brought cuttings with him, as General Vallejo asserted, only to lose them along with the flax and beans. Still, they would have represented the first planting of *Vitis vinifera* in California. There may have been others as well, either unrecorded or recorded but not yet discovered. The search for this historian's prize at the rainbow's end need never cease.

As for the first wine made in California, Roy Brady places this at San Juan Capistrano in 1782. He bases this conclusion upon Father Serra's December 1781 letter complaining about the lack of altar wine, and another of October 1783 complaining that a barrel of wine being sent from San Juan Capistrano had fallen off a mule and broken. That barrel, he believes, contained the previous year's vintage, October being too early for that of 1783.

It is quite certain that, in any case, Father Serra lived to see his efforts rewarded by vintages at two missions, San Juan Capistrano and San Diego, and the planting of vineyards at others. By 1795 seeds brought directly from Spain had been planted at Mission Santa Clara. Had the vines prospered, the history of winemaking in California might have taken a quite different course. They flourished only briefly, however. By 1800 the fathers at Mission Santa Clara were making wine from the usual Mission vines. So were those at missions San Buenaventura, Santa Barbara, San Luis Obispo, and San Gabriel. The last was to become the largest viticultural establishment of them all.

Progress continued, but it was hard going. In 1801 Father Fermín de Lasuén could report that six missions were making wine, but he added rather wistfully, "In most missions, despite our endeavors, we have no success, since we missionaries, being all Europeans, do not know the climate or similar conditions." Nor were these men practical winemakers, although most would have been as familiar with the process as they were with, say, the baking of bread, so that they were able to oversee it.

By 1823, when the last of California's twenty-one Franciscan missions had been established, vineyards had been tried at all of them, and successfully at all but four. One of the four was Mission Dolores at San Francisco, which had to make its wine from grapes sent northward from missions San José and Santa Clara. As California's most flamboyant winemaker, Agoston Haraszthy, was to discover again many years later, grapes will not mature by the cool, foggy shores of San Francisco Bay.

Mission winemaking was done in the traditional Spanish way, but with different dramatis personae. Converted Indians formed the work force. "Neophytes" they were called, and neophytes they were in agriculture as well as religion. The padres taught them to cultivate the vineyards and prune the vines, which were unsupported by stakes or trellises in the Spanish way.

The vintage itself must have been a remarkable spectacle. Indian men, women, and sometimes children as well harvested the grapes and piled them on the crushing platform. This was usually a shallow inclined wooden stage, sometimes simply an area of sloping ground, covered with clean hides. Then, according to one startled observer, well-bathed male Indians wearing *zapetas*—thin loincloths—trampled the grapes. They had mopping cloths wrapped over their hands so they could keep sweat from dripping, and other cloths over their heads to keep their hair from dropping, and they carried poles to keep themselves from falling into the slippery mass.

The juice produced by their bizarre dance drained into pottery jars or leather bottles that were emptied at intervals into wooden tubs. Some of the grape skins were added (the rest were pressed and that juice distilled), and the mixture left to ferment in the vats for two or three months.

This method was, of course, California's most primitive. As time went on, equipment was built or imported, and more sophisticated methods were learned. Today at missions San Gabriel and San Fernando you can see brick vats into which grapes were dumped and trodden. They are well designed for the purpose, and nicely provided with footwashing basins.

Treading was the way all the world's grapes were crushed in that era. Although presses for extracting the remainder of the juice from the trodden grapes were devised early, mechanical crushers were not developed until the mid-nineteenth century, and even then they came into use slowly.

Containers for fermenting, aging, and carrying wine never ceased to be a mission problem. Barrels gradually became common, but there were never enough of them.

"If you have any empty barrels, send them" reads a 1797 plea to the mission suppliers in Baja California. And into the 1820s, letters accompanying mission-to-mission shipments and mission gifts to secular authorities carry urgent requests that the empty casks be returned.

And there were other problems. Crops failed. Wine spoiled, giving the padres more vinegar than they wanted. Vineyards could be protected against some predators by adobe walls or prickly pear hedges, but not against hungry birds. These were combated in a variety of ways, from baiting with nux vomica to setting out snares and even stationing drumbeating Indians on platforms above the ripening grapes. None were of any more avail than equally varied twentieth-century attempts.

Problems notwithstanding, mission winemaking continued, increasing in quantity, improving in quality, and setting its stamp unmistakably upon California viticulture in all the years to come. It reached its peak between 1823, when the last mission was founded, and 1833, when Mexico, having shaken off Spanish rule, ordered the disestablishment of the California Franciscans' religious communities.

By that decade the fathers had stopped listing wine and brandy among their annual requests for supplies to be shipped from the south. Their system was producing enough for its own use, with some left over to sell or barter to the military men of the presidios, the civilians of the pueblos, and the growing number of rancheros. They had even exported a little wine. As early as 1819, the governor of the then-Spanish province of California, who had been the recipient of several barrels of mission wine (and had dutifully returned the casks when they were empty), sent a request to Mission San Diego that must have delighted its winemakers:

His Excellency, Viceroy Count de Venadito, desires to have a dozen bottles of wine from your mission in order to send them to the king, our august monarch, Don Fernando VII. Let each bottle be labeled thus: Wine of New California from Mission San Diego.

Junipero Serra was the father of California winemaking, instigator of its earliest vineyards. Arriving at San Diego in 1769 to establish missions to convert the Indians, he was awaited by the first of the missionary supply ships that were to bring food, clothing, and wine until the establishments should become self-sufficient. During his fifteen years as father-president of the mission chain, the Mallorca-born Franciscan bore his own suffering with saintly patience, but was impatient about New California's lack of wine. He constantly urged that grapes be planted so that there might be a reliable supply of altar wine. In 1783 he complained to his superior in Mexico that he had had to buy at government warehouses, and pay the same price, moreover, as the soldiers from the presidio did. The next year, however, only a few months before his death, he was able to write that "God has provided a way out" of the shortage, and "we are well looked after."

By the 1830s, when the entire mission chain was flourishing, the Franciscans' vineyards were growing more than three hundred thousand vines, most planted from shoots taken from descendants of the original cuttings brought from Baja California through the efforts of Father Serra.

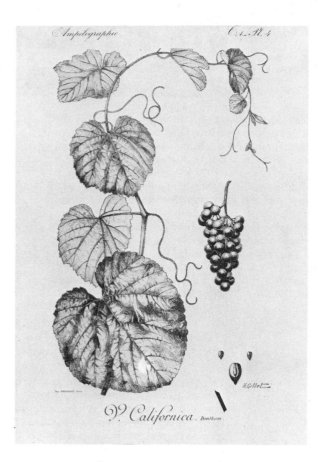

The native grapes of California are *Vitis californica* and *Vitis Girdiana*. The two varieties are similar. *Vitis californica* grows north of the Tehachapi range, *Vitis Girdiana* to the south. This botanical drawing of *V. californica* is from the great early twentieth-century French ampelography of Pierre Viala and Victor Vermorel.

Early European visitors to California were impressed by the bountiful wild grape vines growing along the coast and in the central valley, seeing in them a promise of the state's great agricultural potential. They grew with special abundance around John Augustus Sutter's farm in the Sacramento Valley, and he had characteristically high hopes of making a fortune by fermenting and distilling their juice. The attempt was not notably successful, nor were the attempts of others to make either wine or brandy from the fruit of the native vines. Equally unproductive were later University of California experiments using the vines as pest-resistant rootstock upon which to graft European wine varieties.

The grapes still grow in wooded places and along stream beds, and occasionally they are gathered to be eaten out of hand or made into jelly.

The Mission grape was brought to Alta California, the Spanish colony that became the state, from Baja California. It was first grown there by the Jesuits, then, after their expulsion, by the Franciscans who were put in charge of the Jesuit establishments. The wine made there was said to be excellent; this wine, shipped to San Diego aboard the packet boat *San Antonio* in the spring of 1769, was probably the first consumed on California soil. Just when the name Mission was first applied to this grape is unknown, as is its place of origin. Professor Harold P. Olmo, famed University of California geneticist and plant hunter, has chased it halfway around the world and found similar but not identical grapes. He believes it to have come from southern Europe, and that perhaps it and the *Criolla negra* of Venezuela have a common ancestor; but the ancestor itself remains to be found. Wherever it came from, this variety of *Vitis vinifera* grew and still grows vigorously in California. It was a single Mission vine near Santa Barbara that in one year, 1893, was said to have borne eight tons of grapes.

Mission San Gabriel Arcángel was the leading wine producer of California's mission days. Its four outlying vineyards yielded some nine thousand gallons of wine and three thousand more of brandy annually during its most productive years. Its first vineyard was known as the *viña madre,* probably because cuttings from it were distributed to other missions. This well-preserved structure at Mission San Gabriel is said to be the oldest winery building in California today. On its floor can still be seen the handmade bricks where Indians once trod out the grapes.

This wine press, built on the island of Mallorca in 1770, was the kind in common use in Father Serra's native land when he lived there as a young man. It was used for many years by the ancestors of Mallorcan winemaker José L. Ferrer, who in honor of Father Serra presented it to the Serra Museum at San Diego in 1971. The first wine presses in California were simple improvisations for extracting the remaining juice from the mass of skins, stems, and pulp after the Indians had crushed the grapes. These presses were probably simply two boards hinged together at one end; the mass was squeezed between them. They were supplanted in time by screw presses like this one. In 1810, Father Mariano Payeras at Mission La Purísima wrote to his superior that the wine was being "made here after the Mallorcan method in new winepresses. Hence, if God grants us life, some day Your Reverence will drink it without filminess, without sediments, and without bad taste, pure and clear."

Mission San Juan Capistrano may have been the earliest wine producer in California. "The location of the mission is very pleasant, with a good view," wrote Father Francisco Palou in 1785. "The climate is good, hot in summer and cold in winter, and so far it has proved healthy. . . . Having noticed from the beginning of the mission that the ground was thickly covered with wild vines, of which some appeared to be grape vines, they [the fathers] tried planting cuttings from cultivated grape vines they had brought from Antigua California, and have been able to make wine not alone for the mass, but also for pleasure"—*el gusto.* It is the first wine of Capistrano that Roy Brady believes should have carried a label bearing, in today's style, the winery name followed by the grape variety and vintage date, and the names of its producers:

Mission San Juan Capistrano
Mission 1782
Estate grown and bottled by
Fr. Pablo de Mugártegui and
Fr. Gregorio Amurrio

At the restored winery of Mission San Fernando Rey de España are casks, an animal skin of the kind used by the early missions for storing and carrying wine, and a handsome brass still for making brandy, *aguardiente*.

Father Narciso Durán, a kindly, versatile man, made Mission San José a center of liturgical music and also of viticulture. Its large vineyard yielded, under his guidance, notable wines, and he made brandy described by Hubert Howe Bancroft as "doubly distilled, and as strong as the reverend father's faith." He also wrote the earliest known analysis of California wines.

"I have received your request asking me about the manner of making red wine, brandy, etc.," he wrote in 1833 to the governor of Mexican California. "I have to remark in reply that I can say little or nothing about muscatel, because there is none of it at Mission San José; nor do I know it. The wine at San Luis Rey in my opinion is not the best, nor the best suited to place before a friend. I think there are only two kinds: the red wine and the white wine. The latter, which is used for altar purposes, is rather unpleasant, because it has no sweetness whatever, but is very dry. The best wines I have found in the various missions are those of San Gabriel. There are two kinds of red wine: one is dry, but very good for the table; the other is sweet, resembling the juice pressed from blackberries, and so rather unpleasant. There are also two kinds of white wine. One of them is from pure grapes without fermenting. I mean from pure grape juice without fermenting it with the skins of the pressed grapes. This produces the white wine. The other of the same juice is fermented with a quantity of grape brandy. [This is the wine that came to be known as angelica.] These two make a most delicious drink for the dessert. The wine from the pure grape juice is for the altar, the other for any use whatever. The two would shine at the table of the president of the [Mexican] Republic for smoothness, delicacy and simplicity of composition, but as they make only a small quantity of these, I can offer only a little to you."

2. Pueblos and Ranchos

THE missions were secularized in the mid-1830s. According to the plan the Kingdom of Spain formulated at the time they were established, they were to continue only until California's Indian population was converted. Mexico shook itself and its northern province of Alta California free of Spain in 1822, but the policy was not altered. However, in 1834, although in fact the missions had not completed their task, Governor José Figueroa issued the secularization decree. It was implemented over the next several years. Most of the missions fell into decay. But they left behind them a tradition of religion, culture, and agriculture. Of special importance to winemaking was the fair number of vineyard and winery workers they had trained.

Meanwhile, pueblos and ranchos had been established. The pueblos were agricultural communities created to supply the presidios, or military posts; several acres of land went to each settler. The ranchos were grants of one, two, four, or even more leagues, given to the province's military men for the most part, land where they could settle their families, raise cattle, and, together with the pueblo dwellers, create in New California a permanent society.

Long before the missions were disestablished, grape-growing and wine-making spread to the pueblos and ranchos. Governor Pedro Fages planted vines in his garden at Monterey as early as 1783, to pass away the time until his young wife should come from Mexico City, and to please her when she arrived. He failed to please her with that or anything else in this crude provincial capital, and it took the combined efforts of numerous friars to keep her from demanding a divorce. But he succeeded in becoming the first on record to grow grapes beyond mission lands. When Comte Jean François Galaup de la Pérouse visited Monterey in 1786 on his *voyage autour du monde,* he found Fages' four-acre *huerta* of fruit trees, vegetables, and grape vines flourishing.

The governor sent his visitors a variety of welcome provisions including milk but no wine, so far as accounts show. The Comte's ships had reached Monterey with a good supply of wine remaining, and although Fages by then might well have made wine from his young vines, he might also have thought twice before inviting comparison with French vintages.

Fages departed regretfully in 1791, probably as a result of a letter from his wife to authorities in Mexico City urging that he be recalled. He left behind in a final report a nostalgic description of his *huerta.* Shortly after, it supplied fresh produce to grateful members of another expedition, that of Spanish explorer Alejandro Malaspina. They did drink the wine of the country; it could have come from a mission, or it could have been Pedro Fages' Monterey wine.

Three years later, in 1794, another governor, Diego Borica, granted the Ortega family six leagues of grazing land along the coast west of Santa Barbara, ordering at the same time that grapes and crops be planted. Alta California's economy was based upon cattle hides and tallow, but colonization was important to Spain, and colonists needed food and wine.

The request for the grant of what came to be named Rancho Nuestra Señora del Refugio was made in behalf of Captain José Francisco Ortega, who had been a scout with the Portolá expedition and thus perhaps the first European to lay eyes on San Francisco Bay. He had now fallen onto hard times. His son, José María Ortega, who asked for the land, also asked the governor to relieve him of military duty to help the old gentleman recover his financial equilibrium. The governor, somewhat against his better judgment, made the grant, and José María and his brothers obediently saw to the planting of fields of corn, wheat, and beans, an orchard, and a vineyard of considerable size. These were clustered around the family homes and outbuildings at the mouth of Refugio Canyon. The Ortegas also built a wharf.

In 1829 Yankee trader Alfred Robinson, scouring California ranchos for hides to ship back to Boston, visited Refugio. He found vineyards and some other crops but few signs of vigor. He was told that "it was once a large place and, under the supervision of its proprietor, Don José María Ortega, appeared like a little mission; but that in the year 1819 it was visited by a piratical vessel, under the command of Bouchard, who nearly destroyed it, since when it has never regained its once flourishing condition."

His report was not entirely accurate. In fact the family continued to occupy the land for many years in reasonable comfort. Hypolite de Bouchard had not one but two vessels, and

the date of his arrival was 1818. But the story is an interesting one.

By 1818 Rancho del Refugio had acquired an odd reputation. Both wine and brandy had been made there since before 1800, entirely legal pursuits providing the required taxes were paid, which they may or may not have been. Then, the Ortegas' wharf came to be known as a smugglers' landing place, where both goods and foreigners might come ashore without official scrutiny. Also, several of the Ortega brothers were growing grapes on shares for nearby Mission La Purísima, another entirely legal pursuit, but they were rumored to be "confidential agents" for the friars, who could make irregular arrangements with missions. They were also thought to be directly involved in smuggling and to have treasure stored on the ranch. Bouchard must have heard the rumors.

News of the pirate ships arrived in California long before the vessels themselves did. Orders were given for the men of the coastal settlements and ranchos to be ready to move their women, children, and livestock inland, and to prepare to defend the province. The forewarning was not entirely effective. Late in November Bouchard and his pirate crews sacked Monterey. Early in December they anchored off the wharf at Refugio. In less than twenty-four hours they plundered and burned the by then deserted ranch buildings and sailed on. They left behind, however, a young man who was to have a small but secure place in the history of viticulture in California. He was Joseph Chapman, a carpenter and blacksmith, assertedly pressed into piratical service in the Sandwich Islands.

At Monterey he was captured but treated well and soon released. At Refugio he jumped ship, having, according to family tradition, seen enough of California and Californians to become enamored of both. He made his way up Refugio Canyon toward Mission Santa Inés, where he found asylum. Perhaps this blond young New Englander, passing by the vineyards of Rancho Refugio, may have had a glimmer of his future place in the annals of his adopted land as its first American viticulturist.

Almost immediately upon arriving at Mission Santa Inés, he had proved himself a valuable workman. Moving on to Mission San Gabriel, he used his blacksmithing skills in the winery and distillery and became familiar with the winemaking process.

He owes the distinction of being the first independent American viticulturist to the fact that, New England-born, he did not become a naturalized Mexican citizen until 1831, some years after he had planted a vineyard. According to his own account, Governor José María de Echeandía granted him a piece of land in the pueblo of Los Angeles, along the river, in 1826; on it he planted four thousand vines and a fruit orchard. His statement, given under oath in 1829 when he applied (successfully) for a larger grant near Santa Barbara, was preserved in the official archives of the province. Historian Hubert Howe Bancroft drew upon this document for his *History of California,* but somehow the date of the Los Angeles grant came out as 1824, and that is the one later historians used. In any case, although Chapman's vineyard was planted two years later than has been believed, he remains the first American to grow grape vines in California— so far as still other historians have been able to ascertain. Since the provincial government discouraged foreign settlers, he had not much competition.

The California rancheros of Hispanic origin were by tradition much less energetic. "It is a proverb here," wrote pioneer John Bidwell in 1841, "and I find it a pretty true one, that a Spaniard will not do anything he cannot do on horseback." What he could do, of course, was tend cattle, and since stock-raising formed the real economic base of California in those years, it was just as well.

Nevertheless, many of the ranches did, like Refugio, grow some crops, worked by the Indians trained at the missions. A surprising number had small vineyards and produced wine and brandy for local consumption. Some turned out to be the beginning of enterprises of later significance, while others, like many missions, simply left old vines that encouraged subsequent settlers to plant new ones.

On Rancho Cucamonga, for instance, east of Los Angeles, Tiburcio Tapia planted a vineyard before 1840 that became the nucleus of one of the state's largest. On Rancho El Pinole, along the Carquinez Straits northeast of San Francisco, Ignacio Martínez retired from a long military career to become a ranchero and cultivate vines. He gave his name to a town established later on the edge of the rancho, and planted a vineyard in an area where others in time would set out vines.

On Rancho de las Pulgas, on the peninsula south of San Francisco, José Darío Argüello, *comandante* of the San Francisco presidio, had about two hundred vines planted but was unable to command them to prosper. Like those tried earlier by the padres at the mission in San Francisco, and those tried later by Agoston Haraszthy near Crystal Springs, they were fog-ridden. So probably were those planted earlier by the Russians at Fort Ross on the north coast; they existed, but not for long. Like those grown from imported seeds at San Jose, they too might have changed the course of winemaking in California. They had been brought from Lima, and might well have been a variety quite different from the Mission. But after the Russians left Fort Ross in 1839, the vines gradually disappeared.

Not far south of Fort Ross, but inland, was Rancho Cabeza de Santa Rosa, near what is now the city of Santa Rosa, and here the strong-minded Doña María Ignacia López de Carrillo had a vineyard. She was the widowed mother-in-law of General Mariano G. Vallejo. After her husband's death, she and nine of her twelve children went to Sonoma, where Vallejo lived, and shortly thereafter her son-in-law, who was in charge of making land grants in the area, saw to it that she and her brood could move on to a two-league rancho in the Santa Rosa Valley. She was as good a rider as any man and willing to do any kind of work on or off a horse—and "a handsome woman, queenly in her walk" as well, according to a contemporary. She ran the rancho with a strong hand. She was the first woman viticulturist in what would become an important winegrowing area.

There were other rancho vineyards. The industrious Dr. Jacob N. Bowman found seventy, but he gave out after scanning only 475 of the 853 land-grant cases for grapes. He found that Rancho San Francisco, in what were later Los Angeles and Ventura counties, had a vineyard, but he neglected to mention that Rancho Camulos was originally part of it, perhaps not recalling that there the great historical romance of California, *Ramona,* is centered. On Rancho Camulos the del Valle family early planted a vineyard, and their wine continued famous long after the Americans came. So did its grape arbor.

Helen Hunt Jackson's novel tells a sad story. Tender Ramona, the beautiful adopted daughter of the proud Spanish Señora Moreno, falls in love with the noble Indian Alessandro and, against her foster-mother's wishes, marries him. She remains faithful to him as they are driven first from the rancho, then from pillar to post by the advancing land-hungry Americans, who finally kill her husband. After a respectful pause, however, she and the heir to Rancho Camulos marry and flee from Yankee-ridden Alta California to Mexico. The Rancho Camulos grape arbor figures in the motion pictures, paintings, drawings, and "literary" photographs based upon the Ramona story, which became a California legend.

A real-life heroine was Doña Marcelina Dominguez, who a few years one side or the other of 1800 planted the great Montecito grape vine that produced as much as sixteen thousand pounds of grapes in one year. Her place as California's most famous woman vine grower is secure. A romantic legend attaches to the vine's origin, but there are numerous factual accounts of the vine itself that attest to its abundance and great size: Its trunk measured four feet, four inches in circumference, and its arbor covered more than five thousand square feet. It might still be there had not someone decided that it should be exhibited at the 1876 St. Louis Exposition celebrating the nation's centennial. It was dug up, cut up, crated, and sent off, leaving in the area only a minor echo, a smaller large vine at nearby Carpinteria. Historians have a hard time not mixing up pictures of the two vines, however, for the Carpinteria vine is now gone too. The way to tell them apart is this: The Carpinteria vine had a thick, helically twisted trunk, while the wonderful vine of Doña Marcelina grew almost straight up.

Such bountiful growth was anticipated by many of the early nineteenth-century voyagers to California. Russians, Frenchmen, and Englishmen came to look at the country, most of them covetously, then returned to their homelands to write about it. They reported enthusiastically the great prospects for agricultural production. They were less than unanimous, however, in their appraisals of California's wines. While Count Nikolai Petrovich Rezánov was writing confidential reports from San Francisco to his emperor about California's value as a breadbasket for Russia, his engineer companion, George Heinrich von Langsdorff, was drinking the wine of Mission Santa Clara and judging it to be of only "ordinary quality," although finding at the nearby pueblo of San José a several-year-old vintage that he considered "excellent wine, sweet and resembling Malaga."

It was at San José, some years later, that Rezánov's compatriot, Otto von Kotzebue, observed "hedges of vines bearing luxuriant clusters of the richest grapes," characteristic of the land that he found "extremely fruitful."

Adelbert von Chamisso, naturalist aboard the Russian ship *Rurik,* summed up the Russian view in a lament that "this fine and fruitful country" should "lie entirely useless" because foreign vessels were not allowed to trade the manufactured goods its inhabitants so sorely needed for the agricultural goods they could produce. The *Californios,* however, proved characteristically generous: They gave the departing *Rurik* fruit, vegetables, and a cask of wine.

Great Britain had, like Russia, been watching California from outposts to the north, hoping for a chance to add the Spanish province to its empire. The British visitors themselves were inclined to be condescending, but Captain John Hall, visiting in 1822, reported good wine at San Diego and Mission San Juan Capistrano, the red at the latter being "of a peculiarly fine flavor." He was a merchant seaman, however. Officers of the Royal Navy were more critical. Naval Captain Frederick William Beechey found wine from several missions "resembling claret though not near so palatable" in 1826, and some years after that another naval officer, Sir Edward Belcher, reported huffily the poor quality of both California's inhabitants and its wines.

Sir George Simpson of the Hudson's Bay Company was equally disdainful of California's bad tea, worse wine, and indolent people. He wrote: "What a splendid country, whether we regard its internal resources or its commercial capabilities, to be thrown away on its present possessors." As his ship departed, however, again a cask of wine was put aboard as a parting gift. It came from the mission at Santa Barbara. "Most of the stuff we had tasted we should have carried away without compunction," he later recalled, "thinking that we were doing the owners a service; but we were sorry to deprive the very reverend donor, in the present state of his cellar, of a really good article."

The most often quoted British pronouncement on Alta California wine comes from Alexander Forbes' book, *A History of Upper and Lower California.* "Wine is now made of tolerably good quality, and some even very excellent. Nothing is wanting but intelligent persons to make wine of superior quality." The flaw here is that he had not visited upper California when he wrote it. He had, however, carefully studied the map, and he noted:

> The latitude of the Bay of San Francisco corresponds almost exactly with that of Lisbon, and is consequently not very much northward of Bordeaux; other parts of the country correspond in latitude with Madeira, and, in the opposite hemisphere, with the Cape of Good Hope; so that this country embraces the analogues, at least, of the most celebrated wine countries in the world, and consequently offers a wide and most promising field for the cultivation of the grape in all its varieties.

French visitors came to similar conclusions. They too thought that California could, if it would, make enough wine of reasonably good quality to supply its own needs and create a healthy export market. Auguste Duhaut-Cilly, commanding the merchant ship *Le Héros,* arrived in 1827 and gave an early description of Los Angeles and its viticultural prospects. As he stood on a hill above the community, he later recorded,

> I counted eighty-two houses comprising the pueblo, from which I inferred it might have one thousand inhabitants, including in this number two hundred Indians, servants or laborers. The environs of the village and the low lands dividing the two channels which form the river, appeared to me cultivated with some care. The principal produce consists of maize and grapes. The vine succeeds very well, but wine and brandy extracted from it are very inferior to the exquisite taste of the grape used for it, and I think this inferiority is to be attributed to the making rather than to the growth.

Nevertheless, he carried back to France with him some wine made at San Luis Rey and reported that it tasted, after seven years, like Paxaret, a dark, sweet Spanish wine.

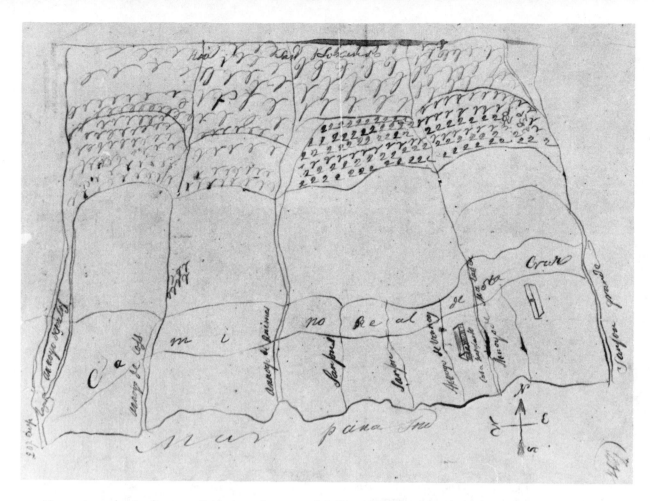

No surveyors having been available to make maps of California land grants, simple drawings like this, called *diseños,* were filed with authorities. Here Rancho del Refugio is shown lying along the coast (the sea is at the bottom) with its narrow canyons running inland across El Camino Real, the crude road that connected the California missions, to the mountains beyond. The houses and ranch buildings of the Ortega family are shown toward the right, with a sort of road running among them to the wharf where Joseph Chapman landed and made his way to freedom at Mission Santa Inés.

Joseph Chapman was baptized José Juan Chapman in 1822 at Mission Santa Inés and married to Guadalupe Ortega. Tradition has it that she was a member of the same Ortega family that owned Rancho Nuestra Señora del Refugio, where he jumped ship, and that they had met at the mission to which both had fled from the pirate Bouchard. The young couple moved to the pueblo of Los Angeles; four years later he was granted land there and planted the vines that established him as the first American viticulturist in Alta California. He was by reputation then and later, when he became a respected member of the Santa Barbara community, a valuable citizen of his adopted land, contributing his skills as a craftsman and even on occasion as a surgeon. A Yankee to the end, he was a hard worker to boot.

This formal portrait, a daguerreotype, is believed to be of José and Guadalupe Chapman at Santa Barbara.

Sir George Simpson inspected California for the Hudson's Bay Company in 1842 and found "nature doing everything and man nothing." He disliked the wine of General Vallejo and most other Californians, approving only of that made at Mission Santa Barbara.

"A wide straight walk shaded by a trellis so knotted and twisted with grape vines that little was to be seen of its trellis woodwork" was the way Helen Hunt Jackson described the grape arbor at Ramona's home. Either her imagination clothed it with more vines than those at Rancho Camulos, which she visited in 1883 with the intention of using it as the setting for her novel, or time had thinned them by the time this photograph was made in the early 1890s.

UNDER DOÑA MARCELINA'S CELEBRATED GRAPE-VINE, AT THE MONTECITO, SANTA BARBARA.

The legend of Doña Marcelina's grape vine relates to its origin. Both the vine and Doña Marcelina were real and accounted for. The story was, however, that around the turn of the nineteenth century, a beautiful young Spanish girl named Marcelina Félix lived near Los Angeles with her poor but proud parents. They wished her to marry a wealthy don, but she fell in love with a tall, handsome young man who was ingenious, though he had no wealth or social pretensions. When her parents decided to take her away to thwart this romance and find her a suitable husband, her beloved, Carlos de Dominguez, arranged a final tryst. There he presented her with a slender riding whip that was in reality a shoot of a Mission grape vine. He told her to plant it in her new home and to remain true to him for two years. The family rode off and settled in Montecito, near Santa Barbara. Just before the time was up, Marcelina's parents told her she was to marry a rich ugly old don. Sadly, on her wedding eve, she stole away to hide under the leaves of the vine she had dutifully planted. (It would have been a precocious vine to have afforded shelter so soon, but in view of its later history, precocious it may have been.) As she sat weeping, who should appear but Carlos. He had brought with him a fortune equal to that of the rich old ugly don, and the next day she married him instead. The vine continued to grow and grow and grow, and after Carlos' death it provided enough grapes for the widow to sell to support their fourteen children. It became one of the wonders of southern California, and there was great local resentment when it was taken away to the St. Louis exposition without leaving as much as a riding-crop-size slip behind.

The Carpinteria vine came to be known as the Largest Grape Vine in the World after Doña Marcelina's was taken away. This was one of the many pictures sold to marveling tourists to show how big it indeed was.

3. Los Angeles, the City of Vineyards

Well before the end of the eighteenth century there were vineyards in the pueblo of Los Angeles, the village that would later be known as the City of Vineyards. Dr. Leonce Hoover, a Swiss physician turned winemaker, said in 1858 that he had some vines eighty years old, but that seems improbable. Others—Matthew Keller, the Sansevain brothers, Manuel Requena—dated their oldest vines to the 1790s, although they did not know who had planted them.

The first identifiable Los Angeles vine grower is Antonio María Lugo, a quintessential Spanish Californian, born at Mission San Antonio de Padua, a soldier in Spain's Alta California army until the age of thirty-four, when he settled in the pueblo. That was 1809, and, shortly after, he planted the vineyard that came to cover eight acres behind his house a few blocks from the Plaza—in what is now downtown Los Angeles but was then open fields. He made wine from grapes grown there, as well as from a vineyard he planted a few years later on his Rancho San Antonio, which adjoined the pueblo lands, and from other ranches he came to own. He continued active well into the 1850s, an increasingly venerable figure, still proud as age advanced. A contemporary described him in his eighties "as he rode into town on horse back, erect, with his sword strapped to his saddle beneath his left leg."

By 1818 Don Antonio had been joined by enough other vineyardists to bring the pueblo's total number of vines up to more than fifty-three thousand, which, as they were planted in those days, covered about fifty-three acres. That number would double in the next thirteen years, and then continue to grow as winemaking at the missions declined.

These early grape growers were, of course, Hispanic, but there arrived surprisingly quickly men from the United States, England, France, Ireland, and even Holland, as local officials gradually relaxed the ban against foreigners. In the end, almost all the Spanish and Mexican California vineyardists would be driven from the field by the newcomers.

These immigrants were a motley crew. There was, of course, the industrious Joseph Chapman, who planted his vineyard in the mid-1820s; it must have grown well, for the years 1827 and 1828 saw unusually good grape harvests in the pueblo and an upsurge of interest in vineyard planting. Perhaps that was why Johann Groningen, a Dutch ship's carpenter shipwrecked at nearby San Pedro, felt the pueblo looked promising, as Duhaut-Cilly had described it, and decided to settle down and plant vines. He changed his name to Juan Domingo but was generally known as Juan Cojo, "Lame Juan," perhaps because of an injury sustained during the shipwreck. Before the end of the decade William Logan, an American carpenter, had planted another vineyard, and a French cooper, Louis Bouchet, had bought an existing one. It was situated on what later became Bauchet Street—his son made the slight change in the name. Bauchet is one of several streets in the old part of Los Angeles that perpetuate the names of early grape growers.

A foretaste of changes to come was the increase in the number of Americans. William L. Hill, a New Yorker, joined Bouchet. Another New Yorker, William Chard, and a New Mexican, Lemuel Carpenter, who became butcher and soapmaker respectively, together planted a vineyard on Alameda Street near the river, the pueblo's choicest vine-growing area. And a Kentucky native, Nathaniel M. Pryor, arrived to divide his time between clockmaking, otter hunting, and vineyard tending. There were others, amd more to come, but they all played only minor parts in the pueblo's viticultural drama. Its heroes were Don Luis Vignes and William Wolfskill. Two men more unalike would be hard to find.

Vignes, born Jean Louis Vignes in the Bordeaux region of France, was California's first full-time professional winemaker. He brought to the unformed Mexican province an image—a reflection of the great wine estates of Europe that was in turn reflected down through the years in vineyard estates in his adopted land. It was an image that included making as good wine as one could, by rational and systematic methods, and sharing with others both its making and its drinking—without, however, neglecting the necessary commercial aspects of a sound business enterprise. He soon had California's major winery, but he continued generous to all, the spirit of uprightness, open-handedness, and hospitality, the better-than-prototype *vigneron*.

Vignes did not leave France until he was forty-seven years old, and he did not reach Los Angeles until five or six years later. At Cadillac, near the city of Bordeaux, he had worked as a cooper and distiller, was married and had a family.

Why he left is a mystery. All we know about the matter is contained in a letter Father Alexis Bachelot sent to his order's headquarters, the Congregation of the Sacred Hearts of Jesus and Mary, in Paris. He wrote that Vignes "had been forced into exile as a result of troubles caused by his loyalty, his misplaced tenderness and his over-zealous desire to be of service." The priest and the cooper-distiller had left France together in 1826 on parallel missionary and agricultural ventures in the Sandwich Islands. There, before both undertakings were abrogated, Vignes grew sugar cane and grape vines and later distilled rum from sugar cane.

Writing as they left the Sandwich Islands, Father Bachelot explained, "Vignes has been our mission's constant friend and has performed numerous services which we alone can appreciate. His family in Cadillac is very religious. They will learn with pleasure that his decent behavior, so rare here, has made him generally liked and respected."

Although decent behavior was perhaps less rare in Los Angeles, Vignes became much liked and respected there too. He took up residence in the pueblo in 1831 or 1832, apparently practicing his crafts of cooper and distiller and buying a 104-acre tract that became his vineyard and orchard. It extended from what is now Los Angeles Street to the river; if you drive east above downtown Los Angeles on the Santa Ana Freeway, you pass along the northern edge of its site.

Much of what we know about Vignes comes from his younger acquaintance, William Heath Davis. Davis was a third-generation Yankee Pacific trader, born in Honolulu but deeply devoted to California, where he spent the greater part of his long life. As a boy of nine he came to California on the same ship that brought Jean Louis Vignes. Davis wrote in his *Seventy-five Years in California:*

> Don Luis, as the Californians called him, was a Frenchman, who came to Monterey in the bark *Louisa* with me in 1831. . . . From Monterey he went to San Pedro, shortly afterward established himself at Los Angeles, and before long had the largest vineyard in California. At that early day he imported cuttings of different varieties of grapes, in small quantities, which were put up with great

care and sent from France to Boston; thence they came out in the vessels trading on this coast, to be experimented with in wine producing.

These were the first grape vines brought to California directly from Europe—the first *viniferas* other than Missions to be grown here—so far as is known. Their arrival was an extremely important step in the progress of viticulture in this state. We do not know what varieties they were or what the results were of Vignes' experiments. There are no clues in the names of Vignes' wines, for they were called, like most other California wines of the time, simply red, white, port, and angelica. We do not know, for that matter, just how he made his wines, although contemporaries indicated his methods were more rational and professional than the usual California procedures. The probability is that as a cooper and especially as a distiller in Bordeaux, he had learned the prevailing winemaking methods and followed them, adapting them as necessary to California's grapes and growing conditions.

One can be quite certain that he performed systematically all the tasks of a conscientious winemaker, tending his vines well, conducting a careful harvest, watching over the crushing and pressing and fermenting, sending to his distillery such material as would lessen the quality of the wine, keeping his casks and barrels clean, racking the wine off the lees with care and frequency, and faithfully checking and topping the casks of aging wine in his cellars.

William Heath Davis continued his account of Vignes: "He took great pride in the business. I regard him as the pioneer not only in winemaking but in the orange cultivation, he being the first man to raise oranges in Los Angeles and the first to establish a vineyard of any pretension."

Two years after Davis and Vignes arrived in California, Davis visited the older man in Los Angeles for the first time:

In 1833, I called to see him at his house and found him well established. My old friend was overjoyed to see me and received me most hospitably; I remained two or three days with him. I was a boy at the time, and he said to me most warmly: "William, I only regret that I am not of your age. With my knowledge of vine and orange cultivation and of the soil and climate of California, I foresee that

these two are to have a great future; this is just the place to grow them to perfection". . . . He was then about fifty years old [actually he was fifty-four], full of zeal and enterprise. He was one of the most valuable men who ever came to California, and the father of the wine industry here.

When in 1839 a nephew, Pierre Sansevain, joined Vignes in Los Angeles, he found a large vineyard, many oak casks made by Vignes from trees he himself had felled, and "a very good cellar" full of wines being aged.

The aging of wines was another of Vignes' important contributions to California viticulture. The practice was common in France but not in California, largely because in California wines were made carelessly and placed in unclean vessels, so that they spoiled before age caught up with them.

By the time Davis visited Vignes again, the winemaker could demonstrate the result of his practices. Wrote Davis:

In 1842, nine years afterward, I again called to see him. He asked me if I remembered what he had said to me when I was last there, about the California wine, its importance and value, and remarked that he would now prove to me that his predictions were correct, and would show me what he could do for California. He then took me and a friend who was with me into his cellar and showed us the different vintages stored there, and brought out several bottles of his old wine, which were tested and commended. He said he had written home to France representing the advantages of California for winemaking, telling them that he believed the day would come when California would rival "la belle France" in wine producing of all varieties, not only in quantity but in quality, not even excepting champagne; and that he had also induced several of his relations and a number of his more intelligent countrymen to come to California to settle near Los Angeles and engage in the business.

Davis, who had by then become an experienced commercial trader, also reported on Vignes' brandy, which, while perhaps not as strong as Father Durán's famous mission *aguardiente*, was undoubtedly a more consistent and mellow beverage.

"He also manufactured *aguardiente* in considerable quantities," wrote Davis,

as did other wine producers. This liquor was considered . . . as a superior article when three or four years old. Beyond that, it still further improved in quality, being of a finer flavor, entirely pure, and was regarded as a wholesome drink. It was made from the old mission grapes. When first produced it was clear and colorless, like gin or alcohol, but gradually assumed a slight tint with age, and when six, eight, or ten years old, became of fine amber color, and was then a rich, oily liquor, very palatable.

The merchants bought the *aguardiente,* and also the wines, in considerable lots, directly from the vineyards, and sold it to their customers at Monterey, Yerba Buena [later renamed San Francisco], and other points along the coast. At that time I was familiar with wines of different kinds, and was regarded as an expert in determining their quality and value, and I considered the *aguardiente* as vastly superior to the [other] brandy made in those days.

Two years earlier, in another forward step for California, Vignes himself had sent the first sizable shipment of local wine and brandy up the coast, aboard a ship with an improbable name, the *Mooson.* At Santa Barbara, Monterey, and Yerba Buena they had fetched four dollars a gallon for the brandy and two dollars a gallon for the white wine, according to Pierre Sansevain, who had gone along to handle the sale. He did not mention red wine; if it was sent, it probably commanded the same sum as the white.

According to Davis, Vignes'

choice old wine could be drunk with impunity. It had an agreeable, exhilarating and strengthening effect, but no unpleasant after-consequences. He was known by everybody in the vicinity of Los Angeles, and appreciated. He was generous to the poor; in their distress he helped them in bread, money and wine. When they came to him he advised the mothers of young children to give them a little wine as an internal antiseptic, so that they might grow up strong, as in his own country.

He was also generous to friends and visitors. Davis told an amusing story about a cask of wine Vignes presented to Mrs. John Paty, who accompanied her husband on his merchant ship when it sailed along the coast of California. She was one of the first American women to visit this rapidly Americanizing province of Mexico, and she charmed everyone.

In 1842, Mrs. Paty was presented by Don Luis Vignes with a cask of California wine, while the captain's bark was at San Pedro, and she had it

put on board for the benefit of sea travel until such time as the vessel should reach Honolulu, when the intention was to have it bottled. Captain Paty and his officers were accustomed to a little wine at dinner, and, after tasting the Vignes wine, they found it so agreeable that they could not resist drinking of it while on the voyage. The good lady, who was aboard, never suspected it was her wine that was disappearing day by day, she herself being a participant in the abstraction. . . . The vessel reaching Honolulu, Mrs. Paty inquired for the cask and was much chagrined to find that the contents had wholly disappeared.

In that same year the commander of the United States Pacific Squadron, Commodore Thomas ap Catesby Jones, under the misapprehension that his country and Mexico were at war, seized Monterey, then gave it back and proceeded to Los Angeles to explain and apologize to Governor Manuel Micheltorena. There he and his officers were widely entertained. The hospitable Don Luis Vignes invited them to drink his wines and visit his El Alisal cellars, and he presented them with "several barrels of his choice wine, which were gratefully accepted," as Davis noted. Then, in the tradition of sending California wine to heads of state, "He remarked that he desired them to preserve some of it to take to Washington to give to the president of the United States, that he might know what excellent wine was produced in California." Nothing further was ever heard of the matter; the president's cask undoubtedly met the same fate as Mrs. Paty's.

Don Luis reached the age of seventy-two in 1851 and decided it was time to retire. He advertised his property for sale. It had two "orange gardens," and a vineyard with forty thousand vines, thirty-two thousand of them bearing grapes that yielded a thousand barrels of wine each year—about fifteen thousand gallons if his barrels were the same size as those of his contemporary, General Mariano G. Vallejo. It was not until 1855, however, that he sold his estate. The buyer was another nephew, Jean Louis Sansevain, who paid forty-two thousand dollars for it. The nephew who had long worked with Don Luis, Pierre Sansevain, joined Jean Louis, and the business continued for nearly a decade to be operated as Sansevain Brothers. They marketed their own wines widely, and others' as well, becoming the state's leading wine merchants. In 1857 they established the state's first commercial manufactory of sparkling wine. Then, rather unaccountably, not long after the death of Don Luis in 1862, the Sansevains dissolved their firm. The brothers went on to other viticultural enterprises, and El Alisal was subdivided, destined to become an indistinguishable part of metropolitan Los Angeles.

Los Angeles' other leading wine man was William Wolfskill. He was an American frontiersman, an unlikely sort to settle down in a dusty little Mexican California village and raise fruit. Born in 1798 in Kentucky on the edge of the mid-American wilderness, he learned reading, writing, and hunting there and in Missouri as his family was buffeted about by skirmishes of the War of 1812. At the age of twenty-three he set out on his own, heading west for Santa Fe with a trailblazing trading expedition. With New Mexico as his headquarters, he hunted, trapped, and traded over a large part of the Southwest. In 1830 he was baptised José Guillermo Wolfskill and granted Mexican citizenship, and he headed for California with a small party, intending to trap beaver in the San Joaquin and Sacramento valleys.

Reaching southern Alta California early in 1831, the group crossed the mountains and stopped, tired and hungry, at Rancho San Antonio. There Don Antonio María Lugo made them comfortable for a day or so, then at Wolfskill's request directed them to Mission San Gabriel so they might visit Father José Sanchez. Why they had chosen Father Sanchez to see is not known, but they rested at the mission for some days, and their visits to Lugo's ranch and the mission undoubtedly gave Wolfskill and his companion, George Yount, their first acquaintance with California vineyards.

Nevertheless, they pursued the fur trade for a time. The season being too far advanced for beaver hunting, they decided to seek sea otter, and at Mission San Gabriel saw to the building of a boat by another *yanqui* Californian, José Chapman. That venture failed. Yount headed north, where he would later make a name as a pioneer Napa Valley winegrower. Wolfskill settled down in the pueblo of Los Angeles to work as a carpenter for enough wages to buy a small vineyard.

Thus in 1836, at the age of thirty-eight, Wolfskill began the career in agriculture that would make him a wealthy and successful man. Industrious and active, he expanded his first vineyard, then in 1838 sold it and bought a larger tract on the pueblo's outskirts, a hundred acres adjacent to Don Luis Vignes' by then well-established vineyard. When that same year Wolfskill's younger brother John rode into town, hot and dusty, to look for him, he was told Don Guillermo was in the mountains cutting trees for barrel staves.

Wolfskill's holdings were nearly as large as those of his French neighbor; he planted what came to be the second largest vineyard in the state, and later the largest. He planted carefully, not, as was noted, in the haphazard rows customarily set out by mission-trained Indians. He built a sizable winery and distillery. Throughout the 1840s he planted, tended, and improved his vineyard and also, having admired his neighbor's orange trees, set out some himself, then more and more until he became the state's most notable citrus grower.

Wolfskill's vineyard and his grapes were much admired. After California became an American state and its citizens organized their interest in agriculture, Wolfskill twice, in 1856 and 1859, was awarded first prize by state fair judges for having the best vineyard in the state. In between, he and his fellow vintner Manuel Requena sent wine to the president of the United States, shepherded across the country to the White House by Henry D. Barrows. It was a large gift, including one case of Wolfskill's "fine old California port," a case of red wine, a case of white wine, some brandy, and some angelica. The Los Angeles *Star* described the angelica, an unique California wine, as "a most palatable and agreeable drink, but woe to him who drinks too deeply." Perhaps Barrows, a conscientious New England schoolmaster, warned President Buchanan as he made the presentation. It was thought to be the first California wine known to have arrived at the White House, but Barrows did not leave Los Angeles until September 1857. Recently a document has come to light proving that the Sansevain Brothers got there earlier. The Wine Museum of San Francisco turned up a letter from James Buchanan to the Sansevains dated "Washington City 14 Jan: 1857" and beginning, "Many thanks for the case of sparkling California wine." He pronounced it the most agreeable American wine he had drunk and predicted that California would soon become "a great wine producing country." Whether or not the wine that Barrows brought him confirmed his view is not known, but perhaps in time a letter from President Buchanan to William Wolfskill will be discovered.

Barrows was soon to become Wolfskill's son-in-law, but he had for several years been part of his household, tutor to his children. It was a large household made up of Wolfskill's two children by his first wife, (who ran off with a fugitive silversmith), his second wife (a niece of Don Antonio María Lugo), and their six children, not to mention innumerable Wolfskill relatives who kept coming west and staying for a while before moving on. The house itself was a commodious, finely furnished adobe, but Wolfskill never opened it to all as did his neighbor Don Luis Vignes.

The ex-trapper got on well with his fellow townsmen, both foreign and Hispanic, cooperated with them in business and civic matters, and was respected for being, as a contemporary put it, "a man of uncommonly sound and correct judgment and temperate habits." But he was apparently rather formal and not outgoing. Few visitors wrote of his hospitality. American Edwin Bryant was welcomed in 1847 and wrote of how clean and comfortable Wolfskill's house was compared to others he had seen in California, how beautiful the gardens, and how the glass of wine he was given "compared favorably with the best French and Madeira wines." But several years later a reporter visiting the area's vineyards was given a chilly reception.

"We were courteously received," he wrote, "but being neither invited to walk over his place or taste his wines, can only say that it [sic] *looked* well at a distance." Another man on a similar tour in 1860 reported simply, "Mr. Wolfskill has the largest orchard and vineyard in the city of Los Angeles. . . . He is a very plain old man, who enjoys life by taking it industriously. He may be seen at work every pleasant day, in a dress clean, but almost as coarse in material as that of any of his laborers."

That year Wolfskill was making no wine. He had become increasingly interested in his vines and his orchards and in making experimental plantings of fruits new to Southern California. He had first switched his commercial emphasis in the early 1850s when, like many other Los Angeles vineyardists, he started shipping grapes north to booming San Francisco, where fresh fruit was more eagerly sought than wine. In time the northern growers came to supply that demand, but by then two southern California firms were not only making their own wine but buying grapes from their neighbors' vineyards, usually making wine from them on the sellers' premises, and merchandising it all statewide. Sansevain Brothers was taking the harvests of numerous vineyards, including those of former Mexican governor Pio Pico and Tennessean Benjamin D. Wilson, while Wolfskill's grapes were among those being made into wine by the enterprising San Francisco-born firm of Kohler, Frohling & Bauck.

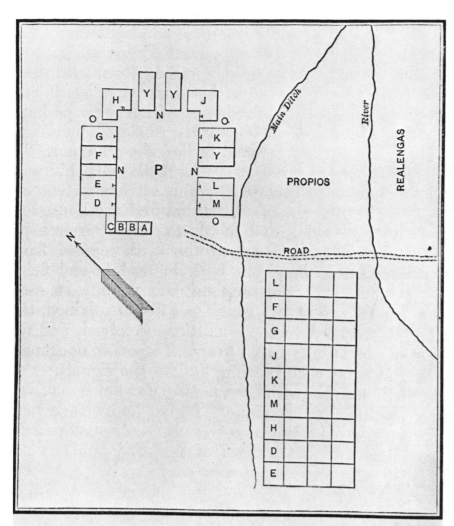

LOS ANGELES IN 1786.

Father Juan Crespi who, like his companion and superior, Father Serra, kept an eye out for grapes as he explored Alta California, noted upon first seeing the site of Los Angeles that "a large vineyard of wild grapes" grew along the river, and that the area appeared capable of growing grain and fruit. A dozen years later, in 1781, a pueblo was established. Home sites surrounding a plaza (labeled *P* on this map) and agricultural lands (lower right on the map, drawn here on a scale one-fifth the size of the home sites) were given to all. The fields lay between what Duhaut-Cilly called "the two channels" of the river, actually the main channel and to its northwest a manmade irrigation ditch. The river was at first called the Porciúncula after the name given the pueblo, Nuestra Señora de la Reina de Los Angeles de Porciúncula. Both names were in time simplified to Los Angeles. Father Crespi's prediction proved accurate. This was the cradle of California viticulture, its center for its first three decades.

Don Antonio María Lugo, one of the earliest pueblo winemakers, was born a Spanish Californian, put up fairly patiently with Mexican rule, but never fully accepted the American government under which he lived the last dozen years of his long life. When his son-in-law Stephen Foster told him he was going as a delegate to a convention at Monterey to formulate a constitution for the new state, Don Antonio replied bitterly, "So the Mexicans have sold California to the Americans for fifteen million dollars, and thrown us natives into the bargain!" When he suggested that Foster stay with his sister, Doña María Antonia, at Monterey, and Foster asked him for a letter to her, the aging *caballero* replied, "A letter? I can't write and she can't read, for we had no schools in California when we were young."

The Dutch ship carpenter who arrived at the pueblo in 1829 took the name Juan Domingo and became a respected citizen and family man. He married a Señorita Reymunda Félix, raised a large family, tended a sizable vineyard, and became a prosperous wine and brandy maker whose establishment was deemed important enough to include among the border illustrations of a famous 1857 lithograph of Los Angeles.

Don Luis Vignes' winery was in the 1840s and '50s the state's major wine and brandy producer. It included a cooperage, a distillery, and, in the words of a contemporary observer, "wine cellars filled with long rows of tierces." (A tierce is a forty-two-gallon cask, a third of a pipe.) The vineyard, and by extension the winery itself, was called El Alisal, after a huge old tree that was a pueblo landmark. *Alisal* means "alder," and the tree was a sycamore, but no one seemed inclined to correct the error. The entrance to the vineyard, which was marked by a great stone gateway (beyond the left edge of this picture), let into a splendid grape arbor that was ten feet wide and ran nearly a quarter of a mile to the river bank. Visitors viewed the arbor with wonder, and local citizens used it for pueblo celebrations.

The lithograph above was made in 1857, shortly after Don Luis had sold the estate to his two Sansevain nephews, the year they began making champagne. Wrote a visitor to El Alisal in Vignes' time, "The place is a perfect Paradise, little, if any, inferior to the Garden of Eden."

24

The year after the Sansevain Brothers bought El Alisal, they determined to try what their uncle, Don Luis Vignes, had long before predicted possible, the making of champagne in California. Pierre Sansevain returned to France to learn about the process and brought back with him a champagne maker. They produced 50,000 bottles in 1857, 150,000 the next year, and established a warehouse in San Francisco, the state's metropolis and the strongest market for such luxuries. This advertisement, from a San Francisco newspaper, reproduces their label carrying one version of the California grizzly, which was to be a favorite subject on wine labels until the end of the century. Although their Sparkling California was widely praised, the venture failed. The Sansevains lost what was a very large sum of money for that time, fifty thousand dollars. It was eight thousand dollars more than they had paid for El Alisal.

SAINSEVAIN'S FIRST PREMIUM WINES.

SAINSEVAIN BROS.

SPARKLING CALIFORNIA

TWO GOLD MEDALS AT STATE FAIR, MARYSVILLE: Two Silver Goblets at Mechanics' Fair, San Francisco.

SPARKLING CALIFORNIA CHAMPAGNE.—We have reduced the price of our Sparkling California at $12 per case, from one to five cases. A liberal discount to the trade.

Superior CALIFORNIA WHITE WINE,   Superior CALIFORNIA ANGELICA,
Superior CALIFORNIA RED WINE,   Superior CALIFORNIA PORT WINE,
SUPERIOR CALIFORNIA BRANDY.

For sale to the trade in lots to suit, by

SAINSEVAIN BROTHERS,

17   No. 188 Montgomery street, basement Pioche & Bayerque's Building.

William Wolfskill's agricultural estate, with its orchards and vines, was almost intact when this drawing was made in the late 1870s, still carefully maintained by his heirs. At its height, its four cellars held cooperage for a hundred thousand gallons of wine. Some years before the time of this picture, the family had given the Southern Pacific a strip of land on which the main railroad line into the city was built, and the side line was put into the estate. By 1900, however, all this was gone, cleared to make way for the new Los Angeles Union passenger terminal and city buildings.

4. The Northern Valleys

NORTHERN California's major winemaking tradition had its source in a small fertile valley north of San Francisco where the last of the missions in the California chain was established. A combination of circumstances unrelated to grapes and wine gave the initial impetus: the need for a new mission in the area, the threat of Russian territorial ambition, and the administrative efficiency of Mariano Vallejo. Yet all these would have meant nothing had not the Sonoma Valley been an excellent place for growing wine grapes.

Seeking a mission site, Father José Altimira found here a combination of good climate, abundance of wood and stone, streams and, most important, springs. Wild grapes abounded as well. In 1823 he established Mission San Francisco Solano in what is now the town of Sonoma, started the construction of a church and living quarters, and planted the usual mission crops. By the end of 1824 well over a thousand young grape vines were thriving. Only nine years later came the order to disestablish the missions. One year after, in 1834, when the young Lieutenant Mariano Guadalupe Vallejo was sent to San Francisco Solano to take over as commissioner of secularization, he found that the establishment had been allowed to fall into near ruin. He cleaned up a few deserted rooms for his family to live in, and set about making an inventory of what was left of the mission's belongings. Of its winemaking paraphernalia all that remained were these: 148 barrel hoops, 2 barrel cocks, 4 vaqueros' leather wine bags, 31 barrels and smaller casks, some 184 barrel staves, and a large copper still. The vineyard itself was completely neglected.

On the heels of secularization came the government's order to the commissioner to establish a military garrison and a pueblo. He quickly advanced to the position of military commander with the title of general, and was made director of colonization of the northern frontier. The Russians held Fort Ross, not many miles to the northwest, and the Mexican government still felt threatened by their imperialism. The technique of colonization combined with military presence was one the Americans would use against Mexico not many years hence.

Vallejo briskly set about laying out a town. Facing its plaza, he built a large adobe home for his growing family and barracks for the soldiers. Behind his home he set out a vineyard, planting cuttings from the mission vines, and in his adobe he started a winery using whatever of the mission equipment he found salvageable. In 1842 the supercilious Sir George Simpson visited Vallejo and found "a small vineyard behind the house of about three hundred feet square," containing five-year-old vines that "have just yielded twenty barrels of wine and four of spirits" (that is, *aguardiente* or brandy). But, characteristically, he found nothing good to say for the wine he was served.

With or without the approval of foreign visitors, Vallejo pursued his winemaking along with his cattle ranching and other agricultural endeavors. By January of 1848 the mission still he had been using to make his *aguardiente* became either inadequate or worn out, and he wrote to John Augustus Sutter to ask if he had a still to sell. Sutter replied early the following month that he did not, but he added: "My sawmill is already finished. All of my other business is advancing rapidly, and I have made the discovery of a gold mine which, as far as we have investigated, is extraordinarily rich."

This was the world-shaking discovery, made not quite three weeks earlier by James Marshall when he was building a sawmill for Sutter at Coloma—the discovery that started the great California gold rush and completely altered the lives of Vallejo, Sutter, and all other old Californians.

A year later Sutter's bumbling son found a still of his father's, which he sold to Vallejo. The sale for some reason infuriated the easily infuriated Sutter, but probably pleased the rather more easily pleased Vallejo. By then he was planning a new home just outside the pueblo, on property where he had already started planting more vines. When he moved to it, he gave the use of the adobe to the Reverend John L. Ver Mehr for a school. It was probably then that the winery was moved to the soldiers' barracks building next door. There in time it was presided over by one of the first technically trained men to bring scientific knowledge to a California winery, a physician educated in France, Dr. Victor Faure.

As a surprising nicety, the cellar was decorated with a group of murals. A visitor described their subjects: "Maidens with baskets of fruit, fruitpieces, and several convivial pieces, all emblematic of the Vine, from the Grape to the Wine made from it."

Although the barracks still stand, the murals and the winery itself have long since disappeared. In the restored Vallejo estate nearby, however, one may still see awards the general won at state fairs in the 1850s and early '60s for his red and white table wines, brandy, vinegar, sherry, and even sparkling wine. Certificates, a silver pitcher, and a silver spoon decorated with grapes are reminders of the prestige achieved by the general's viticultural endeavors.

In these and other ways, Vallejo brought to the attention of his fellow Californians the promise of the Sonoma Valley as a viticultural area. The vines planted on the Rancho Cabeza de Santa Rosa by the general's mother-in-law were probably cuttings from his vineyard. His rough, tough brother Salvador planted vines near the old mission vineyard. His Ohio-born brother-in-law, Jacob Primer Leese, developed a respectable vineyard along Sonoma Creek that yielded twenty-six barrels of wine and eight of *aguardiente* in 1846. Leese gave cuttings to a young Tennesseean named Nicholas Carriger, who set them out nearby in 1847 to begin what in time became a large vineyard and winery that he operated until his death in 1885.

George Yount, William Wolfskill's partner on the overland trek and in the southern California seal-hunting fiasco, came to ask Vallejo for work and stayed to make shingles for him, an alternative to tiles that the general had not seen before. One day Yount borrowed a horse to ride over the hills to take a look at the next valley. It must have been early summer, for as he crossed the ridge he saw before him the Napa Valley covered with golden California poppies, and decided that was where he wanted to spend the rest of his life. The decision was as curious as Wolfskill's decision to settle down in Los Angeles. Yount returned to Sonoma and asked Vallejo for a grant of acreage in the Napa Valley. Vallejo offered him two leagues. Yount wanted to take on no more than half a league, but two leagues he got—nearly twelve hundred acres—granted after he was baptized Jorge de Concepción Yount and given Mexican citizenship. He became the Napa Valley's first American settler and, planting vines from that same Sonoma mission stock, its first viticulturist. By the mid-1830s he had set out crops including the vineyard, which, while never large, he cultivated until close to the year of his death, 1865, making several hundred gallons of wine annually and occasionally winning state fair awards. In 1859 Richard Henry Dana visited him and, writing pontifically, as he often did, noted in his journal: "Old man gave us a bottle of wine of his own make. I like it. It has no spirit, but pure juice, pressed by hand. Better so. The skin and seeds of the grape should not go in."

There were numerous other northern California viticultural ventures before the American conquest. Few were large or lasting, but many were of interest.

At the old pueblo of San Jose, near Mission Santa Clara where winemaking had started at the beginning of the century, many residents had small vineyards and made their own wine. There was at least one commercial winemaker in the Santa Clara Valley by the late 1830s, Spanish-born Antonio M. Suñol, who joined the French navy and jumped ship in California. He became pueblo postmaster, had a grog shop, and planted a sizeable vineyard. A few years later Juan Pablo Bernal, like Vallejo a California-born military man, was growing a thousand vines just south of the pueblo, and Jacob Primer Leese added a Santa Clara Valley vineyard to his Sonoma County holdings in the late 1840s.

In the Livermore Valley, Robert Livermore planted a vineyard in the 1840s on his stock ranch, but not until some decades later would this area become important as a source of fine white wines.

There were two notable ventures in the Sacramento Valley. At New Helvetia, the eleven-league grant at the fork of the Sacramento and American rivers, owner John Augustus Sutter began experimenting with making brandy from wild grapes in 1840. He hoped it would be a profitable venture, but although he continued his distillery for several years, it turned out to be, like all his other ventures, a castle built on sand. Later, driven from New Helvetia by gold-rush immigrant squatters, he planted vines and made wine at Hock Farm on the Feather River, further north in the Sacramento Valley. The vineyard was under the supervision of his son Emil, whose interest in botany and growing things was probably a legacy from his father, who always believed that agriculture, not gold, would be the source of California's prosperity.

When the visiting committee of the California State Agricultural Society inspected Hock Farm in 1858, it found a vineyard that represented a significant advance over those planted in the mission tradition. On some thirty acres there were thirty-four thousand vines planted only five to six feet apart, compared to the traditional seven feet. A five-foot stake was "set by the side of each vine, to which the branches are brought up from near the ground forming a symmetrical pyramid," a contrast to the unstaked vines of the old mission vineyards. From the twelve thousand bearing vines that year, Sutter made four hundred gallons of wine, which, the committee reported—apparently without tasting it—"was said to be of excellent quality." Nevertheless, this venture too failed in the end, probably less because of any lack of merit than because of the luckless Sutter's financial shortcomings.

Toward the western foothills of the Sacramento Valley, John Wolfskill had a vineyard, which prospered for a couple of decades. He had worked with his brother William in Los Angeles, helping him set out his vineyard. Later he decided to apply for a land grant of his own on Putah Creek, which has its source over the hills to the west in Napa County. The land was finally given nominally to William but occupied by John. During the tedious negotiations, he worked for George Yount and perhaps learned something of grape growing in the northern part of the state. In 1842 he stocked the four-league Rancho de los Putos with cattle and planted a vineyard. After the gold rush he found a ready market for fresh grapes in San Francisco and was one of the earliest northern Californians to send his produce there. But he and another brother, Sachel, were more interested in making wine, which they did with moderate success. They were among the few long-term pioneer viticulturists in a valley that was to have a checkered future in winegrowing.

Southward, near the delta formed by the Sacramento and San Joaquin rivers, another American set out a vineyard in the late 1830s. Quirky, bad-tempered, laconic John Marsh, who parlayed a Harvard B.A. into a license to practice medicine, bought a ranch on the east side of Mount Diablo, put cattle on it, and got some of the resident Indians to bring him cuttings from the old vineyard at Mission

San José. Marsh was intelligent and, like others, believed that only able colonists were needed to make this potential Eden bloom.

He was murdered in 1856 for reasons never entirely understood—perhaps simply robbery, perhaps the result of some feud. By then his vineyard was flourishing. Had he lived he might have demonstrated the proof of his conviction that California was capable of producing wine and brandy of excellence.

Mariano G. Vallejo embodied much of the best of Mexican California culture. Although almost as formal and seemingly proud in manner as his uncle, Don Antonio Lugo of Los Angeles, he was nevertheless a humane and thoughtful man. He was born in Monterey in 1808 and adjusted much more easily than did Don Antonio to Mexican and then American sovereignty, for it was California itself to which he was loyal. "Is not the land capable of every product," he once wrote to a Mexican government official, "and yet do not the Californians purchase brandy from Catalonia, tobacco from Virginia, vinegar from Marseille, cloth from Boston, manufactured goods from everywhere?" Much of his effort went to remedying those anomalies, and he continued serving his native land throughout his life. In 1850 the Mexican general served in the first American state constitutional convention, then as a senator in the first state legislature. But he also served with interest and dignity in so small a post as treasurer of the State Board of Horticulture during the last decade of his life, the 1880s.

The Sonoma Plaza is shown here as it looked in the early 1850s, with the mission buildings at the upper right; near the center is General Vallejo's adobe, the two-story building with the tower, known as the Casa Grande. His first winery was in a mission building, his second in his adobe, and his third in the barracks building between the adobe and the mission.

Lachryma Montis, "Tears of the Mountain," was the name Vallejo gave to his estate half a mile from the center of Sonoma, where in 1852 he built an American-style carpenter's gothic home in contrast to his Mexican-style adobe on the plaza. The spring from which the mountain's tears flowed irrigated his vineyard, which was planted mainly with the traditional Mission grapes, but also in the 1850s with imported vines supplied by Antoine Delmas of San José and Agoston Haraszthy, who came to settle in the Sonoma Valley.

Vallejo's wine labels carried a vignette, the home and the adjacent "Swiss chalet" of Lachryma Montis. There were initially two wines, "Sonoma red wine" and "Sonoma white wine"; both won prizes at the state's first fairs. In 1858 at the famous Mechanics' Institute Industrial Exhibition in San Francisco, his red was the only California wine submitted to be officially commended. The judges declared it to be "pure in quality, of a fine ruby color, and more nearly approaching the claret, or Bordeaux wine of France, than any other."

The town of Sutterville was one of John Augustus Sutter's many short-lived enterprises. Situated on the Sacramento River not far from Sutter's Fort, it was intended to be an important shipping point for the cured hides, barley, flour, wine, brandy, and other goods to come from New Helvetia.

Pictures of George C. Yount, the pioneer viticulturist of the Napa Valley, seem to belie his rather gentle character. He was, in fact, fierce only when confronted by hostile Indians or grizzlies, or by portraitists.

John Augustus Sutter, the ill-fated German-Swiss dreamer, might have succeeded in building a successful feudal empire in California if his carpenter, James Marshall, had not discovered the gold that brought the forty-niners who overran his land. Sutter's Fort, the center of his huge New Helvetia grant, was on its way to becoming the nucleus of a self-sustaining military, agricultural, and manufacturing community when the gold rush changed the direction of almost everything in California. The reconstructed fort, in what is now the city of Sacramento, gives evidence of Sutter's dream of making everything from horseshoes and flour to brandy, to supply the citizens of his envisioned empire.

5. The Search for Better Vines

I T is beyond doubt that California will produce as noble wines as any part of Europe" wrote Agoston Haraszthy in 1858. He gave no timetable for this achievement by his adopted state, simply adding with a characteristic blend of practicality and optimism: "When it will have the proper varieties of grapes, the most favored localities in soil and climate will soon be discovered."

The search for varieties was by then underway, started early in the decade by nurserymen and by viticulturists, Haraszthy among them, who realized that the Mission grape did not make noble wine.

The nurserymen must have found in this fertile, untried frontier land as adventuresome a challenge as ever did the gold hunters. They assembled huge collections of fruit, including grape varieties, from both the eastern United States and Europe.

The Santa Clara Valley, with its warm summer days and cool summer nights, drew such notable French horticulturists as Louis Pellier, Antoine Delmas, and Louis Prevost. John Llewelling brought nursery stock from Oregon to the east shore of San Francisco Bay. In the Sacramento Valley, A. P. Smith purchased Hock Farm acreage from Sutter and established Smith's Pomological and Floral Gardens.

Many viticulturists, some known and more unknown, followed the pre-gold-rush lead of Don Luis Vignes and experimented with imported vines. Several Los Angelenos tried Catawbas and Isabellas from the eastern United States without much success and went on with diminished enthusiasm to others. Sutter and Vallejo, in the north, experimented. So did Agoston Haraszthy on acreage he bought in 1852 near Mission Dolores in San Francisco and later on a tract some twenty miles to the south. Their efforts were for the most part unrecorded and unrewarded, but they persisted. It is to the credit of these forebears of the California wine industry that they did so, for the Mission vine was a comfortable one for them. Well adapted to almost all parts of California, it grew well, produced many grapes, and made adequate wine. It was perhaps symbolic of California's easy bounty. But many had a sense of adventure and sought the challenge of growing grapes to make noble wines.

They were also caught up in the general challenge of the 1850s in California. Intelligent men, many with knowledge of one branch or another of science, took it upon themselves to try to systematize what had been learned of agriculture in this state and what could be learned. In 1854 they formed the California State Agricultural Society. It was headed by Frederick W. Macondray, a San Francisco importer, a gentleman-scientist who maintained an experimental greenhouse and "grapery" at his suburban home in San Mateo County. The Society held yearly fairs to exhibit the state's best products and reward excellence. It held meetings to exchange information, and it published papers. It also organized visiting committees to travel around the state, observe progress and report upon it, leaving for posterity vivid first-hand views of pioneer farms and ranches. The committees looked at cattle, sheep, fences, barns, gardens, grain fields, orchards, and vineyards. The 1857 committee visited the Sacramento Valley farms of John Wolfskill and Sutter, noting their grapes, then the town of Marysville to look at a vigorous vine covering the home of one Mr. Linsley, and the nearby nursery of George H. Beach with its five thousand vines. In the Napa area it noted vines on the property of Nathan Coombe, Joseph W. Osborne, Reason T. Tucker, and George Yount, as well as a big planting at the Thompson Brothers' Suscol Nursery and Orchard. In the Sonoma Valley the members made a detailed inspection of the recently purchased vineyard and orchard of Colonel Haraszthy, and the estate of General Vallejo with its thirteen hundred grape vines representing several varieties. They ventured a prediction that the "Napa, Sonoma, Santa Rosa, Petaluma, and the Russian River valleys . . . will, in a few years, become the great vintage ground of the north, with their wine presses dotting the plains, and the vintage time will become an important yearly epoch." Then they went on to the more nearly realized vintage area, southern California, noting on the way "numerous vineyards" in the Santa Clara Valley. In Los Angeles they visited William Wolfskill, the Sansevain brothers, and John Frohling, and they cast especially pleased eyes upon Manuel Requena's "beautiful little vineyard."

The visiting committee of the following year, 1858 took its junketing even more seriously, reporting in greater detail the progress of farms, nurseries, and ranches throughout the state. Although viticulture continued to flourish in southern California, in the northern part of the state the committee found many small vineyards on diversified farms, most of them clearly experimental, and also nurseries with growing collections of grape varieties.

Near Marysville that year they visited the farm of Frenchman Charles Covillaud, who had imported vines. Wrote the committee's scribe:

> The proprietor being absent, his wife volunteered to show us the place; and upon our objecting that the sun was too hot for her comfort, she broke off the branch of a tree, to supply the absence of a parasol, and continued to lead us on, from point to point, explaining the designs, and referring to proposed improvements, and calling our attention to the many objects of interest, with a true womanhood which scorns all aristocracy not founded in the faithful prosecution of some laudable calling.

This was Mary Murphy Covillaud, for whom the city of Marysville was named. The committee members may have known her as a survivor of the Donner party's mountain ordeal.

Of the imported varieties observed by the committee, few were named, but the 1858 report did list some of those at A. P. Smith's nursery: White Sweet Water, Royal Muscadine, Early White Malvasia, Sashmier Seedling, Black Hamburg, Muscat of Alexandria, Chasselas de Fontainebleau, Black Prince, White Frontignan, Grizzly Frontignan, Reine de Nice, and White Syrian.

All were growing well in the open air. In the list of varieties Smith submitted for display at the State Agricultural Society's fair that autumn, more were given: Dutch Sweet-water, Zinfandel, Tokay, Catawba, White Muscadine, and Isabella. Many of these were primarily table grapes, of course, but the range was notable. With these Smith won the first premium for foreign grapes that year—twenty dollars— while Haraszthy won first premium for vineyards—forty dollars.

Agoston Haraszthy so strongly dominated California winemaking for a period of almost a decade that his name is still known today by people who hardly know why they know it. It is, of course, an odd and memorable name, and later generations of Haraszthy winemakers have kept it alive. But Agoston Haraszthy himself, who died in 1869, is still a subject of controversy, having at times been idealized and at other times debunked, and having always eluded the hand of a major biographer.

After the repeal of Prohibition, when the wine industry in California was recreating its image, Haraszthy's career was dramatized, and he was labeled "the father of California viticulture." That was later modified to "the father of modern viticulture in California," yet such a claim was too pat not to draw counterclaims. And, while much is known about him, much remains to be discovered.

Among the things that are known is that he was intelligent, versatile, and energetic. A member of an aristocratic, landed Hungarian family, he was born on an agricultural estate in Futak, Hungary (now in Yugoslavia). He was well educated, and saw both military and government service before coming to the United States on a visit in 1840; he returned with his family to settle in 1842 in Wisconsin, in the area around what came later to be called Sauk City.

He is still a legend there. He created a community in the wilderness, attracted European settlers, and supplied the settlement with roads, bridges, industries, a Humanistic Society, and agriculture. He experimented, growing hops successfully, but was unsuccessful with grapes. Noted Professor Maynard A. Amerine more than a century later, "Any man who did that deserves a place in history for optimism!"

He came west in a wagon train in 1849, having been given a banquet by the Wisconsin state legislature as a send-off. It was a time when most emigrants were heading for the gold mines, but Haraszthy and his family went to southern California and settled in San Diego. He became something of a legend there too. He involved himself in a variety of commercial and real estate enterprises; he was elected to several city offices and later became an assemblyman, serving in the third California state legislature. And he tried again to grow grapes, this time apparently more successfully, joining several others in planting an orchard and vineyard in nearby Mission Valley.

He was in San Francisco as early as 1850 and then back and forth frequently thereafter until probably 1853, when he decided to move to the northern metropolis. He had by then bought acreage near Mission Dolores for a nursery and garden, which he named Los Flores.

San Francisco's Mission district was and is a good area for growing many things. It was there, for instance, that Professor H. P. Olmo, the famed grape geneticist, began his career as a boy gardener in the 1920s. Grapes, however, do not grow well in San Francisco, as the Franciscan fathers had learned, and as Haraszthy learned. So he bought land to the south near what is now Lower Crystal Springs Lake, still today a beautiful area of luxuriant meadows. But his vines did not really prosper there either. Meanwhile, versatile and energetic as he was, he had become partner in the Eureka Gold and Silver Refining Company, and then in 1855 assayer at the recently opened United States branch mint. In 1857 he resigned, asking for an audit of his accounts, and for the next four years the newspapers sporadically carried reports of legal actions against him for alleged embezzlement. By the time he was absolved, he had become as well known to the state's winegrowers as he was to its casual newspaper readers.

Somehow he had come to the Sonoma Valley and found what he had hoped to find first in Wisconsin, then in San Diego (then near San Francisco): a good vineyard location. He could, of course, see the vineyards already there. General Vallejo's biographer, Madie Brown Emperan, indicates that he learned of Sonoma's potential by drinking some of the general's wine at his home. Others have it that he first tasted wine from the vineyard he was to buy as the nucleus of his large viticultural enterprise there. That was the one originally planted by Salvador, the general's brother, in 1834. At any rate, in 1856 Colonel Haraszthy made his first purchase of land to the northeast of the town of Sonoma and had his son Attila, who had been in charge of his vineyard at Crystal Springs, start transplanting the vines. In 1857 the State Agricultural Society visiting committee reported, "This beautiful location, partly in the foothills, overlooking the valley, is admirably adapted to the cultivation of the grape." That statement has been proved over the years; it was and it still is. Mr. Haraszthy had, the committee noted, vine varieties representing "the largest collection, probably, in the state" and was "importing, from Europe, a variety of grape cuttings suited to mountain culture."

He continued buying acreage and setting out vines, and apparently filled his hours and his mind with experimenting and studying viticulture. The next year the committee again visited "Buena Vista Farm," as he had named it, and was supplied with a description of it by its owner, along with details of its operations, expenditures, and income. It was the kind of sharing of knowledge for which the agricultural association had been established.

The farm, wrote Haraszthy, contained 1,000 acres of valley land and 4,000 of pasture land. On 355 acres grain was being grown. There were mineral springs on the property, but through the "vineyard and arable land" ran three creeks, and there were also about a hundred freshwater springs. Among the buildings were a brandy distillery and "a press-house making the front of two rock cellars . . . dug into the mountain." There was also a large nursery of fruit trees.

Haraszthy described in detail his vineyards. They contained 6,830 vines, some twenty-four years old, some seven, and some three. The oldest had yielded three and a half gallons of wine per vine the previous year and were expected to yield five gallons in the current vintage. He was then selling "the larger part" of his grapes fresh in San Francisco (helping to crowd southern California out of this market) but in 1857 had made 6,500 gallons of wine and 120 gallons of brandy, the latter limited by the size of his still.

Haraszthy also had, he reported, 14,000 young foreign grape vines and 12,000 more rooted in the nursery. All together, he reported, he had 165 varieties of foreign grapes.

A visiting committee interpolation in the text of his report added: "The committee have seen the foreign varieties, being one and a half years old . . . bearing splendid grapes from one pound up to thirty pounds to a single vine."

Haraszthy noted that he had also 450,000 rooted "native" vines (as the Mission had become known) and that some of these and some of the foreign vines were for sale.

He concluded with the rather startling proposition that "if we make such good wines already from one quality [i.e., one kind] of our native grapes, how much better wines will we make when we have differently flavored varieties of grapes for it in a certain proportion mixed together? To illustrate it to persons not acquainted with winemaking, I will say that carrots will make a vegetable soup, but it will be a poor one; but take carrots, turnips, celery, parsley, cabbage, potatoes, onions, etc., and you will have a superior vegetable soup. So with grapes: take the proper variety of them, and you will make a splendid wine." Arguments both for and against blending wines continue to this day, but few are so vivid.

Buena Vista Farm was to grow. Haraszthy would plant more vines, build more cellars, create for himself and his family a splendid Italian villa surrounded by ornamental gardens, see two of his sons married to two of General Vallejo's daughters, and create the state's most famous winery of its era. Because of later financial woes, he would finally lose control of Buena Vista. But in 1858 he was doing what he liked to do best, building and creating.

That year the State Agricultural Society asked him to prepare a detailed paper on California grapes and wines. No book or pamphlet existed to which the state's agriculturists and vintners could turn for information. Haraszthy's nineteen-page "Report on Grapes and Wines of California" proved so instructive that the state reprinted hundreds of copies of it for free distribution.

It was the first publication in California of the general practices of grape growing and winemaking then followed in Europe. It served to bring viticulture in California—where in some vineyards, grapes were still being trampled in hides slung from poles—into the mainstream of the nineteenth century. Even after the publication of several books on the subject, the report remained for many years the most practical manual for California grape growers and winemakers. Even today most of its principles and practices are valid.

The northern California press caught Haraszthy's ideas. The *Alta California,* the state's leading daily newspaper, published articles by him and in support of his views on the need for analytical experimentation. So did the *Cali-*

fornia Farmer, a highly influential weekly. Although Haraszthy, enthusiastic and articulate, became the leader of the ferment, others made notable independent contributions. The United States Patent Office published, in its 1859 agriculture reports, two papers that would seem more important had it not been for Haraszthy's 1858 one. Andrew W. McKee of San Francisco discussed grape varieties, locations, and winemaking in concrete, practical terms. And an enthusiastic Irishman, Matthew Keller, one of the leading Los Angeles *vignerons* of the 1850s, contributed a knowledgeable article on the grapes and wines of his area.

That same year the State Agricultural Society published a report by Dr. James Blake that was certainly the first chemical analysis of California wine to appear in print. Simple as it may seem by late twentieth-century technological standards, it was another landmark in the progress of winemaking in California.

Educated in England, Dr. Blake was a physician who found his way to the American West and practiced medicine for some years in Sacramento and San Francisco. But his greatest interest was in scientific research.

In 1859 he was half of a two-man state fair committee on native wines; he took "one of the best exhibited," a table wine, and made a quantitative analysis of its alcohol, "vegetable acids (tartaric and racemic)," sugar, and "free acid," comparing them with quantities in French and German wines analyzed in Gerrit J. Mulder's work *The Chemistry of Wine.* As a result, the two-man committee "believe they are authorized to call the serious attention of our winegrowers to the necessity of an early introduction into this country of varieties of foreign grapes which appear to possess those qualities which are wanting in our own or, in other words, which contain less sugar and more free acid." This gave scientific reinforcement to a conclusion others had reached empirically about the deficiencies in wine made from Mission grapes.

By 1860, Agoston Haraszthy could see that his views were widely shared, but importation of vines proceeded slowly and not on a highly informed or regularized basis. The next year he proposed to the Agricultural Society that three men be delegated to travel wherever grapes were known to prosper, gather infor-

mation, and bring back those varieties considered most promising for California. The proposal was widely supported, and that May, at the suggestion of the state legislature, the governor appointed a "Commission Upon the Ways and Means Best Adapted to Promote the Improvement and Growth of the Grape Vine in California." Colonel J. J. Warner, of Los Angeles, who had published *The Southern Vineyardist,* a Mr. Schell, who has escaped historians' efforts at identification, and Agoston Haraszthy were named members.

The committee men were not to be paid for their time, but Haraszthy, who clearly knew what he wanted to do, asked for formal legislative authorization of a trip to the main viticultural areas of Europe and reimbursement of expenses. The legislature dithered, and finally in June 1861 Haraszthy sailed from San Francisco without the authorization. In Europe from that July to December, he visited vineyards and wineries, corresponded with viticulturists, gathered quantities of information, and bought vines and fruit trees. He carried with him analyses of California soils. He also carried reports of the State Agricultural Society, which "excited surprise that a state so young and so isolated should have already such wealth of agriculture and horticulture," he noted. To Californians he sent fragmentary reports of his activities and observations through articles carried by the *Alta California.* The following year, home again, he presented an organized account in a book published by Harper & Brothers, *Grape Culture, Wines, and Wine Making: With Notes upon Agriculture and Horticulture.*

By the time it appeared in print he had received the hundred thousand vines he had ordered shipped to San Francisco, and made reports to the governor and legislature. His faith in California's future had been sustained and indeed reinforced. "I was gratified to find that of all the countries through which I passed, not one possessed the same advantages that are to be found in California," he wrote, "and I am satisfied that even if the separate advantages of these countries could be combined in one, it would still be surpassed by this state when its now dormant resources shall be developed."

The legislature refused to reimburse him for

his expenses, and the state failed to find a way to distribute the imported vines to the vine-yardists, as was intended. Haraszthy appeared before the California State Senate Committee on Agriculture in January 1862, but he was received coolly. The Civil War was on and he was thought to be a Southern sympathizer. In addition, there was sentiment against state sponsorship of private interests. Haraszthy appealed to the governor, but he remained out of pocket, and the vines remained at Buena Vista Farm. He circulated a catalogue of them and sold some, but few. The main point of his trip was lost. In the end its value lay in the heightened interest in California wine-growing it aroused, and his published observations on European wine growing.

Nevertheless he continued active. He was elected president of the State Agricultural Society, and he gave it much of his abundant energy. A succession of troubles began, however. His son Arpad, who had been studying champagne making at Epernay in France, came home and made first a successful batch at Buena Vista, then a colossally unsuccessful one, leaving his father to pay a debt of honor to the Buena Vista Vinicultural Society—a corporation formed in 1863 with the backing of financier William Chapman Ralston.

Buena Vista had apparently been too successful for the amount of money immediately available to Haraszthy—"undercapitalized" in today's term. Ralston, California's leading capitalist, head of the Bank of California, was investing hand over fist in all kinds of ventures with a faith in the state's future that paralleled Haraszthy's. He was also anticipating the completion of the transcontinental railway, which got underway that same year. It would bring Eastern settlers west and carry Western goods east—surely California wines among them.

Haraszthy entered exuberantly into the new Buena Vista organization, serving as superintendent and using some of the capital to enlarge the vineyards and cellars and to install tanks made of redwood, a new use for this California tree. But something about Buena Vista, as operated, displeased Ralston. Perhaps he, like certain other investors who were to try to participate in California's wine industry in later years, did not understand that wine-

making was not controllable in the same way as furniture manufacturing or whiskey distilling.

Then, as a result of the "wine mania" of the late 1850s, there were more grapes and wine in California than the market could absorb by the mid-1860s. No dividends were forthcoming from Buena Vista. Hindsight suggests that Ralston could and should have held out until the completion of the railroad, but he did not. What he did was force out Agoston Haraszthy.

That was in 1866. Haraszthy busied himself lobbying in Washington in behalf of the California wine industry, and publicizing the state's wines in the East in an effort to expand their market. In Sonoma he began a brandy-making project on property retained by the family, but his distillery boiler exploded. He leaped out of a window and injured an ankle. Worse, the accident upset an arrangement he had with Kohler & Frohling, who were to market his brandy. On top of all that, some investments he had made proved valueless.

Early in 1868 Agoston Haraszthy left California for Nicaragua to look into the possibility of settling there and beginning a new project and a new life. He was fifty-six. The decision to leave must have been bitter for a man who identified himself to the readers of his European tour book as "your Yankee commissioner" and whose heart leaped when he beheld Old Glory flying from a mast in the harbor of Naples.

In Nicaragua he and fellow investors bought a large plantation and started an ambitious undertaking, distilling spirits from sugar cane. Early the next year he returned to San Francisco to buy equipment. A few months later, back on the plantation, he disappeared. His family surmised that he was attempting to sling himself across an alligator-filled stream by a tree branch, and the branch broke.

The Buena Vista Vinicultural Society continued expanding for a few years. Haraszthy's experimental vineyards were, however, soon neglected. The entire enterprise gradually declined and in 1876 it was liquidated. When Frank Bartholomew bought what was left of Buena Vista's old stone buildings in 1941, he had difficulty finding out who had built them.

Agoston Haraszthy, photographed at the height of his viticultural career, looked the intelligent and forceful man that he was.

A drawing of Agoston Haraszthy's formal Pompeiian-style villa, which stood on a knoll overlooking the Buena Vista vineyards, decorated his letterhead. He wrote this letter of February 8, 1862, soon after his return from Europe. It was addressed to the governor of the state of California, then Leland Stanford, and begins, "In accordance with your directions I have taken charge of the grape vines and fruit trees arrived from Europe and purchased for the use of the State; the same came in the very best condition and promise a successful propagation."

He continued, "It would be well that the present Legislature would direct how the distribution should be made, as the propagated vines ought to be taken out of the ground and distributed before the next Legislature will assemble, and would have time to determine the mode of disposing of the named vines." He also asked that an appropriation be made to repay him for the expenses "already incurred for the purchase of the vines and trees, the traveling expense for procuring the same, and collecting all the informations necessary to make our State also a prosperous vine growing district."

And he concluded by noting that "if we put the valuation of the rooted vines at 10 cents (which is less than the nursery men sell fine varieties) it would amount to about $30,000, but to the People of this State it will in time be worth as many millions." Since provisions were never made for the hoped-for distribution of the vines, no one will ever know whether his prophesy was valid. A catalogue of the vines, reprinted many years later by the Board of State Viticultural Commissioners, continues, however, to intrigue ampelographers and historians of a speculative turn of mind.

No 38.

The Buena Vista vineyard was sketched in ink and wash by English artist Frederick Whymper, probably in the early 1860s shortly after he arrived in California. Just left of the center is Agoston Haraszthy's villa. The winery buildings are at the center right.

Little is known about Whymper, but one can guess that he studied in France, for he noted on the back of the sketch three things that he found strange: the vines were "staked as in Europe but farther apart and more luxuriant"; the grapes were picked into boxes rather than into baskets; and the harvesters were "Chinamen," while a "white man or two may be looking on directing the operation."

Haraszthy later revised his views on vineyard layout, concluding that closer planting would result in better grapes for wine. As for the California Chinese, he thought highly of them as laborers, hiring them for field and winery work and also for constructing the caves tunneled into the hillside behind the main winery building. Trained by working on the construction of cuts and tunnels through the mountains for the transcontinental railroad, many Chinese were excellent builders, responsible for much of California's masonry work in the latter part of the nineteenth century.

The Whymper sketch is owned by Frank Bartholomew, the newspaperman who in the 1940s rehabilitated the Buena Vista winery.

A VINTAGE IN CALIFORNIA.
ILLUSTRATED BY EDW. J. MUYBRIDGE.

Transplanting the Young Vine. A hunter with a recently shot hare of unusual size watched a workman planting rooted vines. Haraszthy advocated first putting in a stake at the point where each vine was to be planted, then digging a hole twenty inches square and about two feet deep, then filling it to about six inches from the top, then dipping the vine roots into a "mud-mixture" made of earth, fresh manure, and water before placing the vine in the earth.

Ploughing. Haraszthy advocated, in his 1858 *Report on Grapes and Wine of California,* two ploughings for new vineyard land, the first with a deep tiller drawn by three horses, the second with "a common shovel plough" drawn by two horses, as in this photograph.

Stereoscope views of the Buena Vista vineyard and winery were made by Eadweard Muybridge, the photographer famous for his pioneer motion studies, probably in the early 1870s. Although Agoston Haraszthy had been gone for several years, little had changed visibly. The titles here are those given on the stereoscope cards.

02—BUENA VISTA VINEYARD, SONOMA—Plowing.

A VINTAGE IN CALIFORNIA. ILLUSTRATED BY EDW. J. MUYBRIDGE.

43

Loading Grapes for the Press House. Filled boxes brought from the vineyard to the road's edge were loaded onto the wagon. The man at left in the relatively formal clothing is apparently the overseer. Haraszthy advocated that in small vineyards grapes be gathered before the heat of the day, but that "other remedies" to cool the grapes and prevent "too hasty fermentation" be employed by large vineyards.

The Pomace Heap. After the grapes were crushed and pressed, the residue of stems, skins, and pulp, called *pomace,* was sent out of the Buena Vista winery on this slide.

The Press House and Cellars. The same man who was overseeing the vineyard work was here apparently checking the boxes of grapes as they were carried into the building to be crushed. "When the picked grapes are brought to the press house, they ought to be crushed immediately," wrote Haraszthy, "and not left standing in tubs overnight, or the next day."

0—BUENA VISTA VINEYARD, SONOMA—The Pomace Heap.

Disgorging the Sediment and Re-Corking Sparkling Wines. After the sediment was removed, the bottles had to be filled and recorked. Perhaps all of the men and equipment were moved outside so that the photographer could show the entire process in one picture. The bottles of champagne, like the bottles of wine, went to market in wicker baskets said to have been made by Chinese employees. In spite of all the attention paid to its sparkling wine, Buena Vista had numerous failures with it and no lasting success.

Disgorging the Sediment from Sparkling Wine. This was done in the traditional way at Buena Vista. The man at the left removed the cork and handed the bottle to the man at the right, who discarded the sediment collected in the bottle neck.

Bottling Wine. The man at the right is filling bottles directly from the cask, then passing them in baskets to the man at the left, who is using a hand-powered machine to cork them.

1106—Buena Vista Vineyard, Sonoma—Bottling Wine.

The Cooper Shop. Facilities for both building barrels, as the man at the left was doing, and repairing them were valuable to a winery. If the winemaker bought used barrels, according to Haraszthy, he should have the heads removed and each "barrel itself thoroughly burnt out with shavings or straw, so that its inner parts be charred from one-sixteenth to one-eighth part of an inch all over, then washed out" several times with hot and cold water before being put back together.

1114—Buena Vista Vineyard, Sonoma. The Cooper Shop.

6. The Santa Clara Valley

SOUTH of San Francisco, separated by only one mountain range from the Pacific Ocean, lies the Santa Clara Valley. In the latter part of the nineteenth century it came to be known as "The Garden Spot of the World." Among those who helped make it so, who perhaps may themselves even be credited with establishing its potential as an Eden, were French nurserymen who turned their backs on the mines and settled around San Jose and Santa Clara in the 1850s. They found vineyards of Mission grapes, probably started from Mission Santa Clara's old vines, and added to them. But, more important, they imported European varieties of grapes as well as other fruits, planted them carefully, propagated those that flourished most, and distributed them to farmers and vineyardists in many parts of the state.

One of the earliest was Louis Prevost, who in 1853 assembled a group of like-minded men under a live oak tree on his farm to establish a horticultural society. The members met monthly to compare the fruit and flowers they were growing, and to discuss which were best adapted to their valley.

By 1855 Prevost himself had in his diversified nursery more than 35,000 vines of 18 varieties; three years later he had 80,000 vines of 60 varieties. (He also had 120 varieties of apples, 35 varieties of plums, 40 varieties of cherries, 120 varieties of roses, and even some date palms.) He had a vineyard by then, of both Mission and imported grapes. But he gained his greatest fame for his mulberry bushes and symbiotic cocoonery, for he was the first to propagate silkworms in California—for a time he was loudly acclaimed for his effort to free this nation from the indignity of dependence upon imported silk and, at the same time, to empty California's almshouses into filature workshops.

Another French nurseryman who was a member of the horticultural society was J. R. Bontemps, who astounded a State Agricultural Society visiting committee with a fourteen-foot Chasselas de Fontainebleau vine planted from a cutting only two years earlier. Still another was Louis Pellier, who had started a nursery in San Jose in 1850 and three years later was joined by his brother Pierre, who brought with him French vine cuttings including, it was said, Black Burgundy, Chasselas de Fontainebleau, and Madeleine. That same 1858 visiting committee labeled Louis an "industrious and intelligent French gardener," commented upon his assortment of fruit trees and vines, and reported that he "exhibited to the committee some specimens of pure native wine of the vintage of 1857 which, considering the age, were very good." By then Pierre had made another trip to France to buy more cuttings, which were said on this trip to include Folle blanche, Gray Riesling, and French Colombard.

In 1862 he struck out on his own, starting a sizable vineyard southeast of San Jose in the Evergreen area near the base of the Mount Hamilton range, the same area in which descendants of his son-in-law Pierre Mirassou operate their family winery today.

When he became a naturalized citizen in 1871, Louis Pellier gave his occupation as "gardener," although he had undoubtedly continued making wine, as most French farmers would have. Only gradually did some of the Santa Clara Valley horticulturists begin to specialize, becoming, like Pierre Pellier, first vineyardists, then "wine growers."

Antoine Delmas, who came to the Santa Clara Valley in 1849, early enough to hispanicize his first name to Antonio rather than anglicize it, had a nursery adjacent to that of his countryman Prevost and almost as many fruit trees and ornamental plants, together with a large assortment of grape vines—including those he imported as cuttings from France in 1854. He also imported, perhaps at the same time, one species of French *escargot*, the *Helix aspersa.* It proved excellently adapted to life in northern California and may now be found in every garden, picking its way among the traps and baits, chewing up the tenderest plants. It is the common brown garden snail, and over the years it has eaten vastly more than it has been eaten.

Delmas, like Louis Pellier, listed his occupation as "gardener," although he quickly began making some wine. The 1855 Agricultural Society visiting committee reported that "great praise is due to Mr. Delmas, for his very interesting and admirably located vineyard, the result of his own labor and efforts." It added that "the native wine exhibited to the committee gave evidence of superior skill in its manufacture." In 1859 he submitted some of it at the state fair. "The best red wine that was submitted," stated the committee of judges, "was made by Mr. Delmas, from foreign grapes, and although as appears by his catalogue, these grapes had been selected more as table fruit than for winemaking, yet the sample of wine exhibited by that gentleman only shows what could be done by a judicious selection of proper varieties."

The choice of Delmas' wine is interesting because it was only one year old, and because it was in competition with two- and three-year-old wines made by Sansevain Brothers, B. D. Wilson, Mariano G. Vallejo, and Agoston Haraszthy. It was an early indication of the quality potential of the Santa Clara Valley. Eight years later, in the first full-length practical manual for California viticulturists, *Hyatt's Handbook of Grape Culture,* T. Hart Hyatt would mention "that belt of timbered land stretching around the west and south sides of the valley, from Mountain View to Gilroy; there we find a soil of red clay mixed with gravel and limestone, the very best of soil for producing the finest wines, as all who understand the business will attest." Over a hundred years later, winemaker Louis M. Martini, reflecting upon his sixty-odd years in the California wine industry, would comment, "I think the best wines, over all, going back in history, came from the west side of the Santa Clara Valley, near Mountain View, Saratoga. A long time ago." By then the Santa Clara Valley had been largely paved over, a striking example of California's continuing loss of fine agricultural land to suburban dwellings, factories, supermarkets, and roads to connect them.

Among those who had "a long time ago" helped the valley reach the potential remarked upon by Louis Martini was Frenchman Charles Lefranc. In 1857 he became a partner and son-in-law of another French immigrant, Etienne Bernard Edmond Thée. Thée had planted Mission vines in the hills southwest of San Jose near the famous old New Almaden quicksilver mines, which were still supplying this metal to separate California gold from its ores. Here, on this gently hilly land, Lefranc set about enlarging and diversifying the vineyard, importing many varieties from France; among them, it was said, Cabernet franc, Pinot noir, Muscat Frontignan, Grenache, Carignane, Folle blanche, Semillon, and Malbec. When German-born Frank Stock of San Jose discontinued his nursery, Lefranc acquired his northern

European varieties including Johannisberg Riesling, Sylvaner, and Traminer. And a story, a legend perhaps, has Lefranc planting California's first Verdal when the spirited Mrs. Lefranc, nee Adele Thée, carried several slips home on horseback after a visit to a ranch to the north where they had been presented to her by a Spanish nobleman, who had carried them to these shores.

The vineyard, which Lefranc named New Almaden, became the first real commercial grape-growing enterprise in the valley, and in 1862 he began making wine in commercial quantities. Ten years later the Agricultural Society visiting committee "found it to be one of the best arranged wine houses and cellars we have seen in the state." Its "clean and tidy" winery was a three-story building where crushing was done on the top floor, fermenting on the second, and aging in the bottom. There was also a separate aging cellar. Forty thousand gallons of wine were in storage, some six years old. A good deal of it was in butts made of redwood from trees felled nearby. Two of them held forty-three hundred gallons each. Although redwood had been used earlier, notably by Agoston Haraszthy, it was apparently still little known, for the Agricultural Society visiting committee hailed Charles Lefranc as the pioneer demonstrator of its utility for inexpensive, long-lasting, worm-resistant vessels that impart no flavor or color to the wine they hold.

At his death in 1887, he was also hailed as the pioneer vineyardist of Santa Clara County, perhaps justly since he was the first to devote himself solely to fairly large-scale commercial winegrowing. He died late one October day. "Last evening," read the notice in the *Alta California*, "as Mr. Lefranc came out of his cellar, on his vineyard, on the New Almaden Road, he saw one of his teams running away and attempted to stop it. The horses ran over and trampled on him, badly bruising his head and body, producing concussion of the brain."

He died the next afternoon, aged sixty-two, leaving his widow and three children. One daughter, Louise, followed her mother's example and married her father's young French associate. He was Paul Masson, who had worked for Lefranc for a decade and would become a partner of the son, Henry Lefranc. In time

they parted, Masson to establish a distinguished vineyard and winery nearby, young Lefranc to continue New Almaden. Both names survive in the wine industry today.

There were, to be sure, many other Santa Clara Valley vineyardists who were not born in France. Frank Stock was a German. Victor Speckens (or Speckins, as his name appeared in the Great Register of voters) was born in Belgium; he preceded Pierre Pellier in vine growing in the Evergreen area.

From Italy came Stefano Splivalo, who had first seen California in 1849 from the bridge of the ship he commanded and returned to buy vineyard acreage and a winery that Pierre Sansevain, one of the Sansevain brothers of Los Angeles, had started in 1853. And there were many Americans, among them a Dr. N. H. Stockton, who established the Live Oak vineyard and winery, and D. M. Harwood, whose Lone Hill vineyard was the largest in the county in the mid-1870s.

A surprising number of "old Californians," who had arrived before statehood and settled in the Santa Clara Valley, also became vineyardists—many sooner, some later. Isaac Branham, so revered a pioneer that he was praised in a strong Temperance-flavored twentieth-century book on the valley, settled in San Jose in 1846 and had on his nearby farm a fifty-acre vineyard with foreign and Mission varieties and, in 1872, some 5,000 gallons of brandy he had made from them.

Peter Quivey, who arrived in California the same year as Branham and two years later established the Miners' Home, the first public hostelry in San José, had a vineyard of eight acres and 600 gallons of wine on hand by 1860. Perhaps, like Raffaello Petri in early twentieth-century San Francisco, he wanted a steady source of wine for his hotel dining room.

James Lick, an eccentric Pennsylvania-born piano maker and real estate investor, arrived in California in 1848, bought a tract of more than 500 acres north of San Jose, and in 1860 had seventy-five acres of vines and 150 gallons of wine in storage. He astounded visitors with the beautiful cabinet-work with which he had finished the interior of his flour mill, and the huge piles of manure and old bones and hooves that he amassed to fertilize his orchards and vineyard. He is better remembered today because of his bequest that established the Lick Observatory than is another old Californian, Henry M. Naglee, but Naglee was famous too in his time.

He was born into a well-to-do Pennsylvania family in 1815, went to West Point, resigned his commission soon after graduating, and worked successfully as a civil engineer for more than a decade. When war with Mexico broke out, however, he returned to the army; it was as captain of a company of volunteers that he first saw California. Arriving at San Francisco in April 1847, he and his men were sent directly to Monterey, but in July they were ordered to the Santa Clara Valley to be on hand to evict squatters from Mission Santa Clara in case force should be necessary. It was not. Perhaps while standing by, Captain Naglee decided to buy land in the area. The next year he bought 140 acres in San Jose, and at least by 1859 he was cultivating vines and fighting gophers. Meanwhile, mustered out of the army at the end of the Mexican War, he went into business in San Francisco. Early in 1849 he opened the town's first bank, and he so well survived its closing the following year, paying off all his obligations, that a few years later he was appointed receiver for two other banks that went broke. Business and civic affairs, civil engineering, and his San Jose estate occupied his abundant energies until the Civil War. Then he returned again to the military, serving as lieutenant-colonel of the regular army and brigadier general of volunteers. After his return to California in 1865 he was always General Naglee.

He married, and the home he had built in San Jose became his headquarters. He became increasingly interested in wine and brandy, the latter more than the former, and devoted most of his attention to his vineyards, winery, and distillery, visiting vineyards and wineries and distilleries in France, especially in the Cognac district. He was distracted for a time by the claims of a woman who published a book called *The Love Life of General Naglee,* asserting the letters printed in it to have been written by him to her. Sensational for its time, it even contained a drawing of the general in his tub—its relevance not entirely clear, and its revelations minor since little of his anatomy was visible above the tub side. He countered by demonstrating devotion to his wife and two daughters and his brandy distillery.

He experimented with various varieties of grapes, and finally settled upon two as superior: Riesling and Pinot noir, the grape of Burgundy. From them he distilled only wine newly made from their free-run juice, aging the brandy in oak, and adding nothing to it for color or flavor. And he triumphed.

In 1878 the Reverend John I. Bleasdale, D.D., F.G.S., of Melbourne, Australia, an analytical chemist, mineralogist, as well as clergyman, and a well-known authority on wines, came to San Francisco and participated in the judging of wines at the Thirteenth Industrial Exhibition of the Mechanics' Institute. It was that year devoting special attention to the state's wines. No brandy was included, however, and after it was over, the chairman of the board of wine judges, Professor Eugene W. Hilgard of the University of California, suggested to Dr. Bleasdale, the board's secretary, that the members "consider and report upon certain samples of brandy, made from the pure juice of the Burgundy [i.e. Pinot noir] and Riesling grape, and which had been kept in wood from seven to ten years." The quotation is from the supplementary report to the committee, which did not mention the source of the samples. All the members but one consented; he felt he could not judge brandy and was replaced by someone who believed he could. On December 15, 1878, the group met to consider five brandies, "three of which, viz.: Catawba, Mission and Muscatel, made from grapes of those names, had been sent as matters of curiosity." A system of judging was agreed upon with 100 as "highest award." The results:

Burgundy, over eight years in wood, 100
Riesling, of the same age, 89
the rest in this order, Muscatel, Catawba, Mission.

As if that were not a sufficient triumph for General Naglee, his brandies gained still greater praise from Dr. Bleasdale, who examined them analytically. They were given "every known test of their purity" and found to be "chemically pure spirits, free from any admixture or adulteration whatever." They were free of dreadful "fusel oil so abundant in ordinary liquors of this name," Bleasdale reported.

Their unusual color, greenish yellow, was due only to "a trace of tannic acid extracted from the oak casks," since no coloring or flavoring matter had been added. And the committee members "could easily recognize in these samples the distinctive bouquet of their respective wines, alongside of the brandy flavor proper, derived from the aromatic ethers formed during fermentation."

And finally, triumph upon triumph upon triumph for the general, the committee, assembling again on December 29 to compare the two winners with old French brandy and California commercial brandy, rated the Burgundy 100, the Riesling down to 85 this time, but the French only 67, and the California commercial only 26.

Loud were the commendations gathered together and published by an unidentified individual as a pamphlet early the next year. Letters to General Naglee from "Professors, Physicians, Gentlemen and Experts" who had been sent bottles of the winning brandy were appended to the committee's report. All attested to its excellence. Dr. H. H. Behr wrote:

I have already tried its beneficial influence on a reconvalescent from pneumonia, and have also introduced it to a professional friend, whom I have converted into an ardent admirer of the California grape, and also have begun extensive experiments on this excellent liquid on my own system.

W. G. Tiffany, who had spent many years in the Cognac district, declared it superior to any brandy he had ever tasted and ordered five gallons.

The fact was that the brandy was the best made in California to that date, and in the opinion of many as good as or better than any made since. For rarely if ever have California brandy makers been willing to send through their brandy stills only wine made from fine wine grapes.

The spirit of agricultural fecundity was expressed exuberantly in this vine-bordered decoration for the cover of a Santa Clara County promotional pamphlet.

The vineyard that Pierre Pellier started in the Evergreen area to the east of San Jose in the early 1860s had some three hundred acres of vines stretching across the foothills by the end of that decade.

Charles Lefranc, born in France, retained a Gallic bonhomie throughout his life. At his home, set on a knoll overlooking part of his New Almaden vineyard, he was a genial host to many well-known visitors to California who stopped on their way to see the famous quicksilver mines a few miles beyond.

William Henry Bishop visited California in the autumn of 1881 and described the Lefranc estate in some detail in his travel narrative in *Harper's New Monthly Magazine*. "Here are about 175,000 vines set out—a thousand perhaps to the acre. The large cheerful farm buildings are upon a gentle rise of ground above the area of vines, which is nearly level. An Alsatian foreman shows us through the wine-cellars. A servantmaid bustling about the yard is a thorough French peasant, only lacking the wooden shoes. The long tables set for the forty hands employed in the vintage-time, are spread with viands in the French fashion. Scarcely a word of English is spoken. At other places the surroundings are as exclusively Italian. One feels very much abroad in the scenes of this new industry on American soil. A certain romantic interest attaches to it wherever found. The great tuns in the wine-cellars, and all the processes, seem delightfully clean. It is reassuring to see the pure juice of the grape poured out in such floods, and to know that at this source of supply there is to be no need, founded in scarcity at least, of adulteration.

"Heavy loads of grape[s] are driven up, across a weighing scale, and lifted to an upper story, and put into a hopper, where the stems come off, and the fruit falls through into a crusher. It is lightly crushed at first. It is something of a discovery to find that the first product of grapes of every variety is white wine. Red takes its hue from the coloring matter in the skins, which are utilized in a subsequent rougher treatment. It is not necessary to describe all the various processes of the work, the racking off, the clarifying, and the like, though, having been favored with so much of the company of persons who spoke with authority on these matters, and were continually holding up little glasses to the light with gusto, like the figures in certain popular chromos, I consider myself to yield in knowledge of the subject to but few.

"Immense upright casks containing a warm and audibly fermenting mass, and others lying down, neatly varnished, and with concave ends, are the most salient features in the dimly lighted wine-cellars."

55

General Henry M. Naglee, who was wealthy by both inheritance and effort, devoted himself to brandy-making for pleasure rather than profit. Although a fellow Civil War officer described him as "a sort of thunderbolt in battle," he was described in different terms by a later California acquaintance: "He is of medium stature, trim-built as a race horse, beard frizzled *à la militaire,* voice soft and melodious almost as a woman's, and with a sparkle and vivacity about him, coupled with polished tastes and fine culture that make him one of the liveliest and most genial companions."

In the heart of the city of San Jose there were still in 1872 "establishments which for extent and variety of cultivation would, in many countries, rank with good-sized farms." Among them was that of General Naglee, shown here as it looked three years after the State Agricultural Society visited and described it. "While the General has a place about his residence most gorgeously ornamented with a profusion of trees and vines of almost every variety, both foreign and native to be found in the state," wrote the committee's chronicler, "the principal feature of attraction to us is his vineyard."

Here he had made experiments that would be of value to other vineyardists throughout the state who planted on flat valley land, declared the committee. He had found that by training his vines up four to six feet instead of pruning them low in the usual way, he had "increased the yield from 100,000 pounds a year to 400,000 pounds annually" and improved the quality as well. As to the general's cellars, in 1881 the writer for *Harper's New Monthly Magazine* observed that, in contrast to the spic and span cellars of Charles Lefranc, these were "really charming from an artistic point of view. The cobwebs have been allowed to increase till they hang like tattered banners."

Paul Masson was a rather serious-looking man in middle age when he had this portrait made. He had come to California as a young man, enrolled at a college in San Jose, and gone to work part-time as a book-keeper for his compatriot, Charles Lefranc. He became increasingly important in Lefranc's New Almaden Vineyard, returning to France in 1884 to order champagne-making equipment for the winery and getting back to California in time to receive and install it and make champagne that same autumn. After Lefranc died in 1887, Masson married his daughter and became a partner of her brother in the winery and vineyard. Then, in 1892, he established the Paul Masson Champagne Company and began producing sparkling wines that won prizes and acclaim. He lived until 1938. A flamboyant host, he became in his later years a kind of symbol of America's idea of a high-living Burgundian.

Peter Coutts, "the Frenchman" of Stanford University legends, was a political refugee who, in the six years between 1874 and 1880, managed to create this fine estate, with its big cattle barns, orchard, vineyard, and small winery. His home, which still stands, remodeled, was the L-shaped building at the center of this photograph, and the wine cellar was the structure just beyond it to the right that is partly hidden by a tree. Leland Stanford, who also grew grapes and made wine on his Palo Alto farm just under two miles away, bought the Coutts property and all that lay between for the Stanford University campus.

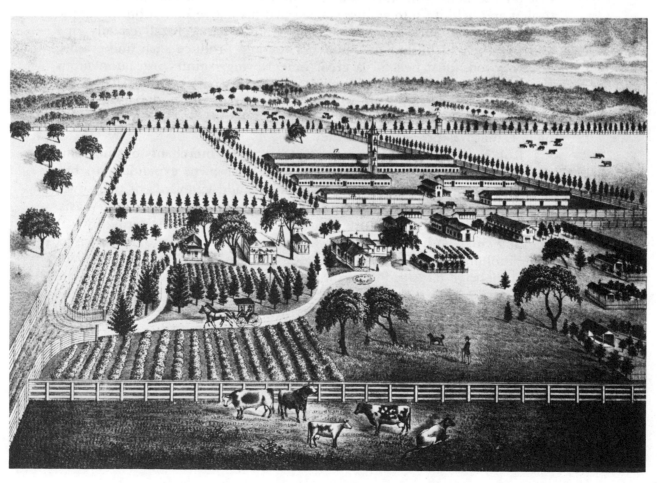

7. "An Altar to the God Bacchus"

ONE fine autumn morning in 1853, three young German musicians walked from their lodgings on Stockton Street in San Francisco out to the ocean beach where the famed Cliff House would later be built. It was a walk they often took, these three young immigrants who had come from different parts of their native land to the music-hungry city of gold rush days. As they walked they customarily speculated upon many things, including the future. On this day either Charles Kohler, the violinist, or John Frohling, the flutist, had brought a bunch of grapes just off the boat from Los Angeles. John Beutler (instrument unknown) took it and held it up to admire, saying that his native Baden on the Rhine never produced such large clusters of grapes that were all equally ripe and without a blemish. Any country that could produce such fine grapes, he proposed, must become a great winegrowing country. An anonymous chronicler, working from now lost notes made by Charles Kohler, had Beutler thereupon exclaim: "We will build an altar to the god Bacchus, and introduce the wine business on this coast!" Whether he said precisely that or not, that was precisely what they did.

Kohler & Frohling became the first successful merchants of California wine, beginning with a single vineyard of their own, expanding to buy others' wine, make wine on others' premises, add vineyards of their own, and send California wines beyond California's border on a regular basis.

In the spring of 1854, the same season that Agoston Haraszthy was planting vines on his recently purchased land just south of San Francisco, John Frohling traveled to Los Angeles to make a beginning. Shortly he sent a message back to his partners. "I have purchased a vineyard. Send me $4,000." They did, and he started re-cultivating some three thousand Mission vines long since planted on a twelve-acre tract by an unrecorded Mexican Californian. He began making wine that same year and, with the initial five hundred gallons, Kohler opened a store on Merchant Street in San Francisco, the first and for three years sole native wine store in that city. Beutler had by then left the firm. The company, first called Chas. Kohler & Co., became Kohler, Frohling & Bauck for a few years, then Kohler & Frohling for the rest of its long, successful existence—although John Frohling died in 1862 and various other partners were in and out of the organization.

For the first four years, Charles Kohler continued working as a musician in the evenings to make up for what the firm lost during the day. But by 1858 the enterprise was on its feet. Kohler had moved the cellar to the basement of the Montgomery Block, San Francisco's most imposing structure. Gradually it expanded to take up the entire basement of that building and overflowed into that of the Center Market a few blocks away.

John Frohling, who had settled easily into southern California's still Hispanic pace, built a two-story winery, and later added a large cellar under the Temple Market in Los Angeles, filling it with more than twenty thousand gallons of wine. In addition, the ever-growing firm rented the entire basement of the Los Angeles City Hall for storage, and took over cellars at Wolfskill's and several other Los Angeles County vineyards where it harvested the owner's grapes and made wine.

In the 1859 vintage season, Henry D. Barrows, William Wolfskill's son-in-law-to-be, wrote for the San Francisco *Bulletin* a description of winemaking in Los Angeles. The firm of Kohler, Frohling & Bauck was just then at work in Wolfskill's vineyard, employing about thirty men to pick the grapes and haul them to the winery, with ten more working around the presses and in the cellars.

> The grapes are cut off by the stem from the vine and carried in baskets to the crossroads running through the vineyard and turned into tubs holding from 150 to 200 pounds (or as large as two men can easily handle) which are hauled in one-horse carts to the press where they are weighed, and then turned into a large "hopper" which has an apron or a strong wire sieve, through which they are "stemmed," the stems being thrown out before the grape is mashed, when the latter is run through a mill consisting of two grooved iron cylinders so gauged as to run as closely as possible together without mashing the seeds. The grooves of one cylinder are longitudinal and of the other spiral. This method is quicker, less laborious and far more decent than the old way of "treading out" the grapes, which in a measure has passed away, as it should.

The machine worked quite well, he added, but Yankee ingenuity could devise a better one. He continued, explaining how wine was made, and also *aguardiente*.

> After being ground, the pomace [the "mashed" mass] runs down into a vat, on the bottom of which is a grating, through which the juice of the grape runs, whence it is conveyed into tubs for white wine. The pomace is taken directly into spiral screw presses and subjected to moderate pressure, the runnings from which make *pale* or *yellow* wine, like sherry. The grape skins are then put into large tubs to ferment six or eight days for *red wine*, or longer, when the residue of their vinous property is extracted in *aguardiente* by distillation.

Cleanliness was important. Two or three men were kept busy "washing, cleaning and sulphuring" the grapes. "Every night," he reported, "all the presses and appliances used are washed out thoroughly to prevent acidity."

Thus in the previous five days ten thousand gallons of wine had been made at Wolfskill's vineyard under John Frohling's supervision. He had also supervised winemaking at the vineyards of John Rowland and William Workman at Puente, twenty miles east of Los Angeles. He would the following week finish making wine from Wolfskill's eighty-five thousand vines and commence at the vineyards of Antonio Coronel and his own firm, which by then had twenty thousand bearing vines.

The wines the firm was marketing, as noted by the visiting committee of the Agricultural Society that year, were "guaranteed to possess a certain uniform standard. This is affected by introducing a portion of 'heavy' wines into casks that are too 'light,' and *vice versa*, until the desired standard is attained." Blending of wines, as advocated by Agoston Haraszthy, had undoubtedly been done experimentally in California, but systematic blending of wines from different vineyards and undoubtedly different vintages to produce a uniform product as done by Frohling was certainly another notable advance. It was a practice that would be adopted in time by most of the state's large winemakers.

The following year, 1860, Kohler & Frohling began shipping California wine east in quantity. It established a sales agency in New York—Perkins, Stern & Co.—which sent its wines up and down the Atlantic seaboard and, moreover, defended them stoutly when New York State and Ohio winegrowers, fearful of losing part of their market, accused the firm of adulterating their wines and, worse, selling Eastern wines under California labels.

Kohler & Frohling also added appreciably

to the volume of California wines sent to foreign countries: South America, China, and the East Indies, and of course the Old World, especially Germany and Denmark. And like California winemakers before them, they could not resist sending gifts of their wines to certain (unspecified) "crowned heads of Europe."

Between 1864 and 1869, the value of California wine exports rose from $100,000 to $400,000 and continued thereafter to increase. The transcontinental railroad was completed in 1869, but these figures were for shipment by sea alone. Shipments by rail started slowly. Rates were high, and perhaps the belief that a sea voyage is beneficial to the quality of wine made the winemakers loyal to the ships. In any case, not until the mid-1870s did they send more wine overland than by water.

Kohler & Frohling constantly expanded its business and its holdings over this period. In 1873 it bought the Tokay Vineyard in the Sonoma Valley. Its existing 35-acre planting was expanded to 150, then 350, with a variety of *viniferas,* among them Zinfandel. California growers had been experimenting with this grape throughout the 1860s; around 1870 Charles Kohler decided it was America's answer to the most popular red wines of France and started planting it extensively. By the mid-1870s he was bottling wine under the label Zinfandel. It proved extremely popular. He also bottled other varietal wines, Riesling and Gutedel. The last was made of the grape that would be often called by the more aesthetic name Chasselas doré.

In the half-dozen years before his death, Charles Kohler, who had by then become sole owner of the company, added further to his vineyard interests. He bought shares in the Italian Swiss Agricultural Colony at Asti, an idealistic immigrant workers' cooperative vineyard venture, which soon had to turn into a corporation. Kohler also bought, with two partners, a 2,080-acre ranch in the Fresno area of the great San Joaquin Valley, where grape growing had started off with a bang in the mid-1870s. Six hundred of this ranch's acres were in vines. And in yet another section of the state, the foothills of the Sacramento Valley, he bought an interest in the Natoma Water and Mining Company; it had been formed in the gold rush to flume water to the mines but by the 1880s had a 200-acre vineyard on its large land holdings.

At his death in 1887, Charles Kohler, the immigrant musician, was widely eulogized as a man who had for more than thirty years exemplified unselfish and sound business leadership in the wine industry.

There are none anywhere to be found to compare
With the wines of Los Angeles County

ran the refrain of the song that carried this decorative drawing, showing Kohler & Frohling's grapes progressing from the vineyard through the press to the casks and (by implication) into the bottles.

61

Charles Kohler was dubbed "The Longworth of the Pacific Coast" after Nicholas Longworth of Ohio, who was America's pre-eminent winegrower for a brief period. Kohler's career was long, and he was steadfast in the successful pursuit of his initial aim: to make good California wines and sell them widely. He was less unswerving in politics. When he came to America he was naturalized and joined the Democratic Party. When the Civil War approached, he became a Republican in protest against slavery. Then in 1880, when the Republican Party showed signs of joining hands with the Prohibitionists, he became once again a Democrat.

Kohler & Frohling's Los Angeles winery and storage cellar, at what would become the busy intersection of Central Avenue and Seventh Street, looked in 1857 like what it was: a substantial building in a rural town. Since John Frohling was the Los Angeles partner, his name came first there. In 1860 he added a cellar under the Temple Market. "In the corner a bar was speedily built," wrote the city's chronicler, Harris Newmark, "and by many Angelenos that day not associated with at least one pilgrimage to Frohling's cool and rather obscure recesses was considered incomplete."

CATALOGUE

OF

CALIFORNIA WINES;

WITH

STATISTICS OF VINES PLANTED, DESCRIPTION
OF VARIETIES, COMMENTS OF
THE PRESS, &c.

PERKINS, STERN & CO.

180 Broadway, New York, 108 Tremont St., Boston.

IMPORTERS AND DEALERS EXCLUSIVELY IN

CALIFORNIA WINES.

Sole Agents for Kohler & Frohling's Celebrated Vintages.

Kohler & Frohling's eastern agents issued this catalogue in 1863. Offered for sale in it were:

"WHITE, OR HOCK WINE, of a light straw color, very delicate, fine flavored, and superior as a dinner wine to [imported] Hock or Rhine.

"ANGELICA, a rich and naturally sweet wine much admired by ladies, and valuable in the sick chamber as it makes fine wheys and jellies. It is a fine dessert wine, and well adapted for Communion purposes.

"MUSCATEL, a light colored, highly aromatic wine, and pronounced by good judges to resemble the celebrated 'Tokay.'

"PORT, deep red color, fine flavor, and in many respects similar to the old wines of Lisbon.

"GRAPE BRANDY, in limited quantities."

One key to the success of the agency may be found in another paragraph in the pamphlet: "Great care is necessary in the handling of these delicate wines after their arrival in New York. Having a partner who was for seven years in the vineyards and cellars of California, and who thoroughly understands the character and nature of the wines, will always enable us to present them to the people as pure and delicate as when they left the vineyard." Later California vintners were to follow this way of ensuring the survival of their wines after they arrived in the East.

This bill dated June 1858 indicated that Kohler, Frohling & Bauck ("late Chas. Kohler & Co.") was remarkably patient. It had sent twelve cases of wine up to the roaring little gold-rush town of Columbia in the Mother Lode in August 1856. Apparently no part of the $69.00 it charged had been paid by the recipient, McHentry & Church, which in January 1858 sent back five cases for a credit of $28.75, leaving a balance which the San Francisco firm asked politely be settled with the Wells Fargo agent in Columbia.

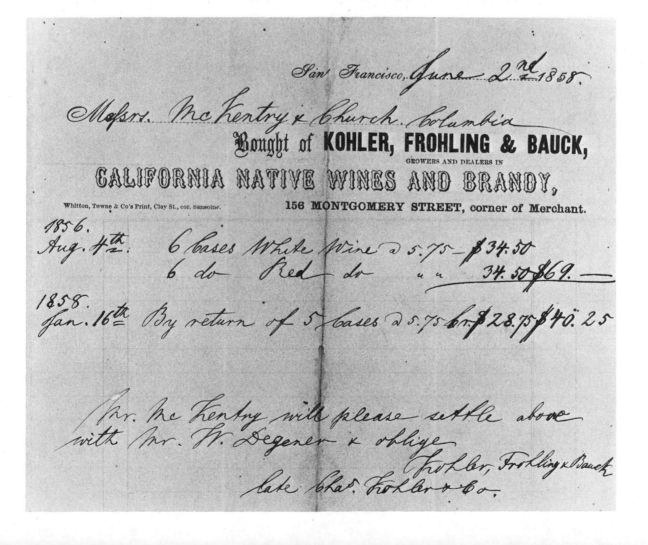

8. Expansion in the South

I N 1863 Los Angeles County had about 205 grape vines for every man, woman, and child living within its borders. Over the next dozen years, both populations would increase, but grapes faster than people. So solid was the viticultural industry there that it was almost unaffected by the slump of the early 1860s. In fact the Los Angeles vineyardists and winemakers substantially alleviated for southern California the economic doldrums that beset the state when tens of thousands of cattle were lost in the great drought of 1863 and 1864. Not until the depression of the latter 1870s were the southern viticulturists even rocked.

The success of Kohler & Frohling was a strong factor, both in dollars and cents and in the encouragement it gave to others. And everyone believed the ringing words of orators north and south who extolled the future of California as the nation's, even the world's, wine land.

Stated a wine merchant, "The more wine we raise [sic] the more we will ship the greater will be our prosperity." A vineyardist added unequivocally that "we have land enough, of the very best quality for winemaking, to produce all the wine that can be consumed in the world for a century to come." And, although a speaker at the state fair of 1868 began, "It seems like repeating an old story to recapitulate the advantages of the soil and climate of California for the cultivation of the grape," he did so, and others continued to without pause.

In the city of Los Angeles, which in 1863 had a population of some four thousand, there were more than 1,000,000 vines. William Wolfskill had the most, 85,000. After him came grower-vintner Matthew Keller with 64,600.

"Don Mateo," as he was known, had a better claim than most to this soubriquet, for he spoke excellent Spanish, in contrast to the "pig" variety picked up by most Anglos. He was an Anglo only in a manner of speaking, for he was born in County Cork, in 1811. He went to Mexico as a young man and attended the University of Guadalajara, then moved north to Texas, and finally in 1849 was drawn to California. After unsuccessful adventures in the gold fields, he settled down in Los Angeles in 1851 and opened a general store. The next year he bought a vineyard adjacent to Wolfskill's, and there he built a home, a winery, and a distillery. He planted more vines, adding eleven varieties to the Missions growing there. He was characteristically open and informative about how he used the varieties. At the 1873 state fair, for instance, he entered white wines that he explained were made "principally from the Mission grape with admixture of two varieties of grapes from the Rhine, the Moscatelle and Orleans," and a sweet wine he named El Dorado "made from the Muscat Frontignan and the Deccan Superbe, half of each." He also entered port made from Tinta Francisca, Touriga and Mission; sherry from "Pedro Ximenes, Maccabeo Araganias," and Mission; and angelica from "Panse Musquie, the Muscat Noir de Jurd [sic: Jura?] and the Mission grape, equals of each, dessicated, and the juice concentrated."

Harris Newmark, the Los Angeles chronicler, characterized Keller as "a quaint personality of real ability." He was intelligent, quick to learn, and had an inquiring mind that probed beyond the practicalities of winemaking. He was articulate, too. It was he who wrote the description of Los Angeles grapes and wines for the 1858 agriculture report of the United States Patent Office. He was an inveterate writer of letters to newspapers on all kinds of subjects related to agriculture. He corresponded, in French, about the chemistry of wine with Louis Pasteur, whose revolutionary *Études sur les vins* was published in 1866. He also translated French wine reports into English for his fellow vintners. Altogether, he was a valuable man, and deservedly successful.

According to family tradition, he got tired of waiting for Leon V. Prudhomme, an assiduous buyer of merchandise, wine and brandy at Keller's store, to pay the fourteen-hundred-dollar bill he had racked up and took in exchange Prudhomme's shaky claim to a nearby 13,315-acre ranch. Keller managed to defend the land title successfully and ended as owner of the Malibu, the prized twenty-two-mile strip along Santa Monica Bay just north of Los Angeles.

Keller also added his pronouncement on the future of California viticulture. "Providence," he stated, "has given us the most extended wine country in the world, as if to complete our means of industry, wealth, and human happiness; and who so insensate as to place obstacles in its development?"

Another noted vineyard in the county, noted less for its size than its historic past and its hospitable *vigneron*, was the former Mission San Fernando of General Andrés Pico, a hero of the Mexican War. He was the brother of Pio Pico, the last governor of Mexican California, a more famous but not more colorful character. When Mission San Fernando was secularized, Andrés Pico was named its commissioner. He liked it so well that he leased it, then bought half interest in it, and settled down there. He rehabilitated one of the crumbling mission buildings to make himself a spacious bachelor's home where he entertained elaborately, singing Spanish songs for his guests, and staging bullfights in the plaza before the church. He maintained an adobe-walled vineyard of thirty thousand vines. In the main mission building were his winery and a cellar that, according to Colonel J. J. Warner, was filled "with that beverage which the gods, in the plentitude of their mercy, bestowed on man," and which Andrés Pico bestowed lavishly upon his guests.

In the San Gabriel Valley, where the Franciscan fathers had planted the largest and most productive vineyards of the entire mission chain, vine growing had a resurgence in the 1860s. Of the mission vines that gentle Father José María de Zalvidea had guarded, with such uncharacteristic ferocity that he was transferred to a less stressful post, few remained, and those merely "black stumps," according to Matthew Keller. But in 1854 Benjamin D. Wilson bought land to the north of the mission and by 1863 had a huge vineyard, the largest in Los Angeles County, a hundred thousand vines. He called it Lake Vineyard after a pastorally pretty small body of water on the property.

Wilson—"Don Benito," inevitably—was a native of Tennessee. Like William Wolfskill, he had paused for a few years on his westward trek to trade and trap in New Mexico. During Mexican California's stormy years, he participated in more military skirmishes than most Americans, winning a position as a leader. He was the second mayor of Los Angeles after statehood but is usually considered the first, his predecessor having been so obscure as to leave little trace, and he held many other positions, including that of Indian agent.

In Los Angeles he tried his hand at raising grapes before selling his home and ten-acre vineyard there at a charitable price to the Sisters of Charity—which is why the Sisters appear on all lists of vineyardists of the period. The ten thousand vines they tended helped support their school and orphanage.

Don Benito's Lake Vineyard home became as famous as General Pico's for its hospitality, which, although it was considerably more decorous, was yet not staid.

"There is no more agreeable place to visit in the southern part of California," wrote a traveler from San Francisco. "A comfortable house, a beautiful landscape, a fine garden and an excellent table contribute, with a large, playful, and pleasant family." He added, "Mr. Wilson makes his own wine, and all that I have tasted of it is excellent."

Wilson is credited with making the first champagne of record in California, although there is a legend that the San Gabriel mission fathers had attempted with some success to duplicate the feat of their Benedictine colleague, Dom Perignon. Several people who tasted Don Benito's sparkling wine in 1855 described it admiringly, but he did not continue making it. Probably, like the Sansevain brothers and other early experimenters with sparkling wine, he found it did not hold up long in the bottle.

Wilson aged his wines more than most California vintners of the 1860s. In 1864 he won prizes at the Mechanics' Institute Industrial Exhibition in San Francisco with 1860 white wine and port. Of the latter, the committee noted, "This wine is of such excellence, and so much superior to any exhibited of this kind of wine, that the committee were inclined to doubt whether it was entirely a California production."

It undoubtedly was California port, for Don Benito was a man of extremely honorable reputation (an actually honest Indian agent, ranger Horace Bell noted with astonishment). *Hyatt's Hand-Book of Grape Culture* of 1867 probably holds the explanation: "The California 'port' is 'poor' simply because the call for it is so great for medicinal purposes, that it has not yet been permitted to acquire age requisite for that class of wine to attain its proper qualities as a beverage of luxury."

Early in the 1860s Wilson began shipping wines to the Eastern states and San Francisco. By 1869 Bela Haraszthy, one of Agoston Haraszthy's sons, was winemaker at Lake Vineyard, and a warehouse had been established in San Francisco. It was apparently an independent agency owned by Carlton Curtis, a United States internal revenue inspector of cigars and tobacco, and James de Barth Shorb, a high-spirited Marylander who, soon after arriving in California, had married one of Wilson's three daughters, bought acreage next to Lake Vineyard, and set out vines of his own. Bright, capable, and active, he would in time become his father-in-law's partner, later merging their estates into one of the largest viticultural establishments in the state.

Wilson died in 1878. By then his vineyard and Shorb's, and that of their neighbor L. J. Rose, were leading an expansion that would make the San Gabriel Valley the major wine-growing area of southern California in the last decades of the century. Wilson's popular fame rests upon one of his earliest activities. As a young winemaker, he blazed a trail up a nearby peak to find wood to make barrel staves, so the mountain that dominates the San Gabriel Valley was named after him, Mount Wilson.

Anaheim, the German viticultural colony with an unusual beginning and a still more unusual end, accounted for about a fifth of the vines of Los Angeles County in 1863. It would contribute a still greater share in the 1870s as the city of Los Angeles gave over more and more of its vineyards to homes.

The idea for a cooperative colony of German immigrant vineyardists was born in 1855, not long after the firm of Kohler & Frohling was started. Its partners had been active in San Francisco's German community, and Charles Kohler continued so after John Frohling moved to Los Angeles. Clearly they were interested not only in helping their compatriots but also in developing a source of supply for grapes. They discussed the matter with Otto Weyse, the editor of the San Francisco German-language newspaper, and George Hansen, the leading surveyor in Los Angeles County. Their plan was to locate a favorable vineyard site and organize a society of fifty equal shareholders to settle on it.

Hansen, vigorous and enthusiastic, scouted

out a tract of 1,165 acres some twenty-six miles southeast of Los Angeles. It was in Los Angeles County then; not until 1889 would Orange County be formed. The tract was a sloping sandy plain that looked like desert land to the first settlers. But Hansen had surveyed in the area earlier and knew of a flourishing little garden carved out of similar land nearby by Don Antonio Yorba. One of his earliest supporters was Yorba's son-in-law, German-born August Langenberger, who became the first to sign the articles incorporating what they named the Los Angeles Vineyard Society. Hansen was instructed to start development of the land, which he did immediately, completing it by the end of 1859 when the first settlers began arriving from San Francisco.

He laid out the colony in a square with fifty 20-acre lots and fifty home sites around a central park, school, and business area. It was not a utopian community, for it was commercial in intent, but it partook of utopian idealism. For instance, no provision was made for churches, as the colonists were of various faiths and they decided to avoid possible causes of factionalism.

Hansen brought water in from the Santa Ana River, laid out a system of ditches, planted a thick willow fence on all four sides of the tract to keep the neighboring cattle out, and put eight thousand Mission vines on each lot. Everything was ready for the settlers to come and build their homes. However, he had gone ahead too intently—so intently that one day a sheriff had to go out and bring him in to testify in a land case that he had forgotten; so intently that he had neglected to tell the shareholders what he was doing while he was spending their money developing their land.

Even before he was finished, the future colonists held a meeting in San Francisco and decided to oust him and turn the colony into not a cooperative but a community of individually owned lands. This it became, but since most of the settlers were sturdy immigrants who anticipated working hard to develop their homes and property, it was a successful community.

Few of the settlers had any experience in agriculture, and only one knew anything first-hand about winemaking, but they set to. At first Kohler & Frohling took most of their grapes, but gradually the settlers planted more vines and developed wine- and brandy-making facilities in the community. They sent wine to San Francisco and the East: hock, claret, port, sparkling angelica, champagne, and "Santa Ana," described as a "white sweet wine" similar to the Italian Lacryma Christi. That many of the wines were poor was undoubtedly due to the predominance of Mission grapes; few others were planted. Nevertheless, Anaheim poured many gallons onto the market, one and a quarter million in 1884.

Early that year something began killing the vines in the southwestern part of the community. Three years later all of them were gone. Anaheim lived on, later devoting itself successfully to orange culture, still later to Disneyland. But viticulture at Anaheim was gone, killed by what came to be known as "the Anaheim disease." Only in recent years have its bacterial cause and probable carrier been discovered, leading to a method of prevention that appears not far off. But it is too late for Anaheim's vineyards. They are now covered by homes and other city buildings.

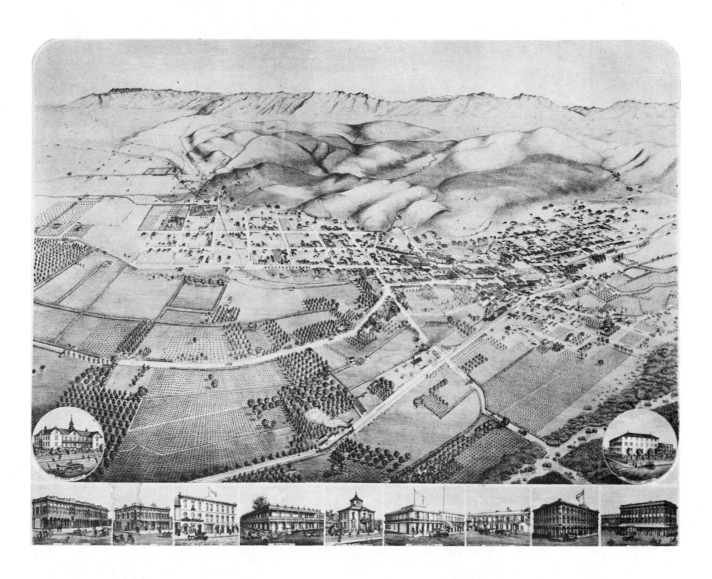

Los Angeles was still a city of vines in 1871, the date of this lithograph. At the bottom, near the center, a train moves along the track on the Alameda, the broad road through the heart of the city's vine-growing area.

The Los Angeles District.

Although Don Mateo Keller did not put on a cheerful expression when he was photographed here with his family, he wrote in an 1866 letter to a newspaper on the subject of California wines: "As a means of restoring cheerfulness when the body and mind have been exhausted or worn out by age or over-exertion, as a means of correction and equalization where disproportionate food has caused irregularities in the human organism, or as a protection against casual derangements produced by inorganic substances, wine is not surpassed by any production of nature or art."

Matthew Keller's bucolic-looking distillery stood, with his house and winery, near Alameda Street on part of the site now occupied by the Los Angeles Union Depot. The workings of the still, with its swan-neck tubes, are visible at the base of the tall chimney, atop the furnace that supplied the heat to vaporize the liquid, in this faded photograph given by the Keller family to the Huntington Library.

It was undoubtedly this still with which Keller was producing brandy he described in 1873 as made "in a plain copper still, heated by steam, distilled and rectified, without any addition of flavoring stuff whatever except a little concentrated grape juice, to give the necessary color." The grapes he used were two varieties from the Cognac district of France, grown in his Rising Sun vineyard, "La Folle Blanc" and "La Folle Noire."

The well-preserved dandy at the right is General Andrés Pico of San Fernando, described by historian Hubert Howe Bancroft as "a brave, reckless, coarse-grained, jovial, kind-hearted, popular man; abler in several respects than his brother Don Pio but not over-burdened with principle." Shaking his finger at the general is another man not noted for an over-supply of principle, Salvador Vallejo. The subject under discussion may have been vine growing, in which both had experience. Less involved was the gentleman at the left, courtly Pablo de la Guerra. A highly respected citizen, whose probity was never questioned, he nevertheless had a notable interest in brandy and cards that might have drawn him into the conversation.

In 1860 Don Benito Wilson had a hundred thousand vines at his Lake Vineyard, the largest planting in Los Angeles County, but most of them were young. In 1864, however, he made 140,000 gallons of wine, more than came from any other individual vineyard. His estate stood in what is now the residential city of San Marino, and his brandy distillery was on the site of the present Huntington Library and Art Gallery.

When construction was started on Benjamin Dreyfus' big winery at Anaheim, its vineyards were flourishing as never before, untouched by the phylloxera that was devastating vines in other parts of California. By the time the building was completed in 1885, however, "the Anaheim disease" had killed nearly half the vines, and in two years more the rest were gone.

"The Anaheim disease," which wiped out the communty's vines within a period of four years, was renamed "Pierce's disease," ironically enough after a blameless United States Department of Agriculture plant pathologist, Newton B. Pierce, who studied it in the hope of finding a means of controlling it. The light areas in these leaves represent the yellow withering that was characteristic of the blight.

9. Sonoma County

THE decade of the 1870s saw, for the first time, more grapes and wine produced in Northern California than in the southern part of the state. The shift had begun in the 1860s. Sonoma and Napa counties contributed most to production in the north, but the western foothills of the Sierra Nevada, the gold mining country, had many vineyards in addition to the Natoma. The most famous was that of James Marshall, who had found the gold that set off the gold rush and settled down where he had found it, at Coloma, to grow vines. Later arriving gold-hunters too stayed close, many continuing to seek bonanzas with part of their time, and grow grapes and other crops with the rest. In the late '60s and early '70s they contributed many gallons of wine to the state's growing total.

The Santa Clara Valley, while less significant statistically, continued making highly important contributions to the state's winegrowing progress through its experimental vineyards and wineries.

It was Sonoma County, however, that dominated, taking the lead in wine production over Los Angeles and all other counties of the state in 1874. That was labeled "an exceptional year" in Sonoma by a contemporary observer, but 1875 proved even more bountiful there, as indeed it was throughout the state.

The same observer gave a lyrical description of the results of this bounty. "Many of the abodes about Sonoma seem to be the abodes of pleasure and comfort," he wrote. "The dwellings are smothered with vines, shrubs, and flowering trees, a fountain sparkles in the yard, gaudy flowers enliven the scene and perfume the air, long and wide avenues lined with fruit trees separate the vineyards from one another, the whole presenting a picture of elegant comfort, the owner of which is to be envied."

Such owners had come from many places, drawn to California for many reasons but to Sonoma County mainly by the viticultural tradition established by Mariano G. Vallejo and Agoston Haraszthy.

Jacob Rink Snyder was one of the earliest, best known, and most popular, an "Old Californian" as reckoning went in this new land. Born in Pennsylvania, he had come west with an overland immigrant party, arriving at Sutter's Fort in 1845. He earned the title of major in Fremont's California Batallion, served in the 1850 state constitutional convention with General

Vallejo and at the San Francisco mint with Colonel Haraszthy, and in middle age decided to settle down near them and spend the rest of his life growing grapes and making wine. His approach was experimental and somewhat scientific, and he was generous with his findings. The visiting committee of the State Agricultural Society called upon him in 1872 and reported:

> The Major is wide awake to whatever may benefit this great industry, to whatever may improve our wines and introduce them into general use instead of the alcoholic and poisonous mixtures heretofore so extensively imported to this country. He is now engaged in testing the wines of the different vineyards in Sonoma County, to ascertain their percentage of alcohol. His cellar contains from 35,000 to 40,000 gallons of wine.

Snyder had named his estate El Cerrito—"the little hill"—and his fine home sat upon it overlooking the Sonoma Valley. There he offered overnight lodging to the visiting committee members, and the next morning he took them on a tour of neighboring establishments. The first was Buena Vista, no longer as hospitable as in Haraszthy's time, but hospitable enough to offer the visitors several glasses of its sparkling wine. That reminded Major Snyder of an anecdote (which the committee appreciatively recorded) about the yokel who, having downed a glass of champagne, remarked, "This is the best way to eat grapes I ever knew, you get so many grapes in so small a compass."

Under Snyder's aegis the committee visited three more Sonoma vineyardists. Oliver W. Craig had well-established plantings and was making notable white wines, among them hock, which he described when he entered it in the 1873 state fair. Its grapes were imported varieties, principally Riesling, Muscatel, and "Tramina"—undoubtedly Traminer. It was clarified with isinglass, bottled, and then sent on a round trip to China for mellowing. Leonard Goss had made his first wine only two years earlier, and was not destined to become widely known. William McPherson Hill, on the other hand, achieved some fame. In 1852 he set out an experimental orchard and some of the county's earliest imported varieties: Rose of Peru, Italia, "Chasselas," and Black Hamburg.

By 1872 he had seventy-five acres in vines, most of them European, and a successful winery. He particularly prized the Zinfandel, the visiting committee reported; many of his contemporaries were coming to believe that this variety would give California a wine to compete with Bordeaux.

The five vineyards the committee members visited formed a typical cross-section of the county's viticultural industry. Most of its members had small holdings. About half were vineyardists who sold their grapes for table grapes or turned them over to others to be made into wine.

Isaac De Turk was the most prominent of the grower-winemakers, and after Buena Vista collapsed his establishment was the largest. Born in Kentucky, of French heritage, De Turk grew up on an Indiana farm where he helped his father make wine. He came to California in 1859 and, after traveling around looking for a place to settle, chose Bennett Valley near Santa Rosa in Sonoma County. A neighbor raised Mission grapes, and De Turk, learning that wine was selling for the rewarding sum of $1.50 a gallon, suggested that the neighbor make some. The neighbor suggested in turn that De Turk do so, and he did. He rigged up a press and the first year made about a hundred and sixty gallons of white wine from the Missions. It sold easily at the nearby town of Petaluma. The next year he made red, "I using my arm to stir up the wine while fermenting. The crushing was done in an improvised crusher of my own, worked by a crank with one hand while the grapes were fed with the other." This wine was sent to a fair at Sonoma presided over by Haraszthy and Vallejo, and "the excellence of that old Mission claret," he recalled, "was remarked by everyone present. It wasn't long until I had a vineyard of my own in Bennett Valley, and was soon embarked in the business for life."

It became a major business. His winery and distillery finally filled an entire city block in Santa Rosa, and spilled across the street where he had a cooper's shop. In contrast to his first improvised equipment, there were in the 1880s two crushers and stemmers "fed by tramway trucks running up from the scales" that weighed the grapes as they entered the winery, and much other advanced equipment.

His own vineyard progressed from Mission to Zinfandel and French varieties.

A reserved but amiable bachelor, De Turk had two major interests in addition to his winery. One was the state's wine industry as a whole; he was a constructive member of the Board of State Viticultural Commissioners. The other was his stable of race horses. His trotting stallion, Silas Skinner, gained at least temporary fame by covering a mile in two minutes and twenty-nine seconds. De Turk died in 1896, but his stable manager carried the winery on into the early 1900s.

Germans were prominent among California's late-nineteenth-century winegrowers and wine merchants. Two, Jacob Gundlach from Bavaria and Emil Dresel from the Rheingau, planted a vineyard on hilly land near their friend Haraszthy's about 1858 and started an enterprise even longer-lived than De Turk's. And, since several generations of several families were involved, considerably more complex in structure.

In a winery they built on the property they called Rhinefarm, they made wines patterned after Germany's Rhine wines that gained much acclaim.

Emil Dresel had had an interesting career before he became a vineyardist. Educated as an architect, he practiced that profession in Germany before coming to the United States. In California in the early 1850s he traveled about and sketched many scenes, which were the basis for a famous series of lithographs published by the firm of which he was a partner, Kuchel & Dresel. It was probably his sketches, for instance, from which the 1857 lithograph of Los Angeles with its wineries was made, and perhaps there he first became interested in California winemaking.

Emil died in 1869, but his brother Julius Dresel took his place in the firm of J. Gundlach & Co. for a time, after which the property was divided and the Gundlach and Dresel holdings each operated independently with its own winery. Dresel's continued until Prohibition under his son Carl. Meanwhile, Charles Bundschu came from Germany, worked for Jacob Gundlach, became a partner in the firm, and married the boss's daughter. After Gundlach's death in 1894, the firm became Gundlach-Bundschu, and many years after that the Dresel property was sold to a member of the Bundschu family. Today other Bundschu descendants are making wine in a building they reconstructed around the remaining walls of the old Rhinefarm winery of 1858.

The most exotic of Sonoma County's winegrowing establishments of the 1870s was the utopian colony of the Brotherhood of the New Life, which in fact gained fame as the producer of very good wines. In 1875 Thomas Lake Harris, whose complex philosophical tenets were based principally upon a combination of Swedenborgianism and certain concepts of spiritualism, brought members of his group to Santa Rosa and set about developing the estate he called Fountain Grove. The keys to its viticultural success were John S. Hyde, an experienced grape grower and winemaker from Missouri, and Kanaye Nagasawa, an intelligent young Japanese who was a student in Scotland when he met Harris and became a sort of adopted son. Together Hyde and Nagasawa planted a vineyard and set about making wine. Harris left in 1892, hounded out of the colony by a woman named Alzire Chevaillier who voiced loud and long accusations against his moral character. (She had once found him sitting with his feet in the lap of his secretary, for instance.) Nagasawa carried on and upon Harris' death in 1906 inherited the property and continued with even greater success. Prohibition put an end to his winemaking. His death in 1934 put an end to his plan to reopen the winery. In time it was bought by a wealthy mining man who put it in the hands of competent viticulturists and started it on its way to renewing its prestige. Then he too died, and the enterprise declined. Today it awaits another reawakening.

The Korbel brothers were among the earliest important vineyardists and winemakers in the northern part of Sonoma County. Not until the mid-1880s would the Russian River area emerge to fulfill the 1857 State Agricultural Society visiting committee's prediction and become the significant winegrowing region it has remained ever since.

De Turk's Santa Rosa winery had a capacity of one million gallons by 1888—second only to Leland Stanford's at Vina in the Sacramento Valley. De Turk aged his wines carefully and sent rail cars of them to Chicago, St. Louis, and New York, as well as San Francisco. He bottled his wines, and he was an advocate of winemakers' selling their wines in bottles rather than casks, thus avoiding the adulteration by wine merchants that was all too common, and allowing each wine to carry its maker's label proudly.

Jacob Gundlach was the son of a Bavarian who combined hotel keeping and winegrowing, but when he arrived in San Francisco in 1850 he became a brewer. With a German partner he established the nostalgically named Bavarian Brewery, which continued into the 1870s. Meanwhile Gundlach and another compatriot, Emil Dresel, had established another nostalgically named enterprise, the Sonoma Valley vineyard and winery they called Rhinefarm.

Joshua Chauvet bought this property near Glen Ellen from General Vallejo in the early 1850s and operated a sawmill and a flour mill. He planted vines and in the 1870s began making wine. In 1881 he built this fine three-story winery and ran his crusher and presses with the same water power that ran his mills.

The Fountain Grove winery, shown here as it looked in the early 1900s, was built in 1882. It made into wine the grapes grown on the estate's four hundred acres of carefully chosen vines, which included Cabernet Sauvignon, Riesling, and Zinfandel.

Kanaye Nagasawa, who smoked cigars incessantly and spoke English with a Scottish accent, was the first but not the last prominent California viticulturist of Japanese ancestry. It was through his direction that Fountain Grove wines gained high prestige. A botanist of broad interests and a friend of Luther Burbank of nearby Santa Rosa, he posed for this photograph in a greenhouse at Fountain Grove.

The first plantings at Ten Oaks Vineyard near Glen Ellen were made by a physician, Dr. J. B. Warfield, in 1859 and were added to steadily. In 1874 he made thirty thousand gallons of wine and in 1876 more than two hundred thousand—which surely included some from grapes of surrounding vineyards. But it was after Dr. Warfield's death in 1878 that Ten Oaks became most famous, for his widow carried the business forward in the tradition of Doña María de Carrillo of nearby Rancho Cabeza de Santa Rosa. Frona Eunice Wait, visiting Ten Oaks in the late 1880s, dubbed her "a woman of rare pluck and energy," and quoted a newspaper characterization: "Mrs. Kate F. Warfield is one of those energetic American ladies who is ready to take her chances with the male vineyardist, and is able to hold her own with the best. The beautiful vineyard, Ten Oaks, Glen Ellen, is 200 acres in extent, and eighty acres are now in the finest class of vines grown in the state. . . . Mrs. Warfield struck out for herself and grafted on the old stock the choicest French varieties. . . . At the Louisville Exposition in 1884 this lady carried off the first prize for Riesling wines, and four years ago [1883] the first premium for brandy was awarded her at the State Fair, to the great discomfiture of many competitors, who insisted upon a second test being made which resulted in a confirmation of the original decision." Lest Mrs. Warfield be thought to be unladylike, it was also pointed out that her home was decorated with "bits of art needlework," that she owned "a score of pretty gowns made according to the mode," and that her wine cellar contained oak barrels with "nickel-plated hoops and lavendar-colored ends with lettering in gold."

The three Korbel brothers, Josef, Anton, and Francis, arrived in San Francisco from Bohemia in the early 1860s and became cigar makers, cigar-box makers, lithographers, and publishers of the famous illustrated satirical weekly *The Wasp*. They bought a redwood timber tract in northern Sonoma County to feed their cigar-box factory; then, after the trees were logged off, asked a scientist at the University of California what to do with the land. Apprised that it would be good for grape growing, they planted vines among the redwood stumps, as this 1890 wintertime view of the vineyard and winery shows. They started making wine in the early 1880s, and their champagne became famous. The Korbel family continued operating the winery until 1954, when they sold it to German-trained champagne maker Adolph Heck and his family, the present owners.

10. Napa County

NAPA County's viticulture began as a direct descendant of Sonoma's when George Yount crossed the western Mayacamas range separating the two parallel valleys and set out cuttings from General Vallejo's Mission vines. Then for more than two decades it slumbered, progressing little, until Charles Krug made the same crossing. Krug brought with him the ideas and ideals of Agoston Haraszthy, and he sparked the Napa Valley's dramatic ascent to pre-eminence in both quantity and, to many palates, quality. It was at first a slow ascent, but between 1870 and 1880 wine production increased nearly ten-fold. By the end of that decade Napa was producing about half as many gallons as the state's leader, Sonoma, and almost as many as second-place Los Angeles County. A decade after that it led them all.

At the Charles Krug winery today there is a small cider press that is one of the California wine industry's historic relics. It is the press that the thirty-three-year-old German immigrant, born Karl Krug, borrowed from Haraszthy to make wine for one John M. Patchett near Napa City in 1858. It is an unremarkable little machine that may or may not be the first European-style press used in the county. Its importance lies in its association with two of the men who contributed most to the state's viticultural progress, and in its part in carrying that progress to the Napa Valley.

Krug had come to the United States as a young man, taught school in Philadelphia, returned to Germany to fight against a reactionary government, and had come back in 1852. From Philadelphia he was called to San Francisco to become editor of its first German newspaper; then, restless, decided to try his hand at agriculture. He took up land south of San Francisco, and there he found as a neighboring tiller of the soil a Hungarian named Agoston Haraszthy. Eight months later he gave up his farm and joined Haraszthy first as an employee of the San Francisco mint, then as a partner in a metallurgy firm, and finally as a vineyardist in Sonoma County. In 1858 he bought land there, and he must have been a fast learner, for that same year he borrowed the small press Haraszthy himself was using that vintage season and carried it across the mountains to make twelve hundred gallons of wine from Patchett's grapes. When in 1888 he reminisced about that first crush, his own winery near St. Helena was making several hundred thousand gallons of wine yearly from his and others' grapes.

In 1860 Krug moved to the Napa Valley, there to remain for the rest of his constructive but not always easy life. The move was probably made as the result of his having met Miss Caroline Bale, a great-niece of General Vallejo and a daughter of Dr. Edward Bale, who had made wine from grapes grown on his Rancho Carne Humana before the gold rush. That autumn Krug made wine for his brother-in-law-to-be, Louis Bruck, and on shares for old George Yount. In December he married Miss Bale, and the next spring he began planting vines on her dowry, part of the Carne Humana.

He built a winery, and in time he became the Napa Valley's most prominent viticulturist, a leader in local and statewide viticultural organizations. He was a kindly, well-liked man, and intelligent. But also frequently unfortunate. His winery was severely damaged by fire in 1874, his vineyards by phylloxera in the 1880s, and once he was forced to file a petition in bankruptcy, due, it was reported, to "the endorsement of notes for friends." He was still in debt at the time of his death in 1892. Nevertheless, neither his wine nor his reputation ever suffered. A later industry leader, John Daniel, Jr., of Inglenook, summed up an important period in the development of viticulture in the Napa Valley, dating as its beginning the year Krug planted his first vines there:

> In 1861, with the coming of Charles Krug to the Napa Valley and the planting of *Vitis vinifera* varieties by him and Dr. George Crane, a most important step in establishing winegrowing commercially was taken. In the next thirty years Krug was the outstanding force in Napa Valley wines, not only because of his own operations but also because of the leadership which he provided for others and the training which key industry figures such as Carl Wente, founder of Wente Brothers, Clarence Wetmore,* founder of Cresta Blanca, the greatest name in pre-Prohibition wines, and Jacob Beringer, one of the founders of Beringer Brothers, all received when working for Krug.

George Crane was a physician who chose St. Helena as a healthful place for his wife to live and moved there in 1857. He continued the practice of medicine, but John Patchett's vineyard caught his attention, and after 1858,

when he planted his first vines, his interest went increasingly to grapes and wine. Following an initial planting of Missions, he became converted to the idea of imported varieties and in 1859 bought some from Agoston Haraszthy and some from Frank Stock, who grew German vines in San Jose. Among the latter were the Napa Valley's earliest Rieslings. He had finally a hundred acres of almost all European varieties, a good-sized cellar, and a distillery. He was apparently a generous man, as Napa winemakers were inclined to be. In 1878 he bankrolled an experiment by a Portuguese immigrant, John Ramos, who had learned how sweet wine was made by the *estufa* or heating process on the island of Madeira. With Crane's money Ramos built a twenty-six-thousand-gallon heater with which he turned wine furnished on credit by the doctor into what was probably California's first baked sherry. Most California sherry since has been made by the baking process.

An even more adventuresome vineyardist was Hamilton Walker Crabb, an Ohioan who came to the Napa Valley in 1865 and, although close to middle age, began planting vines with youthful single-mindedness. He had a passionate interest in experimenting with different varieties, and he bought all he could lay his hands on, frequently ordering them directly from Europe. A decade after he began he had nearly two hundred varieties, by the 1880s some four hundred. It was said that after the phylloxera hit the vines in the Luxembourg Gardens in Paris and before it hit those of Mr. Crabb in the Napa Valley, he had the largest collection of *Vitis vinifera* varieties in the world.

The collection was not just for show. Crabb sold a tremendous number of cuttings to many other growers, enriching California's vineyards. And in his large winery he experimented with wines made from different grapes. Most famous was his Burgundy, described as a brilliant ruby-colored wine of considerable flavor. It was a varietal wine made from the grape known as Crabb's Black Burgundy. Its original name and source had become lost long before phylloxera hit his vineyard, and he did not perpetuate the vine itself. Others did, however, and after Prohibition was repealed and University of California viticulturists began re-examining successful earlier varieties, they investi-

---

*Charles Wetmore founded Cresta Blanca, but Clarence Wetmore carried it on to its greatest prominence.

gated Crabb's Black Burgundy. They found it to be an Italian grape common in the Venice region, Refosco. One might assume that Crabb had imported it from Italy, but later research revealed it to be also the same grape as the Mondeuse of the Savoie region of France. Whatever Crabb's source, it is still available, one of California's useful European imports.

A small, spare man who did not believe much in show, Crabb shared two convictions with De Turk of Santa Rosa: that California wines should at best be sold in bottles bearing the vintagers' label, and that horses are man's best friends. "His one great weakness was horses," wrote a contemporary, "and these he loves with all the warmth of a horseman's heart." He maintained a fine stable and a three-quarter-mile track on his Oakville property.

Of Crabb's winery, writer Frona Eunice Wait noted, "Everything is scrupulously clean, and the storage capacity is immense, but the exact number of gallons could not be ascertained, as the owner has a wholesome dread of the Assessor." The statement suggests an answer to the question, Why are California's nineteenth-century wine statistics so incomplete and inconsistent? Answer: They were compiled from the records of assessors whose sources were not always complete and consistent. Crabb's gallonage for 1880 is known, however. It was three hundred thousand gallons, just twenty thousand more than that of his nearest competitor, Charles Krug.

Jacob Schram was made famous by another writer, Robert Louis Stevenson, but his wines themselves warranted fame. Schram was born in the Rheingau, like Emil Dresel, but while Dresel's first profession was architecture, Schram's was barbering. After operating the grandly named Metropolitan Theatre Tonsorial Parlor in San Francisco, he bought hillside land at the northern end of the Napa Valley in the Calistoga area in 1862, imported Rhine wine varieties and oval tanks, and made wines, especially white wines, that were much praised. The Scotsman Stevenson and his bride, Fanny, visited Schram in 1880, and he wrote a delightful description in *The Silverado Squatters:*

> A California vineyard, one of man's outposts in the wilderness, has features of its own. There is nothing here to remind you of the Rhine or Rhone,

of the low *côte d'or,* or the infamous and scabby deserts of Champagne; but all is green, solitary, covert. We visited two of them, Mr. Schram's and Mr. M'Eckron's sharing the same glen. . . .

> Mr. M'Eckron's [Colin T. McEachron's] is a bachelor establishment . . . but recently begun. . . . Mr. Schram's, on the other hand, is the oldest vineyard in the valley, 18 years old, I think; yet he began as a penniless barber, and even after he had broken ground up here with his black malvoisies, continued for long to tramp the valley with his razor. Now, his place is the picture of prosperity: stuffed birds in the veranda, cellars far dug into the hillside, and resting on pillars like a bandit's cave; all trimness, varnish, flowers, and sunshine, among the tangled wildwood. Stout, smiling Mrs. Schram, who has been to Europe and apparently all about the States for pleasure, entertained Fanny in the veranda, while I was tasting wines in the cellar. To Mr. Schram this was a solemn office; his serious gusto warmed my heart; prosperity had not yet wholly banished a certain neophite and girlish trepidation, and he followed every sip and read my face with proud anxiety. I tasted all. I tasted every variety and shade of Schramberger, red and white Schramberger, Burgundy Schramberger, Schramberger Hock, Schramberger Golden Chasselas, the latter with a notable bouquet, and I fear to think how many more.

Schramsberger with an *s* was the usual spelling, and Schramsberger wine continued being made until Prohibition. After Repeal, several attempts were made to revive its fame, and finally "Schramsberg" champagne achieved the distinction of traveling to China in 1972 for President Nixon's historic visit. It was not, like Oliver W. Craig's hock, sent on a round trip to be mellowed. It was consumed in Peking before television cameras at a great state banquet.

While Jacob Schram's vineyard was hardly the oldest in the Napa Valley, as Stevenson indicated, it could have been the oldest at that time in the Calistoga area, for Sam Brannan's was no longer in operation. Samuel Brannan, the go-getting Mormon pioneer, had bought land there in 1859 and planted an extensive vineyard from which he began making wine a few years later. The place was named Agua Caliente for its hot springs. Determined to make it a fashionable spa, Brannan renamed it "Calistoga." His intention was that it should be called Saratoga of California, but the story is that he had imbibed too much of someone's good wine before he arose at a banquet to announce it, and ended with the portmanteau word, which lasted. His vineyard and winery did not, however; they were gone by the time of Stevenson's visit.

Jacob Beringer was one of the few Napa viticulturists who brought a knowledge of wine with him to the valley. He had had experience first in Germany, then France, then in New York where he and his brother Frederick emigrated in the early 1860s. In 1869, with plans clearly in mind, Jacob climbed aboard a train and traveled to California via the newly completed transcontinental tracks. In Napa he went to work for his countryman Charles Krug, who made him winery foreman. He saved his wages, and in 1875 he bought land near St. Helena from William Daegener, who had retired as Wells Fargo agent in the mother lode town of Columbia and brought his family to the Napa Valley to live. Probably Daegener had intended to join his friend and neighbor John Weinberger in vineyard enterprises, but late in 1874 he was thrown from his buggy and rendered stone deaf. The family moved to San Francisco, selling 160 acres to Jacob Beringer.

There, while continuing to work for Krug, Beringer cleared land, planted vines, and, in partnership with his brother who remained in New York, added more acreage. He supervised the digging of caves and the construction of a large winery. In 1877 he stopped working for Krug, who characteristically joined in the dedication celebration of the new building and placed a twenty-dollar gold piece among the mementos in the cornerstone.

In 1884 Frederick Beringer finally joined Jacob at their vineyards, which they called Los Hermanos, "The Brothers." There he built a home rivaling in fantasy an earlier Napa County residence built by Joseph W. Osborne, whose vineyard the Beringers were later to lease. Osborne's house was described as "English Elizabethan style, applied to a Swiss suburban villa, surrounded by East Indian verandas and topped out by a touch of the Burmese pagoda, covered with a China-built roof." Beringer's, less eclectic, was patterned after his home in Mainz. It remains today a remarkable example of nineteenth-century German gothic architecture.

The Beringer family continued to operate the winery through Prohibition, when it made sacramental wines, and for many years after Repeal. Not until 1971 did it relinquish control. Now the winery is operated by the Nestlé Company of Switzerland, and the vineyard is owned by a French family.

Another winery that remained long in the same family was that established by a sea captain and businessman, tall, handsome, rumpled Gustave Niebaum. Born in Finland, he had been an Alaska trader before joining two German San Franciscans in the Alaska Commercial Company, which finagled exclusive rights to take fur seals in the Pribilof Islands. It was an extremely profitable concession during the twenty years it lasted, and midway, in 1879, Captain Niebaum bought land in the Napa Valley where one William C. Watson had earlier established a small vineyard and a sanatorium. Part of it lay within George Yount's Rancho Caymus. Niebaum, who knew several languages and had apparently nothing against Scottish dialect, let stand Watson's curious name for the property, Inglenook, meaning "cozy chimney corner."

He traveled widely for his company, and in Europe he visited vineyards and began collecting books on grapes and wines in several languages. Later he bought more on standing orders with a Frankfurt bookseller until he had one of the notable nineteenth-century wine libraries in America. When not traveling he visited his San Francisco office only as often as necessary, preferring instead to oversee the ordering and planting of carefully selected vines, the construction of a pilot-plant-sized wine cellar and then a very large one, and frequent white-glove inspections of it when it was completed and in operation. He hired competent managers of which he demanded much. They produced wines that were widely sold outside of California and accorded numerous honors. But if the venture was successful financially Niebaum did not admit it, saying only that his profits lay in the wines he gave his friends. His death in 1908 did not close the winery, but Prohibition did. When it was repealed, however, Carl Bundschu (son of Charles), who was, as he put it, "born in a wine barrel," and educated at the University of California under its first specialist in viticul-

Hamilton W. Crabb, a plain man, gave his estate unexpectedly poetic names: Hermosa, Spanish for "beautiful," and the similar To Kalon. As he explained to writer Frona Eunice Wait, when she visited him in the late 1880s, "The name *To Kalon* is Greek and means the highest beauty, or the highest good, but I try to make it mean the boss vineyard."

The winery building itself, the large structure to the left of the smoke-stacked still house, was "plain and unpretentious," wrote Miss Wait. "In fact, Mr. Crabb is one of the few men who do not believe that fine outsides to a cellar make fine wine." Inside, "the machinery and appliances of To Kalon are of the most approved patterns."

This small press, once owned by Agoston Haraszthy and used by Charles Krug in 1858 to make his first Napa Valley wine, is still on display at the winery near St. Helena that bears Krug's name. In 1888 he reminisced about it: "The grapes were crushed and pressed with a little so-called cider press, which Colonel Agoston Haraszthy, of Sonoma, allowed me to use in Napa, after he had crushed at the Buena Vista Vineyard that portion of the grapes which ripened early and were grown on strong soil. When through with my little vintage work in Napa, the Colonel finished with this returned machine the balance of his crop of grapes. The old pioneer press was about twenty years afterwards presented to me by the then liquidating Buena Vista Vineyard Company. I consider it a valuable ornament of my cellar at present."

Jacob and Anna Schram were here seated, in all probability, upon the same veranda where Anna entertained Fanny Osbourne Stevenson while Robert Louis Stevenson tested wines with Jacob in the cellar below.

The elaborate stone and half-timbered home that Frederick Beringer built in imitation of his family home in Germany was and still remains a showplace of the Napa Valley. It stands in front of the old winery with its deep tunnels, dug into the hillside by Chinese laborers brought to this country originally to dig through the Sierra Nevada range the right-of-way for the transcontinental railroad.

Frederick Beringer was a friend of Grover Cleveland and a strong supporter in his two presidential elections. This photograph, taken at Niagara Falls in the late 1880s, shows the then president sitting at the rear, while Beringer, looking sideways, carefully holds the edge of his top hat.

90

The splendid ivy-covered brick winery building that Niebaum built to produce his Inglenook wines is maintained today as a visitors' center with a small wine museum.

Captain Gustave Niebaum, the handsome Finnish *vigneron* of Inglenook.

Professor George Husmann, the bearded man at the right in this photograph taken at the Talcoa Vineyard in the Napa Valley, was a leading authority on American grapes when, in 1881, he decided to abandon a successful academic career at the University of Missouri in favor of winegrowing in California. He became manager of the Talcoa estate and there not only made distinguished wines but carried out experiments with phylloxera-resistant vines and techniques for grafting wine varieties onto their roots that were of significant value to the state's grape growers. There he also wrote articles on viticulture and revised and amplified his book *American Grape Growing and Wine Making*. That was in 1883 and he had by then become a true Californian, declaring that "We have the finest climate in the world . . . we can raise grapes and make wine cheaper than any other nation or climate . . . we can satisfy every taste." Four years later, at his own Oak Glen Vineyard in the eastern hills of the Napa Valley, he wrote *Grape Culture and Wine Making in California*. Published in San Francisco the next year, it was for many years the pre-eminent practical guide for the state's winegrowers.

Gottlieb Groezinger was a San Francisco commission merchant from the early 1850s until 1866, when his longstanding interest in wine impelled him to open a wine store, and then in 1870 to buy eight hundred acres at Yountville. He turned a small vineyard into a large one, built a big brick winery, which still stands, and was soon an important wine and brandy maker.

This lithograph, produced to advertise the enterprise, was made by F. Korbel & Bros., the northern Sonoma County winery owners.

11. The Phylloxera and the Viticultural Commissioners

O N the 19th of August, 1873, an insect was found on the roots of grape vines by H. Appleton and O. W. Craig, in the vineyard of the latter, situated two miles north from Sonoma town, on the west side of Sonoma creek.

Thus flatly did H. Appleton, who had peered at the insect through his microscope, report the discovery of the phylloxera in California. This was the incident that triggered the opening shot in the two-decade war to control the scourge.

Up to that time, most California vineyardists had ignored the possibility that the root louse that was ravaging the vineyards of Europe could ever come to the Pacific slope. They in fact rather cheerfully anticipated that as European vineyards were destroyed and wine production declined, American wines could rush into the vacuum.

Such was the state of ignorance among California viticulturists that few knew that the *Phylloxera vastatrix* existed harmlessly in Eastern American vineyards and had been carried from them to Europe. Fewer still suspected even dimly that the cause of the decline of certain vines in their vineyards might be the phylloxera, brought from either source. In the Sonoma Valley, however, where the first insect was identified, there was concern if not alarm—and action.

Oliver W. Craig, on whose twenty-four-year-old vineyard the bug had been discovered, did not long retain the distinction of being its sole known possessor. Four days after the discovery, he and Appleton brought damaged roots to the meeting of the Sonoma Viticultural Club, along with Mr. Appleton's suspicions about what had damaged them. The minutes of that meeting, dated "Club Room, August 23rd, 1873," begin:

"Mr. A. F. Haraszthy stated that within the last few days an insect, supposed to be the phylloxera vastatrix, had been found upon the roots of vines in Sonoma Valley. That he had known of vines manifesting every symptom of the disease, as described, for many years in Sonoma Valley." This was Attila Haraszthy, the second of Agoston Haraszthy's four sons, the one who helped him move his vines from Crystal Springs to Buena Vista and subsequently became an independent vineyardist in the Sonoma Valley. He added with characteristic California optimism that the spread of the disease that he had found "was but slow, and that young vines planted in the place of those that had died seemed to do well, and be free from any disease."

In response to this report, the club did what clubs do best, appointed a committee. It included Attila and Craig. (Appleton was asked to stand by with his microscope.) The committee, however, did what few committees do: It acted immediately. Within a week it had traveled around the area inspecting vineyards. It had pulled up sick-looking vines and found insects on roots belonging to Mr. Appleton and Attila Haraszthy themselves, General Vallejo, Major Jacob Rink Snyder, and the Buena Vista Vinicultural Society. It suspected that the insect was indeed the phylloxera, and when it sent a few samples to the entomologist of the United States Department of Agriculture, he verified the suspicion.

Nevertheless, a few months later the president of the California Vine Growers and Wine and Brandy Manufacturers' Association, George G. Blanchard, made light of the matter when he addressed its convention. Having announced that the phylloxera had been discovered in California, he went on to attribute its presence to "atmospheric influences, probably, as some think, from the large amount of magnetism which had been thrown out through the solar system by the sun for the two years past," and added, "I have no fears that any vineyard will be destroyed by insects of any kind where good cultivation and care has [sic] been bestowed." He himself had, however, gone so far as to make an experiment, and it had worked; he had taken a piece of vine root with some *Phylloxera vastatrix* clinging to it, put it in a tumbler full of water, and succeeded in drowning the bugs.

Then, having announced this discovery, which was indeed valid and had been independently found by French viticulturists, he told a sort of a joke about an unidentified member of an unidentified temperance group: "I have heard that one of those meek and lowly hypocrites had exclaimed thank God, the phylloxera bastatrix has got after the vine growers at last."

At the beginning of 1874, Attila Haraszthy and others were busy pulling out ailing vines, inspecting their roots, and experimenting with ways of eradicating the insect. Apparently they made no great progress, for in February of

1876, on motion of Major Snyder, the club created another committee. This one was to demand help from the state legislature.

By 1879 the insect had been identified in other nothern California areas. A San Francisco *Bulletin* reporter traveling through the southeastern hills of the Napa Valley that summer wrote:

> The disease appears in spots over the vineyard, here and there two or three vines showing a poor growth, setting little fruit and slowly dying. It shows itself more after a dry season. We may talk wine and raisins all we please, but phylloxera is a problem for us to wrestle with for a while. A great many vineyards whose owners repose in blissful unconsciousness are suffering from its presence.

Nevertheless, enough vineyardists were barred from blissful unconsciousness by salient present realities—slowly dying vines in their own plots or similarly depressing occurrences in their neighborhoods—and impelled to action. They experimented with methods of eradication that they had heard about and that they invented, they held meetings to discuss the problem, and they added their voices to the Sonoma group's and implored the state for aid. They wanted, in addition to help in fighting the infestation, information on all aspects of grape growing and winemaking, including marketing.

Finally the state acted. On a Friday evening at the end of January 1880, the Assembly Committee on the Culture of the Grapevine held a special meeting at the capital city, Sacramento, in the Golden Eagle Hotel. Fittingly, James Adams of Sonoma was chairman. There was a great deal of ponderous talk. Mr. Reginaldo F. Del Valle, whose family rancho was famous for its grapes and the novel *Ramona*, made an opening statement:

> Mr. Chairman, I will say on behalf of this committee, that we have come to the conclusion that it is now about time that we should do something positive and definite in regard to the culture of the grape, and therefore we have concluded that we should do everything in our power to improve and foster this industry, which seems today the principal one of California; and, therefore, we have called upon those who are not only practical men, but who have made this matter the study of their lives, and I know that they can throw great light upon the subject.

There were two such men. The first to testify was Arpad Haraszthy, another son of Agoston Haraszthy, who had been educated in France and begun his career at his father's Buena Vista vineyard and winery, and who was now a successful wine merchant and champagne maker in San Francisco. He had long been active in formulating federal tax and tariff laws that the wine and brandy makers felt were at least not repressive, and he was president of the State Vinicultural Society. He was considered the foremost spokesman of his industry.

His testimony began with a short oration in the style of Mr. Del Valle's but quickly went on to practical matters. He outlined the effects of the phylloxera in France and Germany, the potentialities of California, assuming it could conquer the infestation, and the need for practical information about the state's soils and climates. He gave as an example of this need the questions a man had asked him the day before. He wanted to know what kinds of grapes to grow in Ventura County. He could not, however, describe the soil, and the only thing he could hazard about the climate was that it was probably warmer than Sacramento's.

What Arpad Haraszthy proposed was a program that would give the Ventura County gentleman the kind of information he needed. The state legislature should appropriate money for a two-pronged program. On the one hand a fund would enable the state university to establish an "analytical department" for viticultural matters and to educate future viticulturists. On the other hand it would enable the Vinicultural Society to set up permanent headquarters as a state institution and disseminate the information its members would gather from their practical experience in their vineyards. Like his brother Attila, he made less of the phylloxera threat than one would have anticipated. Comparing California's infestation to Europe's, he said, "I have not made a study of it as Professor Hilgard has, but I believe that it is not so apt to attack our vines because our soil is richer." He agreed with a committee member's suggestion that the state university should investigate this problem.

The Professor Hilgard to whom he referred was the committee's other scheduled witness. Eugene Woldemar Hilgard had been called to California in 1875 from a position as Professor of Geology and Natural History at the University of Michigan, which had followed a post as Professor of Chemistry and Experimental and Agricultural Chemistry at the University of Mississippi. At the University of California, located at Berkeley across the bay from San Francisco, he was named Professor of Agriculture. It was a newly created position, and he became the first to bring the study of agriculture to higher education in California. He also became the first to make scientific studies of the phylloxera as it attacked vines in the United States, for he immediately realized the gravity of the problem and interested himself in it. He examined vines and met with growers in the Sonoma Valley the year he arrived, and in 1878 he went again to discuss with them their need for "self-preservation as was evidenced by the melancholy piles of costly firewood seen about the vineyards, and even in the public squares"—the diseased vines that they had uprooted.

"Three years ago I found traces of phylloxera in numerous localities, and sounded the alarm," he had then reminded the Sonoma Valley growers. "Sounded too loud, perhaps, for I am pleased to learn that its ravages are not as extensive as I expected they would be; not extending as rapidly as in France; and as it does not spread so rapidly, I think something can be done to stop its devastations." But, he added, "something needs to be done if Sonoma is to continue to be a vine-growing district."

He proceeded to explain to them the life history of "this interesting little insect," which was indeed relevant, since female individuals in only one in four generations, he believed, developed wings that could easily carry them from one vineyard to another, and none of these winged females had yet been found in California.

In his testimony to the 1880 legislative committee, he explained more briefly the life cycle of the *Phylloxera vastatrix* and revised his estimate from four to five generations for the winged form, noting again that it had not yet appeared here.

The two leaders, the academic and the wine man, were in agreement in their recommendations to the legislative committee. Arpad Haraszthy thought an appropriation "in the neighborhood of" $6,000 a year would be needed for the first two years of both university and industry association work; Professor Hilgard estimated the university would need about $2,000 a year.

"Brief addresses were made by Messrs. Krug, Larue, and others, endorsing the views expressed by the principal speakers," read the minutes of the hearing, "and the committee adjourned to make a practical test of some very choice native wines furnished by the chairman."

Two and a half months later, on April 15, 1880, the legislature passed An Act for the Promotion of the Viticultural Industries of the State, creating a board of State Viticultural Commissioners, and also ordering the University of California to initiate studies in viticulture and what we now call enology, and to undertake a broad program of research. Both the board and the university were instructed to make special studies of the phylloxera and other vine pests and diseases, and to disseminate their findings on these and other subjects of importance to viticultural industries.

For all this, the legislature appropriated $7,000, of which $4,000 was for the use of the board and $3,000 for the university, to last some fourteen and a half months until the beginning of the next fiscal year—less than Arpad Haraszthy asked and more than Professor Hilgard thought would be necessary. If there was dissatisfaction among the winemakers at the time, no indication was given. There is, on the contrary, every indication that the industry had a large hand in formulating the act, getting it passed, and selecting the board members.

Among Professor Hilgard's papers at the University of California is a letter to him from Charles A. Wetmore, written on stationery of the Arcade Hotel in Sacramento, apparently in haste and with clear enthusiasm. It begins:

Dear Professor,
I am glad to be able to tell you that our Viticultural bill is passed finally. It has taken a great deal of persistent work to overcome the combined opposition of those who were prejudiced by temperance society appeals and those who oppose everything that costs money. It is a very great moral victory for nearly all the ardent temperance Senators were won over to support the bill. As soon as I can— probably next Sunday—I will have a talk with you about the whole matter. I shall be one of the Commissioners and therefore we can cooperate officially as well as friendly. [sic]

Some years later, when this burst was long forgotten, Professor Hilgard would end a letter to Arpad Haraszthy "Hoping that someon[e] will hunt up in Webster's dictionary for Mr. Wetmore the English meaning of the word cooperation, I remain. . ."

But by then both Wetmore and Hilgard, though at swords' points, had made and were continuing to make notable contributions to the advancement of the industry.

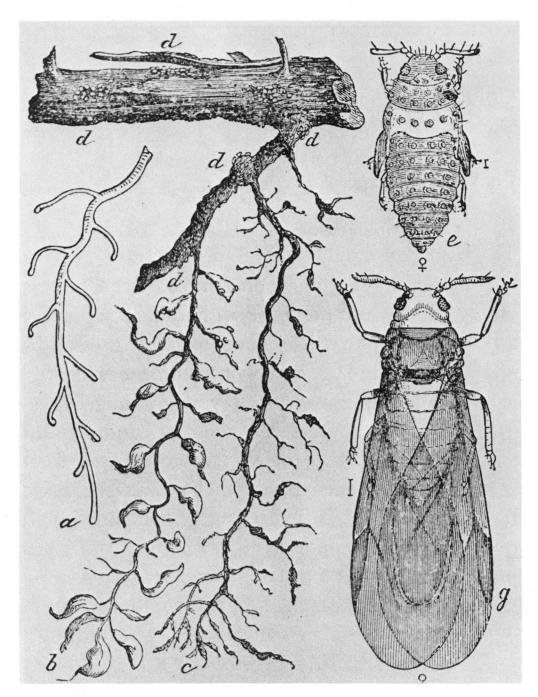

The *Phylloxera vastatrix,* a yellow insect no larger than one twenty-fifth of an inch long and one fiftieth of an inch wide in its greatest moments, destroyed 75 percent of France's vineyards between 1860 and 1890, and ravaged those in all other vine-growing countries of Europe. It laid waste seventy-five thousand acres in California as well. It did not become a recognized problem in California until after 1873, and here it spread slowly, mainly the wingless form migrating on foot or being inadvertantly carried by man. Nevertheless, spread it did, at one time causing damage at the rate of a thousand dollars a day. Not until the mid-1890s was it brought under reasonable control. By then the Board of State Viticultural Commissioners had published valuable material from the French scientists, from its own investigations, and from information it gathered from the state's vineyardists. So had the university, where Dr. Eugene Woldemar Hilgard and his small staff undertook hours of painstaking research. If words could kill, the insect would soon have been laid to rest under an avalanche of papers discussing one aspect and another of its unpleasant habits.

Attila Haraszthy, who was married to Natalia Vallejo, had his vine-yard on land adjacent to Lachryma Montis that General Vallejo had given his daughter soon after their marriage. Ironically, although Attila was one of the first phylloxera-fighters in the Sonoma Valley, the insect completely destroyed his vineyard a few years before his death in 1885.

California's principal 1880 vineyard areas are shown by hatching and cross-hatching on this map, which was issued by the State Viticultural Commission. The phylloxera had by then reached only those areas in northern California marked in black. It would later spread to the others.

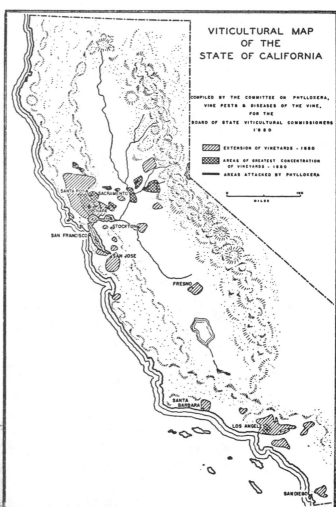

This drawing of treating phylloxera-ridden vines in France, using a steam engine to drive a pump to feed insecticide to the roots of each vine, was published in California in translations of French reports on fighting the insect. It may have gone far toward making California vineyardists try to wait out the plague rather than attack it in so complicated a fashion.

12. A War Within a War

IGHTEEN-EIGHTY can be taken as the year that California wine-growing emerged from a century of pragmatic pioneering to begin a century of increasingly mature investigation and growth. Two major indications were that there were in the state by then nine experienced viticulturists who were willing and able to serve without compensation on a newly created state board that would clearly make heavy demands upon them; and that one of the nation's most brilliant agricultural scientists, Eugene Woldemar Hilgard, was willing to turn his attention for the next dozen years to this relatively small portion of his broad field. Between them, the board and the university led the industry forward, as Arpad Haraszthy hoped they would, at first harmoniously.

Four days after the Act for the Promotion of the Viticultural Industries of the State cleared the legislature, Governor George C. Perkins signed it, and on the same day he named the members of the commission it created. The law specified that they be "specially qualified by practical experience and study in connection with the industries dependent upon the culture of the grapevine in this state." Seven were to be representatives of what were defined as the separate viticultural districts; the remaining two were to be members at large.

Charles Krug was named commissioner for the Napa district, Isaac De Turk for the Sonoma district. Commissioner for the El Dorado district, which included the counties comprising the Sierra Nevada mountains and foothills, was George C. Blanchard, the association president who had drowned the phylloxera in a glass of water. R. B. Blowers represented the Sacramento Valley and George West the San Joaquin Valley. Leonard J. Rose was commissioner for the Los Angeles district, which included all of Southern California and even San Luis Obispo County. Arpad Haraszthy was commissioner for the San Francisco district, which included the Santa Clara Valley and stretched all the way from the city through San Benito and Monterey counties. The two commissioners at large were J. de Barth Shorb, a San Gabriel winegrower, and Charles A. Wetmore.

Wetmore was the only member who did not own a vineyard or winery, although he soon would have both. He was what one would today call a broker and consultant. His letterhead, which was adorned with a bunch of grapes and the words *Ad majorem gloriam boni vini* ("To the greater glory of good wines"), listed the services he offered. He would select, buy, sell, and exchange vineyard land, and plant vines for new owners. He would sell vintages on commission, select wines for private cellars, sell vines, cuttings, and seeds, and assist vineyardists in the legal aspects of settling land titles in both Sacramento and Washington. He was, in fact, bringing together capabilities he had cultivated over the years, a good many capabilities for a man of thirty-three.

Born in New England and brought to San Francisco as a boy, Wetmore entered the College of California in 1864, graduating with both a B.A. and M.A. four years later. Some of his capabilities were cultivated here, for he was an energetic leader, class valedictorian. The summer before his final year he lobbied in the state legislature in behalf of his college to put over the bill establishing the University of California at Berkeley, of which the college was to become a part. He was so successful that the college waived his fees for his senior year.

Upon graduation, having been interested in journalism since grammar school, he went to San Diego to start a newspaper but instead became a successful real estate investor. He also was admitted to the bar and became an equally successful land lawyer at a time when San Diego land ownership was thoroughly unsettled. He again appeared before the state legislature, this time to urge a bill to stabilize the city's early pueblo titles; it was passed. He followed that with a successful lobbying stint in Washington.

Next he went to Peru to work for a year on railroad construction with his father, but in 1872 he returned to San Francisco and became a reporter for the *Alta California.* Perhaps more important to his career in viticulture, he became one of the two dozen charter members of the Bohemian Club. Another was Arpad Haraszthy.

By 1878 Wetmore was well versed enough in California wine affairs to be sent to cover the Paris Exposition as the official representative of the State Vinicultural Society. The trip was arranged by Arpad Haraszthy, who urged him to report everything he could learn about European grape growing and winemaking, wines, and the phylloxera. This he did, in thirty-four long, detailed articles in the *Alta.*

They caught and held the attention of almost everyone interested in wines in California. Their reports of the excellent quality of California's unrecognized vintages compared to the general run of Europe's, and the market potential there, acted as a burr under the saddle of the California industry. To the series was given much of the credit for the passage of the Act for the Promotion of the Viticultural Industries—an act that Wetmore, of course, helped lobby through.

All of these experiences qualified him for his vocation and for what at first seemed a sideline, service on the Board of State Viticultural Commissioners. However, it became his principal occupation for the fifteen years he served it in one capacity and another.

The board held its first meeting in May of 1880 at Mr. Wetmore's office, according to the minutes. Arpad Haraszthy was elected president, Wetmore vice-president, and Charles Krug treasurer. The Reverend Dr. Bleasdale, who had stayed on in California, was named secretary, to be paid a hundred dollars a month, which included some use of his laboratory.

The fight against the phylloxera became the most important order of business. A Committee on Phylloxera, Vine Pests and the Diseases of the Vine was established. In July commissioners journeyed to Sonoma. They inspected stricken vineyards. They talked with vineyardists. They listened to an address by an entomologist on certain obscure beetles, flies, and mites that were possible natural predators of the insect in question. And because there remained so much pigheadedness among the winegrowers, to use the term applied by Dr. Bleasdale, he let everyone look through his microscope at two identical examples of *Phylloxera vastatrix,* one from a local vine root, the other imported from France.

The next month Wetmore and Hilgard together chose as the board's paid inspector Frederick W. Morse, a graduate student assistant of Hilgard's, and directed him to travel throughout the state's vineyards and report on the vine diseases he found "for the use of the board and the university."

The commissioners' *First Annual Report,* published early the next year, carried the results of his search: Phylloxera existed in Napa, Solano, Yolo, El Dorado, and Placer counties as well as Sonoma. The report also carried a proposal by Wetmore for preventing the spread of the insect by quarantine, and papers on various aspects of its control. Since France was far ahead of the United States in studying the matter, Dr. Bleasdale made abstracts of the work of the French Academy of Science's Phylloxera Commission and a French scientist's report on the use of bisulphide of carbon in the vineyard. Anna Louise Wetmore, Charles's sister, translated another French report on the same chemical compound, which was the leading insecticide. In the various other papers that the volume included, other remedies were discussed. The chief ones were flooding vineyards to drown the pest (in the end this proved more injurious to the vines than to the insects); planting vines in sandy soil (if it was so sandy as to be inhospitable to the insect, it often was to the vine as well); various insecticides (most were expensive, hard to use, and unproven); and grafting *Vitis vinifera* varieties upon native American phylloxera-resistant roots. This last had been suggested some years earlier by French viticulturists, who reasoned that if the phylloxera had originally lived on American vine roots without harming them, using those same roots for European varieties would give them resistance. In the end, this proved the solution, and today most of the world's wine grapes grow on native American roots.

The solution was slow to be applied, however. Many of the winegrowers stubbornly refused to do anything but try to wait until the blight disappeared. And no one was sure which of the native American grapes' roots were resistant or how grafts could best be made.

Wetmore and Hilgard came separately to the conclusion that the native *Vitis californica* was the best bet for a resistant plant. It was abundant and easy to procure. Twenty-four years earlier the thrifty Charles Lefranc had grafted European varieties on wild grape roots found near his Santa Clara County vineyard, "desiring to utilize his imported cuttings to the best advantage by cutting them in short pieces"; those vines were still flourishing. This was noted in Wetmore's wide-ranging paper in the first report. He had taken his "commis-

sioner at large" assignment literally, for he seems to have been everywhere and reported on everything. The other commissioners made narrower reports.

A talk that Professor Hilgard had given to Napa viticulturists was also printed in the volume, and it too was wide-ranging, an excellent indication of his scientific knowledge and his ability to put it into practical terms. He discussed the planting of vineyards, and grape varieties especially in relation to soils, for his major field was soil chemistry. But he also discussed fermentation, a subject upon which he was to spend many hours of research resulting in a classic treatise detailing nine different methods. Blending too he commented upon, explaining, "I am not one of the purists who maintain that the juice of each kind of grape must be fermented and swallowed by itself, whether it brings tears to your eyes or not," and urging winemakers to do their own blending rather than leave it to the wine merchants. "In fact," he added, "judicious blending is the height of the art of winemaking."

So full of practical information was this initial volume of the board that a second edition had to be printed, and it set a tradition for bringing to California in subsequent reports the latest viticultural information from Europe and from the state's own investigations.

The next year, 1881, the state legislature passed another act adding to the board's responsibilities. It directed that a paid Chief Viticultural Officer be appointed to formulate quarantine rules so that disease would not be carried from vineyard to vineyard, and to enforce them. (Enforcement proved impossible.) It also directed the board to make practical experiments for control of the phylloxera.

The hand of Charles A. Wetmore, who was named to the full-time job of Chief Viticultural Officer, can be seen here. And the directive for experimentation may have been the opening crack in what became a wide breach between the university and the board. Clearly Hilgard had assumed that the board would, as Arpad Haraszthy had in effect suggested, undertake practical investigation, while the university would do the experimentation, and he had already added first-hand experiments with the phylloxera to his study of the scientific literature. Then there was the question of money, of which there never seemed to be enough for either organization. So a small rift appeared.

By 1885 the Board of State Viticultural Commissioners' inspector, young Morse, had found phylloxera in almost all vineyard areas of northern California. The board published additional papers on how to control it, as well as on other viticultural subjects. There were several notable reports by Hilgard, and Wetmore's landmark ampelography, the first orderly description of wine grape varieties in use in California, a gathering together of a tremendous amount of data both written and observed. The board had also held two successful conventions at which wine and grape men exchanged views on everything from labor to cooperage, and established a small experimental winery in San Francisco under Wetmore's direction.

On the university's part, Professor Hilgard and his small group of assistants had visited vineyards, addressed viticulturists' meetings, and written papers on phylloxera, grape varieties, chemical analysis of wines, and soils suitable for vineyards. Professor Hilgard had also answered hundreds of individual inquiries from winegrowers (as well as wheat growers, mushroom growers, and other farmers with recondite problems, for it must be recalled that his duties included all those of Professor of Agriculture). He had established a viticultural laboratory, pilot winery, and cellar, and he had taken over a small vineyard that someone had earlier planted on the Berkeley campus. Here he was experimenting with *Phylloxera vastatrix,* which he found in it.

Everything seemed to be progressing well on both board and university fronts, but that was the year the rift became a chasm across which insults were hurled. Letters between Hilgard and Wetmore ceased. The points at issue were several, the most salient of them being whether the board should have a hand in controlling the university's experimental work.

Hilgard saw red. On February 17, 1885, he wrote to John T. Doyle, a winegrower and university regent with whom he had long corresponded:

> Wetmore has by a stroke of state—haute politique—captured the appropriation for a vit. labora-

tory as recommended by the vit. convention; and it is therefore quite likely that the univ. vit. laboratory will be finally closed on June 30. Until within a few days, W. wrote the most engaging letters, showing how by his peculiar position he was precluded from working actively for the univ. laboratory. Not a word of dissent or of warning that he had any objection to it.

Then Wetmore had turned perfidious, urging at legislative meetings that the university laboratory be moved to San Francisco and the board take over most of its work, leaving Hilgard only the narrowest academic research.

Clearly furious, Hilgard had conferred with Arpad Haraszthy and Horatio P. Livermore, a Sacramento Valley grape grower, and told them he would "positively decline to act under any such arrangement," as he reported to Doyle in the letter. He told Haraszthy and Livermore that Wetmore had on every occasion "pooh-poohed and belittled" his work "and attempted to tie my hands so that hereafter Wetmore alone should loom up before the admiring gaze of the viticultural multitude. His coup d'etat was managed as astutely as could have been done by Metternich himself, and he holds the field, undoubtedly."

He added ringingly that "the ignorant assumption and censorship of Wetmore, ad majorem gloriam suam, is rather more than I bargained for. He can take the whole of it and manage it as he is able, and if the viticulturists of the state can stand it, I assuredly can."

Wetmore did not, however, hold the field, for the university's laboratory remained on the campus, and in fact Hilgard managed to expand it. But before this was known, another battle broke out. It began just a little more than a month after the row about the laboratory.

On March 24, 1885, the San Francisco *Morning Call* carried under the headline "The Berkeley Phylloxera" the text of letters between W. P. Bartlett, editor of the *Livermore Herald,* and Charles A. Wetmore. Bartlett had read a bulletin of Hilgard's mentioning his phylloxera research in the campus vineyard and had taken fright. He wrote to Wetmore (who had by then established his Cresta Blanca vineyard and winery in the Livermore Valley) to ask if "in your judgment, there is any danger of contagion from this vineyard, which is as yet the only one in this county in which the phylloxera has secured a footing."

The Livermore Valley, with its growing number of so-far phylloxera-free vineyards, and the Berkeley campus were indeed in the same Alameda County, but they were separated by twenty-five miles and a range of hills. Wetmore's response that the campus vineyard might indeed be a danger to both the Livermore Valley and the nearer Contra Costa County vineyards, his suggestion that the university authorities would no doubt order it destroyed, and his observation that phylloxera research would be better carried on in vineyard areas where the disease existed, made Hilgard see red again. It brought up another point of contention, the board's desire to establish experiment stations, and the university's opinion that field experiments and observations could not be made by amateurs.

Hilgard shot off a letter to Arpad Haraszthy explaining why the phylloxera could not spread from the university plot and accusing Wetmore of wanting control of everything and not being "overscrupulous about trying to secure it." Haraszthy replied immediately, beginning "Your favor of the 26th is at hand and I have read its contents with great regret." He assured Professor Hilgard that the commission was working for the best interests of everyone but that it "cannot be intimidated by anyone."

Hilgard had cooled down only slightly by the next day when he received this letter and replied. He repeated an earlier allegation that feuding would harm the entire viticultural community, and concluded with the suggestion that someone hunt up for Wetmore the dictionary definition of cooperation. Haraszthy responded, refusing to pass along to Wetmore "abusive matter" and stating "I still fail to see how a mere matter of personal pique between two enthusiasts in viticulture can prevent the vines from growing, wine from being made and progress continued!"

He was right; it did not, either immediately or in the long run. However, the animosity did not cease but exploded again in 1886, when both Wetmore and Hilgard spoke at the State Viticultural Convention, reported on the progress of their respective experimental laboratories, and exhibited wines made in them.

We have again a first-hand account in a letter from Professor Hilgard to John T. Doyle. It was apparently written in haste without the professor's usual punctillious punctuation, and he left out a few key words:

You have doubtless seen in this morning's papers the final outcome of the game of chess that was being played at Irving Hall for the last two days. On my return to the hall after lunch, hearing sundry excited remarks on the subject of underhand proceedings and the like, I went to De Turk and told him that what was wanted was a state viticultural society in which all would join and be heard, and which the commission, if its meant rightly [sic], ought to desire to have at its back. That we did not care a particle whether it was a new society or an old one revived, but that it must not be a pure Wetmore convocation. I then showed him the paper with the signatures and told him that we had better agree beforehand, privately, what should be done, and avoid a public fracas.

Professor Hilgard did not explain whose signatures were on the paper but apparently he and other anti-Wetmore men had written out a proposal for the new or revived society. Hilgard went on:

De Turk read the paper, . . . said he saw nothing but what was all right, and went to see West and Wetmore about it. But when Wetmore came in he was in a red-hot fury from some cause and said among other things, as De Turk told me, that the commission had been "insulted" by this method of procedure. Just then Haraszthy came in, and I called him aside and told him I thought Wetmore had better not be quite so high and mighty.

Then Wetmore returned and "after glaring at me," led Haraszthy away.

"Well," continued Hilgard,

it is useless to recite all that followed during the afternoon meeting. There was some excessively plain talk, in which Wetmore lost his temper several times, thundering against the "enemies of the commission." I said nothing till toward the end, when Wetmore again referred to the said enemies. I then rose and said the trouble with Mr. W. was that he could not see the difference between himself personally and the commission, and considered everyone who disagreed with him or opposed his particular ideas, as such [an enemy]. As to myself, to whom he had so often referred, the trouble was that I had resisted being reduced [to] the position of his subordinate, doing nothing but what he should dictate, and upon that he had attempted to stop my work, and he had failed. We wanted neither dictation nor dictators—Then I sat down.

The next year's public explosion was detailed in the 1887 meeting report. To another proposal for a resolution to suppress "the public nuisance and danger" at Hilgard's Berkeley vineyard with its experimental phylloxera, the professor responded with dry sarcasm.

"As I am supposed to retain this nuisance at the university, I suppose I am called upon to speak. The good people of Livermore are very much alarmed about a very insignificant matter," he began, then proceeded more caustically. "There is something in the atmosphere of Livermore that causes people to say unpleasant things about matters at the university." He went on to explain, however, that he had only forty infected vines in his plot, that the insect was not carried by wind but mainly by people transporting vines, and that young Morse's studies at the university vineyard of the still rare winged form had proved invaluable in learning under what conditions it might develop in California to hasten the spread of the blight.

Morse reported on his findings on the winged phylloxera, and then Mr. Wetmore arose to make suggestions regarding Hilgard's hoped-for university experiment plots (meddling in the university's business, in Hilgard's view) and to add more sarcasm to the discussion:

> Now, so far as that infected spot on the university being of service to the state, it has been developed by what Professor Hilgard and Mr. Morse have said what it has accomplished: it has taught Mr. Morse how to find the winged phylloxera. That is all. Now if we are to have state institutions maintaining pests for the purpose of educating the professors and their assistants how to find and recognize the insect, I think that our university is working on a very small plane.

The convention voted to again ask the regents to have Professor Hilgard's vineyard destroyed. Again the regents failed to do so. It continued, and the war continued. As Arpad Haraszthy suggested, the viticultural industry appeared not to suffer from the feud. Perhaps it gained, for the controversies were so widely discussed in public print that the citizens of California grew to know more about the state's

wines and look with greater sympathy upon their producers than they would have if Wetmore had been less aggressive and Hilgard less stubborn.

Arpad Haraszthy had maintained a cool head during the controversy, but, as he himself, admitted, he sometimes angered easily. However, if he responded with anger to being in effect dismissed from the Board of State Viticultural Commissioners in 1888, he did so privately. In 1887, Washington Bartlett, the Democratic governor of California, died and was succeeded by the Republican lieutenant-governor, Robert W. Waterman. The following spring Haraszthy's term on the board, which he had served as president since its beginning, ended. There was no reason to believe that he would not be reappointed, for all the members had been reappointed as their terms ended if they wished to be, and there had been few changes in the eight years. So there was amazement when at the end of Arpad Haraszthy's term, Morris M. Estee was named in his place.

Estee was an attorney and one of the most powerful Republican politicians in California. He was a political supporter of Governor Waterman. He also had a vineyard in the Napa Valley, which interested him to the extent that he attended state viticultural conventions. He was in fact an active participant, and so far as is recorded an uncontentious one. But apparently something happened at the 1887 convention that brought him into contention with Arpad Haraszthy.

As it fell out, Estee did not accept the governor's appointment, because he had been named president of the national Republican convention to be held a few months hence. In his place John T. Doyle, Professor Hilgard's longtime correspondent, a regent of the university, and a winegrower, was named. He too was an attorney, but by this time he had retired from the practice of law and was devoting much of his interest to viticulture. He too attended the annual conventions, and he had given the university the use of part of his vineyard in Santa Clara County for its first experimental plot. Both Estee and Doyle were suitable appointments to the board, but they were the first men named who were not primarily viticulturists.

Doyle, for all his conscientiousness, gave far less attention to the board than had Arpad Haraszthy, for Haraszthy had worked tremendously on its affairs. The latter's only known responses to his dismissal were his formal resignation as the board's president and the preparation of a twenty-eight-page final report, filled with facts, figures, and suggestions for future viticultural work.

It contains the only indication of his resentment that appears on the record. In the introductory letter of transmittal to the governor, Haraszthy explained that he felt it necessary to outline the board's activities, "since, in certain quarters there exists, apparently, a determined ignorance regarding the work accomplished by this Commission, as well as a sustained endeavor to cloud the great actual value of its labors."

Its labors continued without him, but his report was referred to time and again. Meetings continued, publications continued, Wetmore continued, but if the loss of Haraszthy's leadership did not lessen its efforts, the economic depression under which the viticultural industry suffered during the last years of the decade certainly dampened its efforts. Conditions did not improve in the vineyards, the wineries, or the state's economy in general in the early 1890s. In 1895 the Board of State Viticultural Commissioners was eliminated. To Charles A. Wetmore, its most constructive and dedicated adherent, was left the bitter task of drawing up the bill detailing its decommissioning.

The board's papers were to be turned over to the Department of Agriculture of the University of California. Whether or not Hilgard treasured them, his possession of most of them was short-lived, for two years later the wooden Agriculture Building went up in smoke. Somehow, however, the board's minutes escaped and are now, along with Hilgard's letter books and other papers, in the Bancroft Library on the campus. (One would wish Wetmore's own papers had been similarly preserved.) The library the board had carefully collected, said to be the finest viticulture library in the United States at the time, had a more mysterious subsequent history. It was supposed to be turned over with the papers, but Professor Maynard

A. Amerine doubts that all the books were transferred, for some made their way to the library at the university's Davis campus, where the Department of Viticulture and Enology, for which Hilgard laid the groundwork and which Amerine later headed, is located.

Wetmore retaliated by forming a group that included Arpad Haraszthy and Isaac De Turk to establish an independent college of viticulture, but it got no further than its papers of incorporation. The university went on to become a world center for the study and teaching of viticulture and enology.

The accomplishments of the board were considerable. Some were concerned with tariff and tax legislation, unglamorous but necessary to the economic health of the industry. It saw a California Pure Wine Law passed, ineffective as it turned out but the only real attempt to control adulteration until the national Pure Food Act of 1906. It also shared credit with the university for controlling phylloxera and improving the grape varieties planted in the state. Following the urging of both entities, as vineyardists replanted vines on phylloxera-resistant roots, they grafted onto them good wine varieties. It was reported that between 1880 and 1890, the ratio of Missions to better wine grapes turned right around; it was 90 percent Mission at the beginning of the decade, only 10 percent at the end.

The university emerged the victor, but Charles A. Wetmore was not vanquished. He went on until Prohibition writing and speaking out in behalf of the state's wine men. He worked effectively and unceasingly on federal legislation crucial to the wine industry. At his death in 1927 his name was added to the list of those called the Father of the California Wine Industry.

As to Professor Eugene Woldemar Hilgard, he too lived happily ever after, or as happily as he had ever before. Having succeeded in establishing university experiment stations and having made tremendous contributions to the cause of viticulture, he turned his attention again to his major interest, soil science, and by the time of his death in 1916 he had written hundreds of scientific papers, of which sixty-four were contributions to our knowledge of grape growing and winemaking.

"Happiness and Thrift in the Land of the Vine" is the title of this 1888 cartoon from the San Francisco weekly, *The Wasp*. The idea that winegrowing equates with a good life seems to be timeless. Cicero wrote, "My delight in the vine is insatiable." In 1870 one of the most unequivocal expressions of the idea was formulated in a viticultural group's report to the state legislature: "It is the universal remark of observant travelers through the vinelands of the world that no communities are so contented and happy and domestic in their tastes and habits, or so strongly attached to home, kindred and country, as the dwellers among the vineyards." A century later similar sentiments brought about a remarkable increase in small new vineyards, as families seeking the idyllic country life fled the cities.

Charles A. Wetmore was an outspoken, often combative crusader for the cause of California wine. A small man, slight in his early years, he grew portly but not from lack of constant activity. Even from his long-standing adversary, Professor Eugene Woldemar Hilgard, he drew grudging admiration: "Let us give Wetmore credit for what he is good for—energy, aggressiveness and inexhaustible cheek; all of which have their uses." While Wetmore's most visible activities were aggressive, more were quietly constructive. He formulated wine laws and lobbied them through. He wrote about California wines in semi-technical terms for viticulturists and in popular terms for general readers. For the latter he could be lyrical: "The vine is a spring of hope, promising gladness" he declared in an article soberly titled "Physical and Moral Influences of the Vine."

"We can foresee the time when pure, natural light wines will become a part of the daily food of the majority of our people," he wrote, and these wines would foster family stability. He reasoned thus: "Wine is a civilizer in the family. It makes the dinner eventful, and prolongs its period of enjoyment. It brings man and wife into full sympathy, and lets the woman into the man's most entertaining moods. He does not save his wit and smiles for the barroom and club. . . . Women fight the saloons partly from fear, partly from jealousy; neither habitual fear nor habitual jealousy are promoters of peace, good will, and contentment. The women then begin to think of rights of all kinds, and women's rights in particular. Wine at the table would make it all right. . . . The vine has been called 'the friend of man'; it should be called the mutual friend of man and wife. It is an anti-divorce prescription."

109

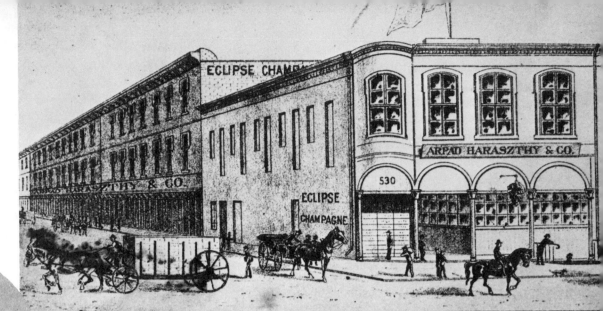

OFFICES AND WAREHOUSES, ARPAD HARASZTHY & CO., 530 WASHINGTON STREET, SAN FRANCISCO

RIESLING

ORLEANS VINEYARD

ARPAD HARASZTHY & CO.
SAN FRANCISCO, CAL.

WINE VAULT, ARPAD HARASZTHY & CO.

Arpad Haraszthy was president of the Board of State Viticultural Commissioners during its most productive years. In his own right, he was the first consistently successful California champagne maker, creator and producer of the famed Eclipse, which he named after an eighteenth-century race horse, a winner as he hoped the champagne would be. It was for many years.

It was made in the bottle in the classic French manner, but the grapes were unlike those used in French Champagne. They were mainly Zinfandel and Burger, with the addition of some Gutedel, Muscatel, and Riesling. They came for the most part from the Orleans Vineyard, from which also came most other wines sold by Haraszthy & Co. The San Francisco cellars, where the champagne was made and the still wines aged and blended, are depicted in this series of drawings from the only known copy of a leaflet, now in the library at Fresno State University.

CHAMPAGNE CELLARS AND RACKS, ARPAD HARASZTHY & CO.

DISGORGING DEPARTMENT, CHAMPAGNE CELLARS, ARPAD HARASZTHY & CO.

BOTTLING DEPARTMENT AND CHAMPAGNE FERMENTING ROOM, ARPAD HARASZTHY & CO.

Eugene Woldemar Hilgard, born in Germany, reared in the American Midwest, educated at the University of Heidelberg, was the first scientist to make a systematic study of wine grapes and winemaking in California. He emphasized, early to late, the importance of wine quality, and he spelled out techniques for achieving it through the right combinations of grape varieties, soil, and climate, in addition to what he called "rational winery practice." His standards were high, his defense of them stubborn and not always tactful. However, he was practical.

Realizing that few vineyardists would come to the university, he carried the university out to the vineyards. Wanting an assistant who could speak with Italian immigrant vine growers, he chose Frederic T. Bioletti on the basis of his name. Bioletti quickly learned Italian and became the man who carried Hilgard's ideas forward across the hiatus of Prohibition.

At the time of Professor Hilgard's death, he was eulogized by his successor as Dean of the College of Agriculture as having been "richly wise, unswervingly true, and deeply patriotic and humanistic, a man whose thinking was as clear and whose motives were as unselfish as his service of them was forceful and effective." The eulogist added, however, a more human note: "Sometimes we thought he fought not wisely but too well. But fighting was recreation for him; it seemed to renew his strength, to deepen his convictions, to freshen his thought."

Most of the papers of the California Board of State Viticultural Commissioners and part of its extensive library, as well as Hilgard's enology laboratory, went up in smoke when the University of California Agriculture Building burned in April of 1897.

13. Alameda County

ALAMEDA County's two major viticultural areas are separate and quite different. The Mission San Jose and Warm Springs district, where Professor Eugene W. Hilgard had his Dos Encinitas summer home and vineyard, is in the southern part of the county, not far to the east of the lower end of San Francisco Bay. The Livermore Valley, where Charles A. Wetmore established his famed Cresta Blanca vineyard estate, lies to its northeast, just over a mountain range from the great San Joaquin Valley but not so far from the bay that it misses its cooling breezes. It was developed principally in the 1880s and has remained to this day a major source of fine California wines, while the area around the old mission and Warm Springs has almost faded from the state's viticultural map, grown over in large part by suburban development.

The county's first winegrowers were of course the mission padres, Father Narciso Durán the most famous. The first known secular vineyardist was Robert Livermore, who some time in the 1840s got cuttings from the mission and planted a small vineyard of no great importance beyond its pioneer status.

The mission's vineyard itself was the source of the first wine made commercially in Alameda County. In 1848 Elias Lyman Beard and a partner bought thirty thousand acres of the secularized mission land, including its vineyard, and in 1851 produced a healthy sixteen thousand dollars' worth of wine. Beard also planted grain and potatoes on a grand scale, and the potatoes themselves were on a grand scale too. A Dr. Willey later wrote that in 1852 he "aided at the sacrifice of one weighing four pounds, which served as a meal for nine persons at the table and three to follow."

Beard bought four thousand acres of ex-mission land, built a fine home, and landscaped its grounds beautifully with palms and other exotic trees and shrubs. He called it Palmdale, and after his death it became the center of a large winegrowing enterprise. It was purchased by Juan Gallegos, who had been a coffee planter in Costa Rica. The ubiquitous Frona Eunice Wait, who saw almost all and told almost all in her 1889 book, *Wines and Vines of California*, wrote of a "lane of gray and solemn olive-trees cleaving its way through a billowy sea of wine grapes owned by the Gallegos Wine Company."

Most of those grapes were Zinfandel, but there were plots devoted to Bordeaux varieties: twenty-five acres of Cabernet Sauvignon, fifteen of Cabernet franc, eight of Merlot. The influence of Gallegos' neighbor, friend, and associate, Professor Hilgard, may be seen here. He sold grapes to Gallegos, too, and he is on record as having bought wine for him from Charles A. Wetmore, a gesture that must indicate faithful friendship.

Gallegos' olive-lined avenue led from his home "nestled cosily in the foothills," wrote Miss Wait, to his winery and distillery nearly a mile away, located with practicality across from the railroad station at the village of Irvington. "The storage capacity is 1,000,000 gallons," she noted, then continuing with a dangling modifier she gave details: "Once inside this enormous cellar, a line of splendid oak cooperage presents itself. There are 507 tanks, holding 1,700 gallons each, saddled by 300 casks, holding 800 gallons apiece, and there are 114 fermenting-vats, with a capacity of 2,500 gallons, all in use during the vintage."

Some of those splendid casks were said to have later made their way to the California Wine Association's huge depot, Winehaven, on San Francisco Bay, through one-time CWA official Henry Lachman. He bought the Gallegos estate in 1905 and spent the last years of his life in peaceful retirement at the Palmdale home that Elias Lyman Beard had built.

In 1852, only three years after Beard's arrival, Charles F. Palmer established the Peak Vineyard. Little is known about him or his winery, which twenty years later had a capacity of a hundred thousand gallons and produced aged wines that commanded premium prices. Palmer is credited with having planted the first foreign varieties in Alameda County in 1852, but one can conjecture that Clement Colombet might have contested that claim.

Colombet, born in Nice, arrived in California in 1844. He worked in San Jose as a tanner, storekeeper, and innkeeper before marrying and settling down at Mission San Jose in 1851. There he grew grapes and made wine, and it is difficult to believe that he might not have brought with him from San Jose vine cuttings shared by some of his fellow Frenchmen, such as Antoine Delmas or Louis Prevost. In 1856 his claret won a first prize at the state fair. That same year he bought from the Spanish grantee the Warm Springs property. Around the mineral springs that had earlier been frequented by the roving Indians of the area, he developed a popular resort, and there is evidence that he planted French varieties of grapes. The resort was heavily damaged in the earthquake of 1868, and the next year Colombet sold the property, one square mile, to lawyer-entrepreneur Alfred A. Cohn, who built a more splendid hotel but almost immediately sold it to Leland Stanford. The hotel became a residence and the extensive acreage was planted in fruit trees and vines. This was the first of Stanford's viticultural ventures, interesting him enough to lead to his later creation of the huge Vina vineyard in the Sacramento Valley. He turned Warm Springs over to his brother Josiah, however, and it was Josiah and, following Josiah's death in 1890, his son Josiah W., who managed it and built it into a viticultural estate of prestige, with its wines on the tables of the even more prestigious Hotel del Monte. But it should be recalled that the hotel was the property of Leland Stanford's Southern Pacific Railroad.

Its vineyards damaged by phylloxera, like most of those in the area, the enterprise declined, the Josiah W. Stanford family continuing however to maintain it as a residence until the 1920s. In 1945 part of the property was bought by Rudolph Weibel, a Swiss, who planted Chardonnay and Pinot noir vines on resistant roots; he revived the old winery buildings and there made Charmat-process champagne and table wines. The Weibel family continues it to this day, but since 1960 the major part of its vineyards and table winemaking have been gradually shifted to Mendocino County, there being now no room for expansion among the housing tracts and industrial plants at Warm Springs.

In the broad, mountain-lined Livermore Valley, wheat was the main crop in 1879 when the earliest notable vineyard was planted, and it was not so notable that much is remembered about the man who established it, Dr. George Bernard. He is recalled principally because his fifty-acre tract with its twenty-eight acres of young vines became the nucleus of the Wente family vineyard and winery.

Carl H. Wente came from his native Germany to the United States around 1870 and in 1881 went to work for his countryman Charles Krug in the Napa Valley. He learned fast, married German-born Barbara Trautwein who knew something of viticulture from her family, and decided to follow the American tradition and start his own enterprise. With two silent partners he bought the Bernard property and settled there the year he married, 1883. His son Ernest Wente gave an interesting autobiographical oral history interview to the Bancroft Library of the University of California in 1969. He knew from his father that the Bernard vineyard was planted mainly to Zinfandel, with some Charbono, Colombard, Mataro, and Gray Riesling.

Carl Wente was, as his son recalled, unhappy about the Gray Riesling, which is interesting in the light of the later popularity of the Wentes' varietal wine made from this grape. In a few years he grafted it over to White Riesling, but meanwhile Ernest Schween took some cuttings and planted them in his family vineyard at nearby Pleasanton.

"After Repeal," recalled Ernest Wente, "when Herman and I started to plant vines again, I went down to get some cuttings from his son, Mr. Will Schween, and he said, 'Well, well, well! The old Gray Rieslings are going back home!'"

Ernest and Herman, who later became the owners under the name Wente Bros., had not yet come into the world when Carl H. Wente built a winery on the Bernard property and began adding more French varieties. Through a neighbor, Louis Mel, he got Sauvignon blanc cuttings from Chateau d'Yquem, famous then as now for its Sauternes. Another neighbor, Charles A. Wetmore, spent weeks with him teaching him how to make Livermore Valley sauternes from the grapes.

The recollection of the imported cuttings brought up another anecdote. Just after repeal, the Marquis de Lur-Saluces of Chateau d'Yquem came to visit the Wentes. "I spent several days with him," Ernest Wente recalled, "taking him around, and he was very inquisitive. Wanted to know all about winds and so forth and the culture of grapes and whether we had wind damage and why we planted straight varieties instead of blending them as they do in France in the vineyards."

Then Herman Wente brought in seven consecutive vintages of Sauvignon blanc. The marquis tasted them very carefully and said, "They are all very much alike and very good. We cannot do this in France. I do not say that perhaps we do not have a vintage which is probably better than these, but we cannot have consecutive vintages like these."

As he left he said, "I am glad to find my children doing so well in California."

Ernest Wente became the second student to enroll at the University of California's new campus at Davis. There he came to know a young Frenchman, a graduate of the National School of Agriculture at Montpellier, Leon O. Bonnet, who was to become a well-known professor of viticulture. He brought Bonnet home, and Bonnet talked Carl Wente into ordering vines from the Montpellier nursery—Ugni blanc among them, a grape that would become useful in another popular Wente wine.

Until Prohibition, Wente wines were sold in bulk. At the 1915 Panama-Pacific International Exposition wine exhibition, Carl Wente said, "I'm probably the proudest man here at this fair because I've won four gold medals, all on the white wines. I've won four gold medals and none of them were in my name."

Prohibition took the heart out of Carl Wente, and he told his sons Herman and Ernest that he was through and they could take over if they wished. They did, and through the dry years they made only what wine they sold to Beaulieu Vineyard, which had a Prohibition Department license and a large business in altar wines. Upon Repeal, the two brothers—Herman, the wine man and Ernest, the field man—started bottling under their own labels. Herman, a selfless industry leader as well as an excellent winemaker, died in 1961. Ernest's son Karl succeeded to active partnership with his father, and after he too became an industry leader and after he too died young, his two sons, Eric and Philip, became the new Wente Bros.

Many of Carl H. Wente's neighbors were not wine men by trade but people who were drawn to winegrowing as a pleasant, perhaps idyllic, perhaps profitable venture into which to sink money they had made through other pursuits. One was Julius Paul Smith, a dapper cosmopolite who, with his better remembered brother, "Borax" Smith, made a fair-sized fortune mining in Death Valley. In 1881 he invested some of that fortune in the two thousand-acre Livermore Valley ranch known as Olivina. He studied vine growing and winemaking on frequent trips to Europe, clearly reflected in the grape varieties in the six hundred-odd-acre vineyard he planted. According to the directory of California vine growers and winemakers that the Viticultural Commission published in 1891, he had thirty-one varieties. There was not a single Mission vine, and to fifty-five acres of Zinfandel there were sixty-seven of Petit Pinot, fifty of Folle blanche, eighty of "Colombar"—probably the grape that we know today as the Sauvignon vert, according to Ernest Wente—and others, many imported directly. He built a winery, bottled his own wines and champagne, and sold them widely. At his death in 1904, however, he left an estate of only a hundred dollars, and Olivina was heavily mortgaged. Fortunately he had married a wife who was not only beautiful but able, and she succeeded in wresting the property from the "greedy" bankers, according to a note on the back of Julius Paul Smith's portrait in the California State Library, and returned it to prosperous activity.

The Louis Mel who gave Carl Wente the Sauvignon blanc was a Frenchman, a successful insurance man in America, who in 1884 bought as a home for himself and his wife a 107-acre tract of rolling land a few miles south of Livermore. And, as he explained later, "as the Wentes and Concannons and other neighbors around us had vineyards, I decided to plant vines too." His estate was called by various names at various times, sometimes Le Bocage, "the shady grove," sometimes Olea Vista, sometimes El Mocho after the stream that ran through the property.

Charles A. Wetmore came from his nearby Cresta Blanca vineyards one day to call on Mr. and Mrs. Mel. "He said he was going to Europe and wondered if we could help him secure some vines from the Chateau vineyards of France. I told him I believed he could get cuttings from the famous Chateau d'Yquem vineyard owned by the Marquis de Lur-Saluces, as my wife was a good friend of the Marquise and had through the years kept up a correspondence with her." Mrs. Mel gave Wetmore a letter of introduction. Mel recalled:

When he visited the great feudal castle, the Marquis and his wife were absent. But the superintendent read Mrs. Mel's letter and when he saw her signature, "née Bire," he remembered her and said, "I'm sure the Marquis will let you have anything you want if you are a friend of Mrs. Mel." So, in due time, cuttings of the Semillon, Sauvignon vert, Sauvignon blanc, and Muscadelle de Bordelais arrived in Livermore. These varieties combined make the blend used in producing the far-famed wines that rank among the most costly in the world. Mr. Wetmore kept a part of the cuttings and turned the rest over to me. I planted those cuttings, and today some of the original vines are still growing in El Mocho vineyard, which is now owned by Mrs. Margaret Aldrich.

This reminiscence took place in 1935, on Louis Mel's ninety-seventh birthday, when Herman Wente and H. F. Stoll, then editor of *Wines & Vines*, visited him. As they were about to leave, Mr. Mel suggested that they join him in a glass of wine, and Herman Wente countered by asking if he would like a glass made from Sauvignon blanc grapes grown on his old vineyard, grapes that Wente Bros. had been buying for the past decade. He had, in fact, brought Mr. Mel a case. So they toasted each other and El Mocho.

Other Frenchmen found the Livermore Valley to their liking: San Francisco wine merchant Adrien G. Chauché, whose Mont-Rouge Vineyard made its first crush in 1885 and won a gold medal at the Paris Exposition in 1889, and whose later partner was Charles A. Bon; Alexander Duvall, wealthy from building railroads in Peru, whose Bellevue Vineyard had almost as many imported varieties as Julius Paul Smith's Olivina; and Eugene Paris, who patiently cleared thirty-five acres of oak-studded land for his vineyards, built a 150,000-gallon capacity winery, and, like most of those in the district, made a greater quantity of Zinfandel than wines of more prestige. Among the others there were also Austrian Joseph Altschul, who like Smith maintained his principal residence in New York but built a palatial home overlooking his hundred-acre Vienna Vineyard; American John Crellin, whose Ruby Hill Vineyard, nearer Pleasanton than Livermore, was planned by Captain H. W. McIntyre, manager of Leland Stanford's big Vina vineyard; and German-born Theodore Gier, an Oakland wine merchant and business leader who made about 50,000 gallons of wine a year at his Giersburg estate. Some was from vines brought from France by that same indefatigable Charles A. Wetmore. Gier would later figure as one of the few California wine men who fought Prohibition in the courts.

Wetmore came to the Livermore Valley as a land-owner in the early spring of 1882, when he bought 480 acres near Arroyo del Valle for two hundred dollars in gold coin, according to a not impossible story. There he planted vines, built a home and a winery, dug storage tunnels, and in 1886 bottled the first wines under the Cresta Blanca label. The name was taken from a white patch on a mountain crest visible from the vineyard. He may well have made wine there earlier, however, for once at a winemakers' convention, pointing out the value of practical experience, he boasted that he and his wife had made wine in a cow shed, and it was good wine. (Professor Hilgard, against whose belief in the value of scientific knowledge the statement was directed, never let Wetmore forget it, referring sarcastically through the years to wine made in cow sheds.)

By then well acquainted with all aspects of the industry, Wetmore set out only fine grape varieties, grafted them on native American roots, and established careful winemaking practices. His ability was confirmed in 1889 when he won gold medals at the Paris exposition for wines he called by the names of their French counterparts, Médoc and Sauternes. What he lacked, however, was business ability. As early as 1887 he was trying to sell the by then well-developed Cresta Blanca estate. To wealthy Adolph Sutro, of San Francisco, he wrote, "Unless some one takes it entire to perfect it according to its true merits—I may find it more advantageous to cut it into small pieces and place it on the market after the Southern California plan." It was worth fifty thousand dollars, he believed, even placing no value on its "esthetic charms." There was a fifteen thousand-dollar mortgage on it. If Mr. Sutro was interested, he could have it for thirty-five thousand dollars cash. Mr. Sutro was not, and somehow Wetmore managed to hang on for a few years longer, until his brother Clarence J. Wetmore, with the help of relatives and associates, took it over.

Clarence, who was famous for being the first student to register at the University of California in Berkeley and then years later for being the oldest living grad, also became famous as the highly successful manager of Cresta Blanca. He maintained it as the prestigious source of wine that years later John Daniel of Inglenook referred to with such respect. The prestige carried over even to the post-Prohibition period, when it came under the ownership of Clarence Wetmore's salesman, Lucien Johnson. Early in World War II Schenley Distillers bought Cresta Blanca. Then, in one of those curious migrations, the Cresta Blanca label became the property of a cooperative, Guild Wineries, which today uses the name on wines produced in Ukiah from grapes grown in Mendocino, Santa Barbara, and San Luis Obispo counties. The Cresta Blanca winery and tunnels and the vineyards that Charles A. Wetmore planted so hopefully and his brother nurtured so carefully, remained unused under Schenley ownership for more than a decade. Then in 1981 they were bought by nearby Wente Bros.

Another winery started only one year later than Cresta Blanca, the same year that Carl Wente came to the Livermore Valley, was that of the Concannon family. How the Irishman James Concannon made the long jump from a potato farm on the Aran Islands to a vineyard in the Livermore Valley is in a way an improbable sounding story, but the beginning is probable enough. He was born in a time of fearful famine in Ireland due to successive failures of the potato crop, and his decision to emigrate to America in 1865 mirrored the decisions already made by thousands of his compatriots. He was eighteen when he arrived in Boston, and he did what many a young Irish immigrant did, took a job in one of the factories hungry for low-cost labor. He worked for the Singer Sewing Machine Company for a time, then he moved on to Augusta, Maine, and became a hotel clerk. It was there that, bright, ambitious Aran man that he was, he began to depart from the pattern. He went to night school to improve his education, and he meanwhile proved himself as an employee as well, for he became manager of the hotel before moving on further west. He took with him to San Francisco in 1874 a bride and continued determination. Working as a salesman for a well-known bookseller, then agent for the manufacturer of a relatively new product, the rubber stamp, he traveled to Mexico. There, it was said, he came to know the head of state, Porfirio Diaz, and—here the story becomes more curious—procured from him a ten-year contract to keep Mexico City's dirty streets cleaned up. Shortly after, he sold the contract to a French firm and returned to California with his gains, seeking a new enterprise.

One was suggested by Joseph Sadoc Alemany, Archbishop of California, whom Concannon, a devout Catholic, had come to know. The suggestion was that there was a need for good sacramental wine, and Concannon should make it. This he began doing in 1883, buying land not far from the Bernard Vineyard that Carl H. Wente bought that same year.

He must have been a fast learner. Having established his vineyard of fine French varieties and started making sacramental wines, he received another concession from Porfirio Diaz. This time he was commissioned to plant good wine grapes in Mexico. So, with cuttings from his Livermore Valley vines he directed the planting of numerous vineyards there.

James Concannon died in 1911, leaving the family vineyard and winery to continue supplying wine to various religious groups through Prohibition under his son Joseph, a colorful World War I cavalryman who continued riding horseback across the Livermore Valley hills and running the winery almost until his death in 1965. In the late 1930s Joseph began selling increasingly to secular wine lovers, and the Concannon family winery continued as a highly respected, conservatively operated family enterprise until it was sold almost a hundred years after its foundation.

State Viticultural Commission member Charles Bundschu, looking back on the decade between 1883 and 1893, could report, "Alameda County, and especially Livermore Valley, appears to have made the most formidable progress in the general rivalry for the production of the higher types of fine table wines."

The three-and-a-half-story stone and brick Gallegos winery, completed in 1885, was built against a cut in a hill so that wagonloads of grapes could be unloaded on the top level where the fermenters were located, and the wine could proceed by gravity to finally reach the ground floor for aging and shipping. Additional aging space was provided in tunnels dug into the hill; they were almost all that remained of the winery after the building itself was shaken down in the earthquake of 1906.

The Gallegos Wine Company claimed, in the late 1880s, to have been "the first in California to adopt and carry on in strict accordance with the principles of Dr. Pasteur" apparatus for pasteurizing wine. The process kept the wines sound, the company stated, "without the use of drugs to prevent the second fermentation or pricking."

Josiah W. Stanford was in charge of the Warm Springs winery when this photograph was taken in the 1890s. The winery itself was far more sophisticated than the grape varieties that went into it. The Swiss cellarmaster in charge when Frona Eunice Wait visited a few years earlier kept everything neat and clean. The interior walls of the buildings were whitewashed, and water was readily available to sluice down the cement floors. There were even "telephones and speaking tubes" connecting the cellars, the office, and the Stanford residence, which is the mansard-roofed building at the far right.

The Stanford vineyard was not as advanced as many others in planting fine wine grape varieties. In 1891 it had 182 acres of Missions (undoubtedly the source of its generally acclaimed angelica) to 75 of Zinfandel and only one or two each of Cabernet Sauvignon, Cabernet franc, Semillon, and Sauvignon blanc. The grapes were picked into what appear to be bushel baskets, which were emptied into the barrel-like containers in the foreground to be carted to the winery.

In 1893 the Carl H. Wente family posed in front of the winery for this group portrait. Ernest Wente is at the left end atop a cask, then his sister Carolyn, then his mother holding Herman, the youngest. Leaning on the upended barrel is the *pater familias,* then Mary, and perched on the barrel at the right is young Carl Wente, who left the family vineyard to become a banker and finally president of the Bank of America. Two more girls were born later. The Oriental rug in the foreground was brought out by Mrs. Wente to dress up the picture.

The second, third, and fourth generations of Wentes in America were photographed in 1954 in the vineyard: Ernest, his son Karl, and Karl's sons, Philip and Eric.

◄ Unloaded at the winery, at the rear of the main structure in the overall view, the grapes were carried up to the crushers at the top of the building. Powered inclined conveyors were fairly common by the 1890s, and several can still be seen in old wineries.

◀ Bordeaux-born Louis Mel, who was instrumental in introducing Sauterne varieties in the Livermore Valley, retained his love of life and good wine into his late nineties.

▶ Clarence J. Wetmore and his foreman stood at two of the entrances of Cresta Blanca's tunnels, in which its wines were aged, for this photograph. Clarence, the slightly younger and considerably quieter brother of Charles A. Wetmore, led the Cresta Blanca winery in its greatest years. Before Prohibition its Souvenir wines were sold throughout the United States and held in high esteem, often introduced to the public by Clarence Wetmore himself. A less intense man than his brother and probably not so hard a worker, he nevertheless served in various capacities on the first Board of State Viticultural Commissioners and then led the second when it was created in 1913. He was also in the forefront of the fight against Prohibition, and after Repeal he gave generously of his time and encouragement to aid the revival of winemaking in California. This picture and those of Cresta Blanca that follow were taken in 1911 by San Francisco photographer Howard C. Tibbitts.

◀ "Olivina Wine Slumbering in Tierage" is the title of this photograph of Julius Paul Smith's champagne cellar. The mustachioed cellarman at left is turning the bottles, which usually contained, according to Smith's neighbor Ernest Wente, exceptionally good champagne.

▶ Chris Buckley, San Francisco's much-lampooned blind political boss of the 1880s, sunk some of his "boodle," as the satirists called it, in a Livermore Valley estate called Ravenswood. There in 1884 he established a vineyard, built a winery and brandy distillery, and advised other vineyardists to plant for quantity, not quality. A lampoon in the *San Francisco Examiner* in 1892 was the form of a letter to Buckley in France from a political henchman, who was his winery foreman. It began: "Dear Chris: Am getting along finely with the vineyard. The grapes are almost ready to dig," and continued, "I went down to the cellar today to get a little wine. When I dipped it up I found it full of pickles . . . Bob explained that a pickle plant had taken root in the cellar and pickled that cask before he knew it. By the way, what do you keep in those big tubs with hoops around them in the cellar? Are they full of boodle?" This cartoon in the satirical weekly *The Wasp* shows Buckley sitting on a keg labeled "Boodle," with his foot on a damsel whose headband reads "Democratic Party."

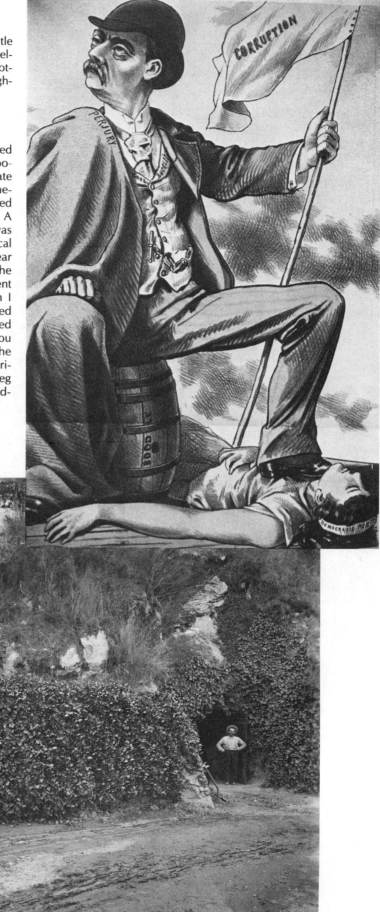

Brought into the Cresta Blanca winery, the grapes were dumped from the field boxes into a shallow screen trough visible here at the upper left, and crushed by hand.

By 1911, multiple-head bottle fillers were in use, as shown here, but filling and corking were still hand operations at Cresta Blanca as elsewhere.

The original Concannon winery continued in use into the 1980s, little changed except for the loss of the windmill and the exterior stairway. Following the death of James Concannon's grandson, Joseph Concannon, Jr., in 1978, the vineyard and winery were sold but continued under the management of Joseph's brother and partner, James Concannon.

At Cresta Blanca, wine was transferred from cask to cask with what was known as an "Armstrong pump."

14. The San Joaquin Valley

THE great San Joaquin Valley, which today produces more than 80 percent of California's wine grapes, is a broad plain between the coastal range and the Sierra Nevada, running south from the delta formed by the meeting of the Sacramento and San Joaquin rivers. Until the 1870s most of it was desert, some swampland. A pair of assiduous researchers, Ernest Peninou and Sidney Greenleaf, could find only two winegrowers in the entire valley to list in their *Directory of California Wine Growers and Winemakers in 1860*. Both were at the north end, where there were more swamps than deserts. One, James H. Commins, had his eighty acres and fifty-nine-gallon inventory of wine actually in the delta, in what is now known as the Lodi area. The other, the partnership of brothers George and William B. West, was not many miles to the south at the city of Stockton, which had grown up on the San Joaquin River during the gold rush as the supply center for the mines of the southern mother lode.

The first man known to grow grapes in the San Joaquin Valley was a Stockton man, its founder in fact, Captain Charles M. Weber. He is said to have planted vines in 1850 in the garden of his home. They were important in demonstrating that Stockton was hospitable to the grape and perhaps suggested as much to young George West, who for two years mined in Tuolumne County. He had arrived in San Francisco in 1850, and he would have not only gone through Stockton to reach the mines but returned to it from time to time for supplies before settling there in 1852. Unlike most gold-seekers, he had made some money, and he and his younger brother, William, who was interested in horticulture, bought land near the city and that year started a nursery and vineyard. The vines they planted were Mission, possibly from Captain Weber's garden. The next year they sent off to their native New England, to the Boston firm of Hovey & Co., for more— some forty varieties, many of them table grapes. Included, however, were unlabeled vines of a wine variety that came to be famous as West's White Prolific. In his 1884 ampelography, Charles A. Wetmore explained that the grape of that name had come to California many years earlier in a collection sent from the Hovey nursery to the Wests.

"There were two vines in the lot, and for years they attracted attention on account of their great vigor and constant fertility. For these reasons," he wrote, "Mr. George West propagated a considerable lot of this variety, and made up the fruit into wine for distillation, together with Rieslings and sometimes Missions. The quality of the brandy began to attract attention, and finally the improvement was traced to this grape, which was then named West's White Prolific, to avoid confusion." Brandy from that grape alone came to be much admired, and the wine made from it had, in Wetmore's view, "a peculiar flavor, but very agreeable."

He believed the grape to be similar to the Colombard, and in recent years his belief has been confirmed. It has been identified as the grape now called the French Colombard, today the most widely grown white wine grape in the San Joaquin Valley.

The West brothers came to devote themselves primarily to grapes, and in 1858 they made their first wine, a small quantity. Production increased steadily year by year after that. William dropped out of the partnership in 1868, and George led the enterprise on to become one of the state's foremost wineries. He himself became one of the state's foremost wine men. As commissioner for the San Joaquin district, he was one of three (Isaac De Turk and J. de Barth Shorb were the others) who were members of the Board of State Viticultural Commissioners for the full fifteen years of its existence.

In 1872, when West entered a number of wines in an exhibition at Sacramento, not many of the grapes he had imported were being used in them. As he explained in his accompanying letter, all of his sweet wines were made from what he called "the California grape," the Mission. Of the three sherries he entered without the addition of "spirit" for fortification, the 1866 was from grapes "dried several days and made in the usual way of making white wine"; the others had "one fourth boiled juice added to common California white wine." The three ports were made similarly, the 1871 with and the others without "boiled juice," the must fermented six to seven days. Another entry, called simply "white sweet wine," was made "in the usual way of making white wine" from the "California grape, well dried." And still another which he called Malaga was apparently the result of luck. It was made from "common red wine," fermented

on the skins ten days, "no spirit added," and "the change took place after the fifth year."

The three dry wines West entered were made from blends of Mission and other grapes. The white was one-quarter "Frontignan," (Muscat Frontignan). One red was partly "Red Frontignan," amount unspecified, and the other was half Zinfandel. He won Special Diplomas for the 1866 sherry and 1871 port, and twenty-five-dollar prizes for the half Zinfandel and for one of the white wines, probably the Frontignan and Mission.

West's Stockton vineyard and winery, which he called El Pinal, came to be, under his guidance and that of his son Frank, the center of one of the state's largest wine businesses. In 1876 he had fifty acres of vines there and fifty more to the northeast on the Calaveras River. One of his cellars held forty thousand gallons of port and sherry, the other twenty thousand of "light wines," probably blended from his own wines and others bought from cooler coastal valleys. Later the Wests built wineries to the south, at Hanford, Selma, and Fresno, and acquired part interest in the big Sierra Vista winery at Minturn—all south of Stockton in the heart of the San Joaquin Valley.

After George West's death in 1899, Frank West added three more wineries. By 1913 he was said to have the largest wine business in the state, with five million gallons of cooperage and thirty-six thousand acres of grapes, from some eleven thousand of Zinfandel to under two thousand each of the next largest plantings, Carignane, Alicante Bouschet, and "the California grape."

The West winery continued until Prohibition. Throughout its history it won prizes and made generally admired sweet wines and brandy. And it trained men who became important in the California wine industry in later years. One was Louis Wetmore, son of Charles, a hero of the 1906 earthquake (See Chapter 18), who served for a time as general manager of the California Wine Association, and for a few years during Prohibition leased the El Pinal winery to make cooking wine. He was one of the experienced pre-Prohibition wine tasters who set standards of judging at the state fairs of the 1930s.

In 1881 George West, surveying the San Joaquin Valley from his vantage point as its representative on the Board of State Viticultural Commissioners, wrote, "Fresno promises to become in the near future the largest grape-growing county in the state, no other, within my knowledge, having made such gigantic strides during the past year." He found that its vineyard acreage had increased more than ten-fold since 1879.

What had started the planting of grapes was a pair of gifts to the valley: irrigation water and a railroad line. They brought fertility to its dry land and access to markets for its produce. Most of the grapes were made into raisins or shipped fresh, but by 1881 Francis T. Eisen was making his sixth vintage.

Eisen is credited with having planted Fresno County's first commercial vineyard, in 1873. The land had been until then, in his own words, "a barren and dreary waste" that "needed only the magic power of water to cause it to yield up its treasures of wealth and develop the lustre of physical beauty which now adorns the fields of Fresno." He wrote these words in 1885. He had by then planted three hundred acres with "the choicest foreign varieties," which, "when not disturbed by the effects of insects or climatic changes," yielded seven tons an acre. That was not a great yield when compared to West's harvest of ten to twelve tons from his Mission plantings, but remarkably good for "choicest foreign varieties."

Legend has it that it was Eisen's wine grapes that began the San Joaquin Valley raisin industry by drying on the vine one torrid autumn and being sent to market in San Francisco where they were sold as exotic Peruvian delicacies at an exotic price. But he himself remained faithful to winegrowing.

A prosperous, seasoned businessman, he seems to have set the pattern for valley winegrowers. Most were moneyed men and drawn, like him, by the idea of cheap land waiting to be developed.

In 1872, having made a "handsome fortune" in San Francisco, he had gone looking for valley land to buy along the newly completed railroad line. Fresno was little more than a railroad station when he first saw it; he bought 650 nearby acres at ten dollars apiece and started developing them. He planted grapes the next year, and in 1875 he made a small experimental crush. In 1876, in time for the vintage, he built a two-story winery with forty thousand gallons of cooperage. It was insulated with adobe, like West's in Stockton. It was, in Eisen's words, "constructed of wood, surrounded with walls of adobe and covered with shingles." This is another 1885 quotation—from the prospectus he prepared for sale of shares in the Eisen Vineyard, when, good businessman that he was, he deemed it necessary to bring in more capital than he could or wished to contribute. In the prospectus he noted that he had experimented with two hundred varieties of wine grapes and was growing those he had found best adapted, but was continuing a small experimental plot; that the winery (by now enlarged more than four-fold) had a storage capacity of five hundred thousand gallons; that its crushers, elevators, and pumps were driven by a water-powered turbine; and that there was a steam engine for the distillery. The success of the enterprise had drawn others to the area, he noted, which was indeed true. His estate, with its splendid avenues and fine residence, had drawn visitors and future settlers by the hundreds, and by 1885 half a dozen large winemaking estates had been established on its pattern.

It was not only moneyed men who had been drawn to the Fresno area. Speculators had bought large tracts, developed them, and sold small farm parcels to people of like mind or common origin who formed agricultural colonies—the Nevada Colony for one, the Church Temperance Colony for another. Most of these colonizers grew grapes, and many supplied them to the wineries.

Next to Eisen's land on the west was the Easterby Rancho, managed by "M. Theo. Kearney," who came to be a leader, albeit a not very popular one, in the viticultural development of Fresno County. He had appeared in San Francisco, background unknown, listed in the 1869 city directory as "capitalist." He first saw Fresno when he was sent there as the agent of one of the earliest developers, and so successful was he that he next was put in charge of promoting and selling parcels of the county's first notably bountiful irrigated cropland, Anthony Y. Easterby's 2,560-acre tract. He advertised it as "the best vineyard land in California," capable of producing ten tons of grapes per acre. He also pointed out that here irrigation water was plentiful and flooding of vineyards would bring "sure death to the phylloxera."

When the Fresno Vineyard Company was incorporated in December 1880 with 450 acres of Easterby Rancho land, Kearney was an investor and in charge of selling its stock. He took credit for having put together the company with the backing of a wealthy Nevadan and several San Francisco businessmen, including the partners in the important wine firm of Lachman & Jacobi, who had inspected Eisen's vineyard. Kearney oversaw the planting of the company's first 220 acres of vines and in 1882 the completion of its two-hundred-thousand-gallon winery. Six or seven years later, when Frona Eunice Wait visited, the vineyard had grown to 360 acres, the winery capacity to five hundred thousand gallons, and the winemakers had "found by experiments that if grapes are picked early a lighter quality of wine is made"—something Hilgard had suggested and which valley winemakers learned all over again many decades later.

So successful was M. Theo. (for Martin Theodore) Kearney with these ventures that he was able to buy 7,000 acres of his own, which he named the Fruit Vale Estate. Here he built a fine residence for himself, surrounded by a landscaped park, and from it to Fresno eleven miles away he thrust a broad avenue lined by palms, magnolias, oleanders, and acacia trees. He furnished his mansion with fine appointments imported from Paris, which he often visited. However, few of his Fresno neighbors and associates—he apparently had no friends there—were ever invited inside. He was haughty, imperious, and uncommunicative, especially about himself and his past. His speech must have been British, for there was speculation that he was (1) the son of a London dock worker pretending he was an aristocrat or (2) a high-born remittance man. His resemblance to Edward VII was remarked upon.

He subdivided most of the Fruit Vale Estate, improving much of the acreage, selling it at $250 an acre with small down payments and long eight-percent mortgages. On some plots he planted fruit and vines and charged more. The buyers were apparently able to gain enough from their crops to make their payments regularly until the general economic slump of 1893, when prices for everything, including grapes and wine, fell as they had periodically since the 1850s. This time raisins were included in the slump, as the three were by then economically interdependent. Of 1893, George West reported wryly, "Had it not been for the diversion of the second-crop Muscats from raisin to winemaking, the raisin markets would have been flooded with low-grade products, while the wine market would have been in much better condition."

Many who had settled on M. Theo. Kearney's estate could not keep up their payments. Without pausing, he foreclosed, getting much of his land back, enhanced by the buyers' improvements.

He was recognized as an able businessman, and his toughness was valued by raisin growers who turned to him for leadership in hard times. In an attempt to stabilize the market, he spoke at Fresno raisin growers' meetings, a curious anticipation of similar meetings of the 1940s addressed by the deceptively emotional, and at least equally able, "Sox" Setrakian.

Kearney became president of the growers' association and served very effectively until ill health sent him off to Bad Nauheim for the cure. On his return he demanded his salary for the months of his absence, but the association refused to pay him. So, having achieved both private and public success but embittered over the loss of a few thousand dollars, he left again, this time for Hawaii. He died at sea in May of 1906.

Kearney is remembered today in Fresno County place names, especially Kearney Park, the site of his home, and the broad avenue leading from it to the center of the city. He is also remembered by researchers in viticulture and the vineyardists who profit by their work, for he left his Fruit Vale Estate to the University of California, which named the Kearney Horticultural Field Station in his memory. There various crops, including grapes, are developed and tested. Among those tested have been new varieties of grapes created by plant geneticist Harold P. Olmo and his associates that have given the traditionally sweet-wine-producing San Joaquin Valley valuable raw material for better table wines.

Among the other early real estate investors drawn to the Fresno area was August Weihe, who bought a two-and-a-half-square-mile tract on another perimeter of the Eisen estate, named it the Henrietta Ranch, and in 1879 sold it to a man who made it the nucleus of a long-famous winery.

He was George Malter, who incorporated his name into those of the property and its headquarters: St. George Vineyard, at Malter-moro. Born in Silesia and well educated, he had come to the United States after the political upheavals of 1848 and in time put his education to good use, becoming a highly successful mining engineer and builder of mining machinery. San Francisco remained his headquarters after he bought the Fresno property, but like most of the other absentee vineyardists of the area, he developed and operated his property with close attention. In 1884 he completed a winery, having planted an extensive vineyard of wine varieties and a smaller one of raisin grapes, and having bought an interest in additional Easterby Rancho acreage nearby. Over the next fifteen years he added more land, more grape vines, enlarged the winery at Maltermoro, and had a wooden tank built for it that held ninety-six thousand gallons—said to have been the largest wine vat in the world in its time, twice as big as the Great Tun of Heidelberg—the wonder of all who visited the winery. It was destroyed in 1902 when the winery itself was almost totally razed by fire. Nearly a million gallons of wine and brandy were lost. Relatively undaunted, Malter rebuilt this and added another winery to his holdings. It was in Antioch in the Delta region, and from grapes grown mainly in the cooler valleys it supplied St. George with dry wines and some additional brandy. So good a businessman was George Malter that he was able to remain independent of the California Wine Association, which dominated the industry from the mid-1890s until Prohibition.

One reason Malter continued successful was that he had his own warehouses in San Francisco and Eastern cities. Another was his inventiveness. He had earlier developed, with his winemaker, a process for making grape syrup, a by-product that has since given viticulturists an additional market, and he attempted to make an unfortified sweet wine. (How it differed from George West's has not been discovered). Furthermore, he made and advertised a variety of unusual products: sherry bitters, for which he did not claim novelty but only that they contained "the proper proportion of extracts of Cinchona, Gentian, Quasia, and Cascara Sagrada, in a pure, well-matured sherry wine of 18 percent strength, grape spirits"; concentrated grape juice, "a refreshing temperance drink for young people" labeled variously Champagne Mist, Claret Punch, and Cherry Phosphate; special Red Cross Brand table wines for medicinal use; and—at the same price as the bitters, ten dollars for a case of a dozen quarts—bathing brandy.

However, neither these nor its altar wines kept St. George Vineyard operating through Prohibition. Along with most of the other large wineries that had been built up and down the San Joaquin Valley before 1920, it closed down. Some wineries were destroyed one way or another. But many, including some of those which had been dismantled, became the homes of new winery ventures in the 1930s, and, remarkably enough, are still in use today. St. George itself, however, though revived for a time, was finally razed for a housing tract.

The first grape vines planted in the San Joaquin Valley, so far as is known, were Mission vines that Captain Charles M. Weber set out in the garden of his gracious home on the Stockton Slough.

At West's El Pinal in 1910, these young men were clearly bracing themselves for the blinding burst of the photographer's flash powder. On the ladder is government gauger Lee Jones, who was soon to become an employee of El Pinal and then after Repeal the builder of the first winery to make full use of the latest engineering and technological advances of the 1930s. At the left is Louis Wetmore, then manager of West's winery and distillery. The year before, in a spectacular attempt to fight a fire that destroyed part of El Pinal, he had fought unsuccessfully to save what was then the largest brandy still on the Pacific Coast.

El Pinal, the West winery, had grown to great size by 1913, when this photograph was proudly printed in a Stockton boosters' booklet. It shows carloads of Tokay grapes waiting to go into the winery. West's storage cellars were built of siding-covered adobe, which gave good insulation against summer heat. Part of one remains standing in Stockton today.

133

The year Francis T. Eisen planted his first five acres of grapes, skeptical observers joked that one person would be able to eat his whole vintage. By 1890 the vineyard had some 285 acres bearing vigorously. This picture of a part of it shows its grape vines stretching across the flat land of the valley, the winery buildings halfway along at the left.

M. Theo Kearney, a recluse and a hard businessman, was nevertheless a considerable contributor to the development of the San Joaquin Valley. He looked like the English aristocrat that he was rumored either to be or to wish to be taken for, and when he traveled abroad he apparently threw off his solitude and attended many a fine social gathering. Here he is setting out from his Fresno home in his elegant chauffeur-driven limousine.

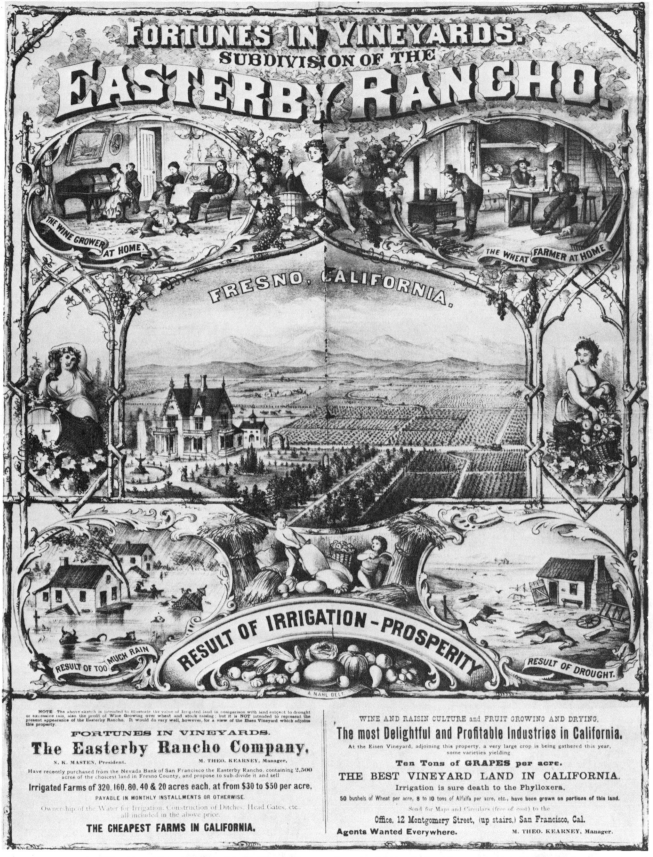

"The Best Vineyard Land in California" was advertised for sale in this poster-sized lithograph drawn by well-known California artist Arthur Nahl. Neither too much nor too little water but precisely the necessary amount would, it indicated, be supplied by irrigation. And prosperity would be the prize for those wise enough to buy Easterby Rancho land. Too small to read easily even in the original is the note explaining that the center picture is not the Easterby Rancho itself but is similar to an adjoining one. The comfortable parlor shown in the picture in the upper left corner, "The Wine Grower at Home," is in contrast to the bare cabin interior of "The Wheat Farmer at Home" in the upper right corner.

The Fresno Vineyard Company winery that Kearney oversaw produced 35,500 gallons of wine in 1883, mainly sherry, port, angelica and Madeira, which it shipped in bulk to San Francisco, undoubtedly to Lachman & Jacobi. In 1887 it was enlarged by one-fourth, and that year Kearney went to England in search of new capital. He succeeded in enlisting the aid of George Baden-Powell, British M.P., publicist, and author of the book *Protection and Bad Times,* for the proposed Anglo-California Vineyard Company. Baden-Powell even wrote a persuasive prospectus, but it was either not persuasive enough or Bad Times took over, for nothing came of it. In 1900 Kearney led another group in the construction of another nearby winery, but after his death in 1906 it was taken over by the California Wine Association.   *Fresno City and County Historical Society*

Palm-loving Benjamin Woodworth started Las Palmas as a grape-growing and raisin-packing enterprise, but when the San Joaquin Valley Railroad laid tracks past the property in 1891 he added a winery. After his death it came into the hands of the California Wine Association; then, during Prohibition and for some years after, it was owned by the Cribari family. In 1954 Las Palmas was acquired by E. & J. Gallo and became the nucleus of its present winery there. This photograph of it was taken in about 1913.

The Thompson Seedless grape, which accounts for a large part of California's total wine production and is the dominant variety for brandy, raisins, and table grapes as well, did not become important until the 1890s when it was taken to the San Joaquin Valley from the Sacramento Valley. About 1872, William Thompson of Sutter County sent to a New York State nursery for some vines called Lady deCoverly. He pruned them short in the usual way and was unimpressed by their yield. Then he happened to neglect pruning one vine at all, and its luxuriance astounded him. Neighbors who got cuttings from it renamed it Thompson's Seedless and learned to leave long shoots when pruning. From a single vine in one grower's vineyard came the grapes in this picture, posed after the fashion of the biblical Joshua and Caleb carrying the Big Grape to the Promised Land.

A curiosity of its time and a forecast of the future was this octagonal fermenting house with its three rings of tanks into which the must flowed from the high platform in the center. It was built by C. K. Kirby, who had been an architect in Boston before becoming the overseer of four hundred acres of vines in the San Joaquin Valley. The grapes were carried to the crusher by the conveyor running up at an angle from the ground at the left in this cross-section drawing. The juice from them was then fed into the tanks by a revolving pipe "not unlike a boom derrick," according to the description that accompanied the drawing in the San Francisco *Examiner* in 1890. Here it is shown in position over the tank at the far left. Eighty-odd years later, the Christian Brothers would devise a remarkably similar circle design (but without using gravity flow) for their "fermenting-in-the-round" champagne cellar at St. Helena in the Napa Valley.

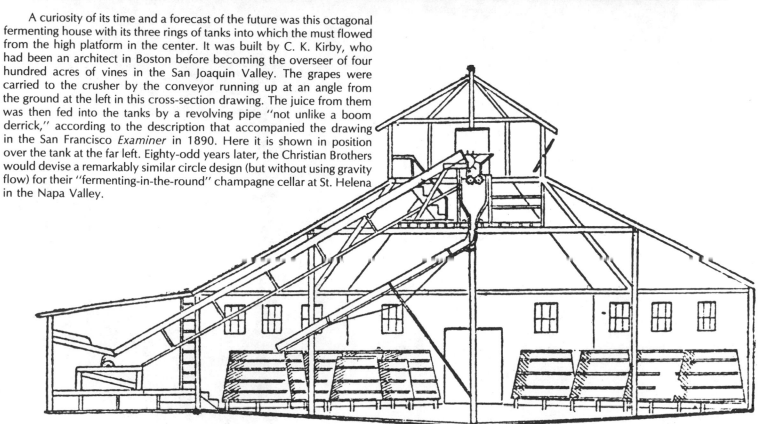

Bathing Brandy

Grape brandy, rich in essential oils, for the use of the bath, is a medical innovation and modern luxury.

Every bath should certainly contain a supply of this grape brandy.

Brandy used on the skin after the taking of a cold or hot water bath, has a strangely pleasant and greatly beneficial effect on the body and mind.

Grape brandy containing a large percentage of fine essential oils of the grape, will be found of much more medical value in the external application to the the skin than ordinary alcohol. Alcohol stimulates the nerves, essential oils serve to strengthen the muscles. These oils not only nourish and improve the skin but they impart direct nourishment to the flesh through the skin. It will be found that parts of the body treated with grape brandy rich in grape oils, will be perceptibly developed and strengthened.

Massage treatment with this brandy will physically improve the condition of the skin, render it soft, glossy, clear and almost translucent, hence the use of grape brandy for sponge bath purposes, is not only one of the greatest luxuries of the age, but it is also one of the most beneficial of the

uses of stimulants, serving as it does to sustain and restore the strength of body and mind. Alcoholic stimulants cannot in all cases be taken to advantage through the stomach, whilst some diseases, ailments and weaknesses call for internal use of alcoholic stimulants; other disorders are sometimes aggravated thereby; more over the abuse of strong drink is to be feared, since the nerves are easily over-stimulated. On the other hand, the external use of alcohol, or better, grape brandy, is not subject to these objections.

The ancient Romans knew of no luxuries as great as that of the use of grape brandy for the bath. No bath can be more beneficial than the brandy bath. The expense of using brandy at the bath is not by any means great since a quart costing a dollar will last a month, reasonably used by one person. Our bathing brandy is almost twice as strong in grape spirits than the brandy for internal use and it contains about 10 per cent of the essential oils of the grape.

Price per case of 12 qts $10 00

George Malter was inventive and original. His bathing brandy was intended to and may have created a new market.

Raisins in boxes with decorative labels like this carried Fresno's fame throughout the United States.

15. Big Wineries

BIGNESS came to the wine industry in the 1880s and increased almost until Prohibition. Of course there had always been a "biggest" wine estate. Mission San Gabriel was in the earliest period. Buena Vista was in its day, and as others caught up with it and surpassed it, they too claimed pre-eminence in size.

It is a difficult factor to measure, as comparable statistics for winegrowing estates do not exist. We have acreage in wine grapes for some, for other wine storage capacity, or wine actually in storage. For still others we have crushing capacity. And all at random dates. Nevertheless, it is clear that in the latter decades of the nineteenth century George West built up a big wine estate, and so did each of several Fresno County viticulturists. So did winegrowers in southern California, notably Leonard J. Rose and J. de Barth Shorb of the San Gabriel Valley, and so did the financiers who owned the Cucamonga Vineyard Company. All these, and the Asti estate of Italian Swiss Agricultural Colony, were unequivocally dwarfed, however, by Leland Stanford's huge winegrowing estate at Vina in Tehama County; it in turn was surpassed early in this century by the Italian Vineyard Company that Secondo Guasti created in the Cucamonga area.

Sunny Slope was the vineyard and orange grove that Leonard J. Rose established in 1861, a few months after he arrived in Los Angeles with fourteen thousand dollars he had made as a hotel keeper in Albuquerque. He bought 160 acres just northeast of Mission San Gabriel from William Wolfskill, added to it until its vineyards surpassed those of his neighbor Benjamin D. Wilson, and in time had the most famous showplace and largest vineyard estate in California. He became an authority on winegrowing, the mentor of Lucky Baldwin who shared his enthusiasm for that and thoroughbred horses. He served on the Board of State Viticultural Commissioners as the Los Angeles district representative. And, unfortunately, he went into politics.

His friend Harris Newmark, Los Angeles businessman and chronicler, told the story of his downfall. In 1887 he ran for the State Senate and won. Thereafter he increasingly neglected his business affairs, until his sizable fortune melted away. First he had to sell his New York wine agency, then Sunny Slope itself. The English syndicate that bought it gave him

$75,000 in cash, the remainder of the $1,-250,000 selling price in stock. The cash went, and the syndicate failed. In 1899, almost penniless, he took his own life.

A happier story is that of another of his neighboring winegrowers, J. de Barth Shorb, who had married B. D. Wilson's daughter and bought land next to Wilson's Lake Vineyard for his own vineyard. After his father-in-law's death he in effect consolidated the two and established the San Gabriel Wine Company. He too got capital from England, but without disaster, and built what was in its time the state's largest winery, with a storage capacity of fifteen million gallons. There was also a distillery, and only Folle blanche grapes went into its highly esteemed brandy.

Shorb died in 1896, not as wealthy as he should have been for all his energy, but full of honors for having served on the Board of State Viticultural Commissioners with leadership and enthusiasm during its entire span of years, and having, by both precept and public endeavor, upheld and advanced the quality of California wine.

In 1905 Henry E. Huntington bought the Shorb family's property. Today the Huntington Library, Art Gallery, and magnificent Botanical Gardens occupy part of the Shorb estate, an echo of the quality of J. de Barth Shorb.

The California wine industry had attracted capital from the state's bankers and businessmen-financiers for several decades. William C. Ralston of the powerful Bank of California, it may be recalled, had invested in Agoston Haraszthy's Buena Vista, and there was many a wealthy silent partner in many another winery. In 1871 Isaias W. Hellman, a leading Los Angeles banker, together with a banking partner, John G. Downey (later to be governor of California), and wine man Benjamin Dreyfus, bought five thousand acres of Rancho Cucamonga, where grapes had been grown and wine had been made since before the American conquest. They put Jean Sansevain in charge, and in 1873 he produced angelica that would sell at auction 106 years later for $212.50 a bottle—still sound. Hellman himself would, before that, play a larger part in the state's wine industry, but meanwhile the Cucamonga winegrowing estate held for a time the title of biggest in California. That was challenged for a few years by the short-lived vineyard of Los Angeles businessman and entrepreneur Remi Nadeau. But it was left to another individual, Leland Stanford, to create the enterprise that for many years went unchallenged by any. Perhaps it was the name Vina on the railroad station in the Sacramento Valley that first drew Leland Stanford's attention to it as a potential vineyard area, for in 1872 his Southern Pacific completed its line that far north from San Francisco. In later years, after he bought the ranch there, he and his family lived in their private car whenever they visited it.

The name Vina undoubtedly had its origin much earlier. Peter Lassen, the Danish pioneer, had planted Mission vines there shortly after he was granted the Rancho Bosquejo in 1843 or 1844, and it was said to be "the extraordinary thrift and energy" of those same old vines that made Stanford decide to buy the land. Most of the original rancho had passed in 1852 to Henry Gerke, another pioneer, a German who about the time Lassen was harvesting his first grapes was building himself a fine two-story house, way out in the unsettled sand hills of San Francisco near what is now the crowded intersection of Mason and Eddy streets. At the ranch Gerke planted imported grape varieties that must also have caught Stanford's eye, for when he bought the ranch he was determined to make fine table wines, and he had some knowledge of the subject.

As governor of California in 1862 and 1863, he had been the recipient of communications from Agoston Haraszthy about the value to California winemakers of imported grapes, and the importance of the state's taking the lead in distributing those Haraszthy had ordered sent from Europe (and also repaying his expenses while collecting them there). Of course the Warm Springs vineyard and winery had furnished Stanford with first-hand observation, and furthermore during his travels he had compared Europe's wines to California's, to the disadvantage of the former. Nevertheless, after he bought the Vina ranch, he brought Frenchmen with vineyard and winemaking experience to work there.

By 1881 when Stanford bought the first part

of what became a fifty-five thousand-acre holding, Gerke had planted seventy-five acres in
vines and built a winery with a storage capacity
of a hundred thousand gallons and an annual
production of ninety thousand gallons of
claret, Riesling, angelica, and sherry, all said
to have been popular. In the next two years,
Stanford planted more than a hundred thousand vines, mainly Burger, "Blaue Elben,"
Charbono, Black Malvoisie, and Zinfandel,
later adding more table wine varieties and then
sweet wine grapes from the San Gabriel Valley.
He poured hundreds of thousands of dollars
into the enterprise, and the same kind of enthusiasm and determination that he lavished
upon Eadweard Muybridge's less expensive
but more successful experiment in making se-
quential photographs of the horse in motion
at Stanford's Palo Alto farm. In spite of the
death of Leland Stanford, Jr., in 1884, which
ended the governor's interest in building a
million-dollar home at Vina, he continued to
expand its vineyards and its plantings of many
other crops as well. In 1886 he built a huge
winery, reminiscent in details of that at Warm
Springs. He then had both the largest winery
and the largest vineyard in the world. But
money and size failed to produce the fine dry
wines he wanted. In the end his sweet wines
were considered good, but it was only his
brandy that achieved real success. In 1890, according to one source, the entire vintage from

Vina's 3,825 acres of wine grapes went to the
ranch's distillery—and Leland Stanford then
became known as the world's largest distiller
of grape brandy. This in spite of the fact that
he had embarked upon the winegrowing project stating that it was in the interest of temperance and that wine was the best protection
against the habit of drinking spirits.

When Leland and Jane Lathrop Stanford decided to establish a university in memory of
their son, the Vina property was turned over
to it as a source of perpetual income. Leland
Stanford died in 1893, the year the market
hit bottom, and his widow cut back the Vina
operations. A teetotaler, she liked the jelly
made from the wild grapes on the ranch and
she believed brandy useful for medicinal purposes, but that was the extent of her viticultural interest. David Starr Jordan, the university president, complained that Vina was
costing five hundred dollars a day, and although before the end of the decade it was
at least breaking even, the gathering Prohibitionist sentiment militated against having
profits from a winery and distillery go toward
educating the young. In 1915 and 1916 the
vines were pulled out. In 1919 Vina was sold.
The two million dollars it sold for went into
the Stanford University endowment, which
would have been seven million dollars to the
good if the founder had put all the money
into it that went into his Vina ranch.

Leonard J. Rose's Sunny Slope vineyard covered more than five hundred acres of land in what is now the cities of Pasadena and San Marino. In the late 1870s Rose and a partner, Charles Stern, were making more than a hundred thousand gallons of wine each year and some thirty-five thousand gallons of brandy. It took fifteen pounds of grapes to make a gallon of their wine and forty-five to make a gallon of their brandy.

Elias J. Baldwin won the nickname "Lucky" fair and square in a manner of speaking, having almost always come out ahead of his speculations in business, mining, real estate, and horse racing. He was a dedicated booster of Southern California, pointing out to a balky prospective buyer of a lot in one of his developments, "Hell, we're giving away the land. We're selling the climate!" In 1875 he bought the Santa Anita Ranch in the San Gabriel Valley, paying for it out of a tin box he carried with him containing several million dollars he had just made on a Nevada mine. A magnificent estate to begin with, he developed it even more magnificently, planting exotic gardens, laying out a race track, and establishing a large vineyard that a contemporary described as "fairly weeping with the fruity juices" of an eclectic collection of grapes. In the winery he built were "hundreds of thousands of gallons of burgundy, claret, Riesling, Muscat, Tokay, Gutedel, Madeira and other wines, together with excellent brandies." By the end of the 1880s, when Frona Eunice Wait reported upon Santa Anita's "vinous products," they had won eleven gold medals in various expositions, and Baldwin's viticultural enterprise, while far from the state's biggest, had become one of the most famous.

An unromantic but necessary winery task, getting rid of the pomace left after the grapes have been crushed and pressed, was the subject of this unusual photograph showing workers loading the material into containers and onto a cart to be carried away. The photograph, in the Huntington Library collection, was made by Carleton E. Watkins at an unidentified winery in the San Gabriel area about 1880.

An old-school gentleman, kind and courteous, sometimes too generous for his own good, but always high-minded and an honor to the California wine industry—such was the general characterization of J. de Barth Shorb. This portrait of him and others as well attest to the accuracy of Frona Eunice Wait's statement that he was the handsomest vine grower in the state.

Leland Stanford's fame rested on more than being the world's biggest winegrower and brandy distiller in the late nineteenth century. He had been first an indifferently successful lawyer in New York State and Wisconsin, then a successful merchant in California, then a reasonably effective governor of the state, then a member of the highly successful "big four" who built the transcontinental railroad and gained for themselves great fortunes. He spent part of his on his Palo Alto farm, where he bred famous race horses, and on his huge Vina Ranch, but more on the university that he and his wife established in memory of their son on land near their home. A Republican party stalwart, he spent his final years as a member of the United States Senate.

Leland Stanford's winery at Palo Alto was supplied by 158 acres of wine grapes, which, together with eight acres of table grapes, yielded 620 tons in 1890—less than four tons to the acre. The varieties included Zinfandel, Riesling, Mission, Muscat, Trousseau, Charbono, and Verdal. No vines are left today, and the winery building is part of a shopping center.

▶ J. de Barth Shorb called his vineyard estate San Marino, after his Maryland birthplace. In 1903 Henry E. Huntington bought the property and built the Huntington Library and Art Gallery on part of it, retaining the name and passing it on to the city created around it.

◀ Created by a long-forgotten artist, this romantic oil painting shows the Shorb San Gabriel Wine Company buildings against a backdrop of the Sierra Madre, with a connecting conveyor reminiscent of an aqueduct crossing the Roman *campagna.* From the winery came port that was said, in an 1890 article in the highly pro-California-wine San Francisco *Examiner,* to be vastly superior to Portugal's dreadfully adulterated wine of the same name, and cognac that was highly superior to the dubious beverage made in France. Many others also praised Shorb's wines and brandy, however. In 1955 a bottle of the port of 1893 was pronounced "a benediction" by connoisseur Lindley Bynum, who also found an 1891 San Gabriel Cabernet Sauvignon still "to be savored with pleasure and respect."

145

Stanford's winery at Vina, depicted here on one panel of a four-part panorama of the ranch, was painted by an unknown artist. The panels were given by the widowed Jane Lathrop Stanford to the Stanford University museum.

Inside the Vina fermenting house, must was delivered to the sixteen-hundred-gallon vats through a movable pipe system somewhat similar to that used in the octagonal Sierra Park fermenting house. The stemmers and crushers were located above, and the conveyor that carried the boxes of grapes up to them is visible here at the left just beyond the slanting pipe.

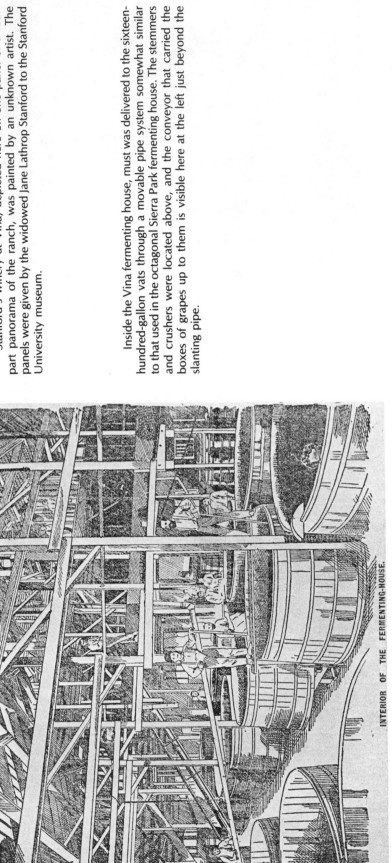

INTERIOR OF THE FERMENTING-HOUSE.

16. And Asti and Guasti

I N 1881 there were some seventy-five hundred Italians in California, many of them recent immigrants who had traveled to America not for political reasons but to improve their condition. Because so many had come from poor rural areas, and they were poorly educated, the stereotype of all Italians in California was of illiterates good only for digging ditches. Even the educated who came had to combat this general prejudice. One graduate of a school of enology in Italy found himself discriminated against in a curious way by another Italian immigrant of an earlier period who had gained a position of authority. He was an official of the Italian Swiss Agricultural Colony who ordered the young immigrant to pay a new assistant more than he himself was getting because "you know, he is an American, and if we don't pay them good wages they criticize us."

The Italian Swiss Agricultural Colony was established in 1881 for the purpose of giving rural-born Italian and Swiss—mainly Italian—immigrants a chance to earn land by working on it. That is a simplification of the plan conceived by Andrea Sbarboro on the general idea of the building and loan societies that he had been instrumental in starting, organizations designed to provide pay-as-you-go homes for San Francisco Bay Area workers. Sbarboro, himself an immigrant who had worked as a grocery clerk, gone to school nights, and become an important financier in the San Francisco Italian community, raised the initial capital for the Italian Swiss Agricultural Colony to buy vineyard land. He invited all interested immigrants to an open meeting and made these proposals to them: In return for board, room, wine for personal consumption, and wages of thirty-five dollars a month, they would work in the vineyards. Each man would take five dollars out of his wages each month for the purchase of five shares of stock in the association. In twenty-five years each would own enough stock to turn in for full ownership of his plot of land.

But actual cooperative ownership of the association's properties would have to wait many years until they passed into the hands of the organization known as Allied Grape Growers; that was far in the future. In 1881 Andrea Sbarboro's proposal thudded. Explained Edmund Rossi, a second-generation member of the family most active in Italian Swiss, "Those people, immigrants, didn't have even those few dollars to put aside . . . and they couldn't be expected to live on future prospects, because they were poor."

They were interested in working, however, so Sbarboro forged ahead, dug up more capital from his well-to-do Italian associates, formed a corporation, and put the immigrants to work as employees clearing the land he and two of the other shareholder-directors had chosen. It was a fifteen-hundred-acre tract of gently rolling hills in the Russian River Valley of northern Sonoma County, much like vineyard land in Piedmont in northern Italy. Houses and work buildings were constructed, and the community was named after that famous Piedmont wine city, Asti. Many of the immigrants were still there twenty-five years later, still working for wages.

In the beginning they set out grapes, mainly Zinfandel and Riesling, although Italian and some other European vines were imported by Dr. Giuseppe Ollino, a physician who became secretary of the organization. No winery was planned at first, as the grapes were to be sold, but when the vines started bearing, the price for grapes had fallen from thirty dollars to eight dollars a ton. Again it seemed better to go forward than retreat, so it was decided that in the future the organization itself would give its grapes a home. More money was raised, and in 1886 a winery was started. By autumn of 1887 it was ready for its first vintage. It was a disaster. From the fine big new stone plant came vinegar.

When Antonio Perelli-Minetti went to work at Italian Swiss in 1902, he was told that the first winemaker was a Swiss Italian from a cold clime, "and the story went that in Switzerland they had to close the windows and doors and sometimes heat up the place in order to ferment, and this fellow did the same thing over there in Asti." He made a hundred thousand gallons of vinegar.

Enter Pietro C. Rossi who, curiously enough, was later to install in that same winery one of the first winery refrigeration systems in California. A friend of Dr. Ollino, he was a pharmacist who had studied chemistry at the University of Turin, the owner of a drug store in San Francisco. Asked to come to Asti as a part-time troubleshooter, he ended by giving up his drug store and taking full charge. It was said there was never again a vintage disaster.

Rossi became president and general manager of the corporation, and in time its largest stockholder. He was a good complement to Sbarboro. P. C. Rossi's son Edmund recalled Sbarboro as pleasant, affable, "a smooth talker, very polished," while "my father was purely the businessman; he never made talks."

He acted, however. Although not until 1897 did the corporation stop ploughing its profits back into the enterprise and start paying dividends, its wines had started winning prizes in 1892, when they were awarded gold medals at expositions in Genoa and Dublin. More gold medals came from the 1893 Columbian World's Fair in Chicago and its echo, the San Francisco 1894 Midwinter Fair. The next year one came from Bordeaux, and the following year "grand diplomas of honor" from Turin and Asti in Italy. In 1900 came the glory of another gold medal from that year's great Paris exposition.

Meanwhile Sbarboro was writing, speaking, publicizing not only Italian Swiss wines but the wines of California as a whole. He knew how to use a combination of facts, logic, and common sense persuasively. Typical was a letter he composed just before America's Great White Fleet made its triumphal visit to San Francisco in 1908. With an Americanized immigrant's zeal, he wrote, "We believe the time opportune for one and all to show their loyalty and patriotism by using only CALIFORNIA products in the entertainment of our distinguished visitors during their stay in this City," and pointing out that recently both King Victor Emanuel and Emperor William of Germany had decreed that only their countries' wines be served at their tables. Had he been as effective in his equally vigorous campaign against Prohibition, the wine industry would never have experienced a thirteen-year hiatus.

Until 1901 Italian Swiss kept forging ahead toward self-sufficiency. Instead of depending upon others to market its wines, it established its own vaults and sales offices in New York, Chicago, and San Francisco. In 1897, after a break between the rival organizations, the California Wine Association and the California Winemakers' Corporation, of which it was a leading member, it decided upon another big step. To avoid having to sell its wines for lack of storage facilities, it expanded the capacity of its cellars in San Francisco to two million gallons, and built a huge tank at Asti that became another of California's wonders.

Then in 1901 it gave in and joined with the ever more dominant California Wine Association, which took a half interest in Italian Swiss. It was at this time that "Agricultural" was dropped from the name. As simply Italian Swiss Colony, it continued functioning independently under Rossi's leadership, so competitive with other wineries of the Association that even some members of the wine industry did not know of the affiliation.

And it continued growing. It increased its plantings so that it could claim the "largest vineyard of choice European wine grapes in the United States." It bought more vineyards and built or bought additional wineries—two in Sonoma County, four in the San Joaquin Valley. By 1911 it had a storage capacity of over fourteen million gallons, equal to a third of California's entire annual wine production.

Then came a critical blow. In October P. C. Rossi was killed. His son recalled the Sunday morning. "He'd just finished breakfast. Went down the road. The stableman came with the horse that he wanted to try out." It was harnessed to a small carriage. Rossi got in and took the reins. "The horse began to get skittish. My father got nervous, went to jump, and he fell on his head. That was it." He was fifty-six and had expected to live much longer, but fortunately he had seen his twin sons, Edmund and Robert, through college, taken them to Europe and North Africa to observe winemaking, and trained them at Asti for two years.

Both had graduated from the University of San Francisco, then studied viticulture and enology for a year at the University of California, long enough to have learned theoretically about some of the advanced practices they would see in use in Europe. That trip with their father was cut off by news that several of the key men at Asti had left to form their own company. The Rossis hurried home, and the day after they arrived Robert went to work as winery manager and Edmund went to work as winemaker.

In France, wine people had been talking about the use of pure yeast culture and sulfur dioxide in winemaking, and that became "one of the modern techniques that was of the greatest value to the quality of California wines,"

Edmund recalled. His father had ordered some sulfur dioxide sent to California, and it arrived just in time for the vintage.

"The first thing I did was to put into fermentation practice the use of the sulphur dioxide, together with pure yeast cultures, and did that among the company's different wineries." He had to do it surreptitiously, for it was not yet generally accepted. After his father's death and the sale of the family's remaining shares in the corporation in 1914 to the California Wine Association, Edmund continued his practice of what has since come to be the standard and approved method of using controlled quantities of sulphur dioxide to inactivate undesirable organisms on the grapes, as well as pure yeast cultures. He continued in secret, however, and the legendary Almond R. Morrow, under whom he worked, never learned what he was doing. "I used to ship this sulfur dioxide from the winery at Asti where I was, and I used to ship it out as cleaning solution to different wineries," he recalled. When he submitted to Morrow samples of the wines he had made, "he complimented me. I never told him one of the principal reasons why the wines were so good. They were excellent! Sound fermentation, beautiful color, fine flavor and all that."

Secondo Guasti's Italian Vineyard Company was in some ways like, but in more ways unlike, the Italian Swiss Agricultural Colony. It was established in 1900 by a man who had begun his life in America as a coal heaver before becoming a cook. He was from Italy—Piedmont—and he had some background, whether through family or environment, in the wine trade. So he progressed somehow from cook to winemaker, buying grapes and making wine—five thousand gallons his first year, which would have been some time in the late 1880s. Details of his early activities are not easily found, but—again somehow—he became interested in the viticultural potentiality of a strip of land called the Cucamonga Desert, an infertile-looking southern California tract surrounded by irrigated orange groves and occasionally intruded upon by small half-tended vineyards. It had been laid out optimistically, when the railroad came through, into lots still marked by stakes. There was one house on the tract, but it was deserted. Guasti examined the sandy surface, and here and there he, with equal optimism, dug below it and found damp loam that he thought would support vine roots very well without irrigation. (As Antonio Perelli-Minetti noted, recalling Secondo Guasti, "You know the Italians, all they see is wine, any place they go.") So, as a 1909 article put it, "He led forth many men of finance into the sands" in an effort to get them to invest. He succeeded, by the harvest, but then had to chase down owners of the lots in order to put the vast tract back together in a single holding. He succeeded in that too, only to face hordes of jackrabbits that could not be eradicated through the frequent rabbit hunts he organized. Four thousand dollars' worth of rabbit-proof fence was the only answer. Within nine years the venture was a recognized success.

"Today," stated the 1909 article in that earnest magazine, *The World's Work*, "the great wine-ranch, with its stone buildings, private railroad and modern wine-making machinery, represents an investment of more than a million dollars."

A community similar to that at Asti had been created around the winery, with a school and a church. The town was named Guasti, the church San Secondo d'Asti. Homes were built for permanent employees, most from Italy, Spain, and France, "where the best vineyard workers are to be found. The company provides them with model quarters—neat cottages for the married folk, and a club house with two dormitories, shower and tub baths, and a large social hall for the single men." During the harvest season Japanese workers were brought in, since, although Indians still harvested grapes in small southern California vineyards, there were not enough of them to supply the Italian Vineyard Company, which needed 250 to 300 men. For this was then "the largest vineyard in the world," with four thousand acres in vines, about the same size as Vina had been at its height. Later Guasti grew to five thousand acres.

The winery, completed in 1904, was huge. It is almost intact today. The main building, six hundred feet long and one hundred feet wide, is built of granite blocks brought from the mountains a dozen miles away. It is divided into three two-hundred- by one-hundred-foot cellars, one of them without interior posts. According to Philo Biane, who was in charge of the winery just after Prohibition and whose Brookside Vineyard Company later owned it, the unobstructed space and the twenty-three-foot-high walls allowed huge tanks to be built in that cellar. A fourth two-hundred- by one-hundred-foot cellar is underground, and until about 1916 barrels were hauled up out of it on a ramp by ropes pulled by mules.

In 1915 the Italian Vineyard Company could claim five million gallons of cooperage, and a one-million-gallon fermenting cellar. It was by then, and continued to be until Prohibition, a major factor in the California wine market, sending its vintages across the country and once even beating the giant California Wine Association in a price war.

Pietro C. Rossi, who directed Italian Swiss Colony's activities from 1888 until his death in 1911, was, in the words of another Italian who became a successful winemaker, "a wonderful man, dynamic, very handsome, very polished, a big man, a man who would impress you. . . . He was strict because you have to be strict in business, but he was very kind and very generous. I never heard him talk loud to a man. I remember one time they had two tanks for sherry, made out of oak. The tanks had been idle the year, probably, and when the wine was being pumped in them, you couldn't stop it from leaking on the floor. And Mr. Rossi came over there and he was pretty excited, but he wasn't rough at all with the men, and I was one of them. Anybody else might have just taken a stave and—But he didn't do it. He said, 'You shouldn't have put the wine in.' "

The largest wine tank in the world was the claim Italian Swiss Colony made for the five-hundred-thousand-gallon concrete vat partly sunk into the earth amidst its Asti vineyards. "Giving each person a quart," a company booklet noted, "it would supply two million people at dinner." It still exists today, but it holds now only a little more than three hundred thousand gallons. The mystery of the missing gallonage was cleared up by a note on a photograph in the California Historical Society. It explained that the 1906 earthquake, which hit Sonoma County hard, cracked the tank. When it was repaired it was divided into three sections and its total capacity reduced by nearly 40 percent.

Andrea Sbarboro, who built at Asti a summer home modeled, like Agoston Haraszthy's, after a Pompeiian villa, sits on the ground holding his dog in this 1894 photograph of what appears to have been a weekend hunting party. Dr. Giuseppe Ollino stands at the right end, with Louis Profumo of the company's New York office next to him, and a Mr. Kucich, foreman of the cooperage department, at the left end. Ettore Patrizi, editor of the San Francisco newspaper *L'Italia,* sits with the Rossi twins, Robert D. at left, Edmund A. at right. They were to succeed to management of Italian Swiss Colony until Prohibition, operate it through the dry years, and then pursue parallel careers in the industry until Robert's death in 1961. After that, Edmund Rossi went on to become manager of a state winegrowers' organization.

▶ Big, short-necked, round-headed, broad-shouldered, and bluff-mannered Secondo Guasti was jolly with his friends, but according to an admiring description, "tremendously American in his adherence to the national motto: Business is business." So successful was he in business that the one-time cook came to dine upon golden plates.

◀ "Hundred Couples Dance in Big Wine Vault," read a headline in the San Francisco *Morning Call* of May 15, 1898, the day after Italian Swiss threw a party to inaugurate its big new tank. The guests, after being welcomed with a drive through the vineyards and a sumptuous luncheon served under Andrea Sbarboro's grape arbors, spent the afternoon dancing to a sixteen-piece band inside the tank—"an event never before witnessed in the history of the world," according to the *Call.*

Over these big Italian Vineyard Company fermenting tanks, young Louis M. Martini presided for three months in 1919. Called to take over temporarily for the winemaker, he at one point confounded everyone by ordering winery work completely stopped for four days. James Barlotti, the manager, was distressed. "Why don't you do something?" he asked. Answered Martini, "When I'm ready to go, I'll tell everybody. If they don't like it, I'll go away." They followed his orders, and according to Martini, "I made at least five hundred thousand gallons in three months, and all was perfect." Apparently Secondo Guasti found it so too, for when Martini left he gave him "a nice dinner at Delmonico's in Los Angeles and a $100 present, and thanked me."

At harvest time the grapes were moved from the Guasti vineyards to the winery in gondola cars hauled by a fifteen-ton locomotive named the Italia. The gondolas themselves could be tipped sideways to slide the grapes directly into the crushers.

The vast Guasti vineyards stretched across the sandy Cucamonga plain. Here stacked along the edge are sections of the railroad track that were laid in place at harvest time so that the gondolas could be pulled through the vineyards to receive the freshly picked grapes.

17. The California Wine Association

THE California Wine Association, which, it was said, never bottled either a great wine or a bad wine, dominated the state's industry from the year of its formation, 1894, until Prohibition took effect in 1920. Its reason for existence and also its strength lay in stabilization—stabilization of wine quality, and especially stabilization of prices. That it was able to control the market was perhaps an indication of the need for such an organization as well as a testimonial to the evenly good quality of its wines. That it was able to operate without running afoul of antitrust laws was undoubtedly an indication of its careful management. It did not rule without opposition, but rule it did.

To understand how it came into existence, one must go back to the economic conditions of the state's wine industry in the 1880s. The first three years of that decade were, as Arpad Haraszthy later wrote, "halcyon days for everyone possessed of a vineyard," and it seemed as if everyone who was not so possessed bought one. There was a boom in the northern part of the state that rivaled the southern California wine mania of the late 1850s—and it was of course followed by another bust. Although prices for wine and grapes rose briefly in 1885, production then once again overran consumption, and thus it continued for what must have seemed forever to the beleaguered vineyardists and winemakers. A few of the large, well-financed viticultural estates could ride it out comfortably; the rest squirmed.

"Wine Is Too Cheap" read a headline in the San Francisco *Examiner* of July 23, 1889, causing no surprise among winegrowers but catching the attention of the general community. "A California Industry Threatened with Destructive Low Prices," read the subheads. "Sold at Less Than Cost. What Prominent Winemakers Say Must Be Done to Rescue the Industry."

The article, which ran to four full columns and was the first of a series, began with the statement "The wine industry is depressed." It noted that wine that cost twelve and thirteen cents a gallon to make was selling in the vineyards for seven to nine cents a gallon. Then it revealed that the *Examiner*'s publisher, William Randolph Hearst (whose father had in 1885 bought a vineyard), had sent an inquiry to most of the state's leading wine men and to many little-known ones as well, asking their opinions as to causes and remedies. A few had also been interviewed in person.

More than a hundred grape growers and winemakers and two wine dealers answered Hearst's inquiries, which included specific (and leading) questions about the desirability of cooperative brandy distilleries, cooperative wine depots, evidence of dealers' combinations to control prices, and opinions as to any innate faults in California wines that might prevent them from "having a ready sale abroad."

Most of those who replied believed overproduction and poor quality to be the main problems. To combat overproduction they suggested planting no new vineyards, pulling out existing ones, and making wine grapes into raisins—although one man pointed out that raisins could be made back into wine and further depress the market. Most were in favor of controlling the wine supply by "turning all the slops into brandy," as one put it. The idea of distilling the oversupply had many adherents, but not until the 1930s, when there was a similar oversupply of grapes, was it actually tried.

Promoting increased consumption was the other main proposal for attacking overproduction. There were various suggestions: educate hotel keepers and restaurant owners to serve more California wines and charge less for them; combat whiskey drinking, beer drinking, coffee drinking, and temperance fanatics; promote the regular use of wine with meals at home.

Noting the difficulties in regard to the last, B. Ehlers of Napa County declared, "The majority do not like wine or are afraid to use it in the house on account of the women." Alleged Charles Detoy of the Santa Clara Valley, "Nine-tenths of the winegrowers will not use their own product nor induce their farm hands to use it. They prefer to supply teas and coffees at meal times." His remedy, fraught with logic: "that people who are afraid to use their own product quit raising grapes."

Pure wine laws to control the allegedly widespread adulteration of California wines were suggested, as they had been often before. So were the planting of only the best varieties of grapes, and confining varieties to areas where they grew best.

A number of respondents mentioned that much California wine was put on the market too young because the makers had to sell it almost as soon as it had finished fermenting

in order to get necessary funds, or if not then, before it was a year old in order to free cooperage for the next year's vintage, since they could not afford to buy more. Thus "more capital" was a frequently suggested remedy. Cooperative warehouses that would give partial payment to winemakers when they brought their wine in, then age it before selling it, were approved by some. Others believed that cooperatives would fail because of competition among their users and also a probable lack of the expert care needed to keep the wines healthy. It was left to Professor Hilgard to contribute, at the end of the series, a letter spelling out step by step just how quality could be improved by careful viticultural and enological practices.

But most of the blame for whatever quality defects California wine had, and indeed finally for most the problems of the industry, was directed at the wine merchants, "the Frisco dealers."

The only man to be specific about them, however, was W. W. Waterman, who had twenty-four acres of vineyards in Santa Cruz County from which he made four thousand gallons of wine a year—the kind of winegrower who, other things being equal, would be most vulnerable to market problems.

"I am convinced that there is a dealers' ring working against the growers," he stated. "A man cannot go to San Francisco with a sample of wine and offer it at one house without its being known all over the city in less than ten hours, and the price offered will be the same at every house."

Declared Isaac De Turk, "There is no real necessity for this depression in the wine trade, and it is all brought about by an unnatural condition of the wine market, caused by a combination of dealers. You cannot buy a small bottle of wine in San Francisco of any kind for less than twelve and a half cents. That is $1.25 per gallon. Allow six cents per small bottle for glass, labels, packing, handling and cases, and you find you are paying fifty-three cents a gallon for the wine. Surely the dealer can afford to pay more than seven cents for a gallon of wine that nets him fifty-three cents." Those figures, he explained, were based on the cheapest wine and the highest supplementary expenses. For "good claret" the gap was even greater, with the cost to the dealer ten cents a gallon but the cost to the buyer $2.00.

"The middleman is making all the profit," he alleged, "while the grape grower is sustaining a heavy loss. One would think that the dealers would hesitate to kill the business that was making them rich, but they do not seem to have any care for the future. They buy a little good wine here, a little bad wine there, make large purchases of aniline dyes for coloring, and, finding that the consumption of wine is increasing, are confident that they will be able to get along anyhow."

The two dealers who responded to the *Examiner*'s inquiry were hunted down by reporters. One, Henry Brune, said the problem was due to "trashy stuff" rather than good wine being put on the market. The other, Isaac Landsberger, stated his unalterable belief in the laws of supply and demand and denied that any combination existed, but he suggested that "if a combination of large wine dealers was formed it would be a good thing for producers, especially when wine is in excessive supply." He added, "A combination now would relieve each merchant from fears of his rivals' competition in buying cheaply, and make the dealers feel more confidence in their ability to meet the demands of the producers."

Just such a combination was created five years later and named the California Wine Association.

It is probable that a bright young Englishman named Percy T. Morgan read with interest the *Examiner* series, including Landsberger's forthright opinions. Morgan had been in San Francisco since 1886, and had been putting to work his considerable skill in accountancy and financial management. He and a partner, William Hanson, listed themselves in the 1892 city directory as "accountants and financial agents." In addition, Morgan himself was auditor for both the Pacific Telephone and Telegraph Company and the Sunset Telephone and Telegraph Company, vice president of the Pacific Fire Alarm Company, and vice president of the Nevada Gypsum and Fertilizer Company, while his partner held several similar positions including secretary of M. Theodore Kearney's San Joaquin Valley Fruit Vale Estate. Among the firm's clients was or soon came to be S. Lachman & Company, one of the state's leading and oldest firms of wine dealers. According to Ernest Peninou and Sidney Greenleaf, whose handsome small volume about the California Wine Association (the second volume in their California winemaking series) was published in 1954, it was through his connection with this firm that Percy T. Morgan conceived and implemented the idea of the organization of dealers that was incorporated as the California Wine Association.

In August of 1894, seven firms agreed to join together in a corporation. Each put into it everything it owned and received in return a proportionate number of shares, a little more than three million dollars' worth. The companies were all primarily wine dealers, although some owned production facilities that supplied part of their needs. All were well established, well known. They were S. Lachman & Company, the Napa Valley Wine Company, B. Dreyfus & Company, Kohler & Frohling, Kohler & Van Bergen, C. Carpy & Company, and Arpad Haraszthy & Company.

It was expected that three more, Lachman & Jacobi, C. Schilling & Company, and Gundlach & Company, would join immediately, but they did not, and the next spring Arpad Haraszthy pulled out. Meanwhile, Pietro C. Rossi and Andrea Sbarboro of the Italian Swiss Agricultural Colony led the formation of a separate organization, the California Winemakers' Corporation. The intention was that the corporation should be a parallel organization to the C.W.A., as the Association came to be called. The Corporation would represent the wine producers *vis à vis* the dealers' group, bargaining in their behalf. This it did successfully at first.

The C.W.A.'s annual report to its stockholders for 1895 told one side of the story. A "combination" had been arranged. "During the past year your Directors, by maintaining amicable relations with other large wine houses, have been able to gradually raise the selling price of wines." It did not detail, however, how it had got the wine to sell.

From the Corporation, to which it had leased some of its members' production facilities, it had bought four million gallons of mainly dry wines for twelve and a half cents a gallon, a triumph for the producers, since the C.W.A.'s opening offer had been six cents, well below the dismal level of 1889. The Association had also agreed to buy five million gallons a year for the next five years, the price to be set annually.

The next year, however, what the C.W.A.'s annual report called "more or less friction" had arisen between the two organizations. The Association begrudgingly paid fifteen cents a gallon for some of the Corporation's wine but refused to take the full five million gallons. Then in 1897 the Corporation asked for twenty cents a gallon, and the Association refused to buy any. Litigation ensued. So also did a price war.

That May the C.W.A. reduced the price of the "Calwa" wine it was sending to New Orleans to twenty-two cents a gallon delivered, killing profits for other California shippers to that important market, principally Lachman & Jacobi. Then it reduced prices of its wines in New York to a level below what a major buyer there had just paid the California Winemakers' Corporation for a million-gallon purchase. The Corporation fought back by installing a million and a half gallons of cooperage in a leased San Francisco warehouse, and Italian Swiss built its huge tank at Asti so they could hold wine until they could sell it profitably. But that was not enough to stem the disintegration of the Winemakers' Corporation. It hung on until 1899. Then it was dissolved. The California Wine Association issued bland condolences and continued its ever more successful campaign toward industry domination.

That year, as the directors of the C.W.A. informed the stockholders, the Association was "obliged to engage more and more in Wine-Making, so that the large stock of Wine necessary to carry on our business might be secured at the lowest possible cost." The next year they announced that they had decided to abandon "price agreements, since others will not hold to them," and to "engage in Wine-Making on a very extensive scale." By then the C.W.A. had bought and leased several wineries. But the next year, 1900, it went on a real shopping spree.

The annual report covering that year noted that "large and conservative financiers" had "become interested in this Association." It was their infusion of money that made the shopping spree possible. According to C.W.A. chroniclers Peninou and Greenleaf, Percy T. Morgan one day complained to Jacob Frowenfeld that unless the C.W.A. could secure more capital it could not control the state's wine industry.

The leaders in the various wine organizations that formed the C.W.A. were board members, and Frowenfeld, a partner in the firm of B. Dreyfus & Company, was a director and treasurer of the C.W.A. He carried the word to three San Francisco bankers. One was Isaias W. Hellman, Benjamin Dreyfus' partner in the Cucamonga vineyard. Another was Daniel Meyer, who held C.W.A. stock as trustee for an estate. The third was Meyer's investment firm partner, Antoine Borel. Of the three, Hellman became the largest investor, and his son frequently presided over executive committee meetings in the years to follow, during which many of the wine men were replaced by moneymen on the board.

But to return to the 1900 shopping spree that resulted in Percy T. Morgan's longed-for control of the California wine industry: According to the annual report, which he signed as president, toward the end of 1900 it became apparent "to all" that stocks of wine were in short enough supply to justify discontinuing "a struggle for business at the expense of legitimate profits." Continued the report, "A conference was therefore held among the leading merchants engaged in the business, which has happily resulted in the establishment of a 'community of interest' which, without necessitating any illegal agreements to maintain prices, should result naturally in all obtaining such a fair margin of profit as is commensurate with the risk."

Which was to say that the C.W.A. had finally been able to pull in the three major "outside concerns," Italian Swiss, Lachman & Jacobi, and C. Schilling & Company, evading antitrust restrictions by using the "community of interests" concept developed by J. P. Morgan. It completed negotiations to buy half interest in each of the firms early in 1901. In March the San Francisco *Examiner* found out what had been going on.

"Hellman Controls the Trade in Wine" read the headline. Confronted by a reporter, Hellman did not deny the premise. "It is a legitimate enterprise," he said somewhat defensively. "Had it not been we would not have gone into it." He added, in reference to antitrust laws, "We have not formed a combination to raise the price of wine. That must be regulated by supply and demand." And, "We want to assist the winegrower as well as the manufacturer, and propose, as far as we are able, to keep the price of the grape up, so as to encourage the production of good grapes. We deal only in California wines, and our ambition is to put the industry on a solid basis, which we believe we have accomplished." They had indeed, by putting in what Hellman called "something over $1,000,000," placed the C.W.A. on a solid basis. As the *Examiner* noted, "there are no big dealers left to fight." The C.W.A. had also bought a number of other wineries along the way, some small and some large, leased still others, and made contracts with yet others. By 1902 it could report that the "community of interest" plan was working well. That year it produced, through its own wineries and those it controlled, two-thirds of all the wine made in California.

Although mention of the C.W.A.'s acquisition of the three large firms was made in the 1901 *Examiner* article, it was for some reason not generally known, and there was surprise when it was publicly confirmed after the death of P. C. Rossi in 1911. That was the year the C.W.A. bought the other half interest in both Italian Swiss and Lachman & Jacobi. In 1915 it completed its purchase of Schilling as well.

The three firms had continued operating with considerable autonomy, using their own labels. In New Orleans, where Lachman & Jacobi held the major share of the California wine market through its brokers, Joseph and Sydney Block, father and son, word came through only dimly, and rivalry between the L. & J. and C.W.A. labels continued vigorously.

"It's hard to understand," recalled Sydney Block many years later. "I didn't know who I was working for. I had Lachman & Jacobi, but frankly Mr. Morrow was my superior officer. We were all in a combine in those days, and I did not know it."

A. R. Morrow was by then in charge of production for the C.W.A., and the way young Block found out the reality of the situation was by going to San Francisco to settle a disagreement about his commission.

"When I got there, Mr. Morrow said, 'They're very sore at you, Syd. You'll have to go over to see Mr. Sutro at Pillsbury, Madison & Sutro.'" By inquiring, Block learned that Alfred Sutro was the attorney who was currently chairman of the board of the C.W.A., a rather formidable figure to San Franciscans. Block went bravely in to see him.

"There's a little disagreement about money," Block told him, "and I'm about ready to leave you."

"Where are you going?" asked Sutro.

"Well, I'm going with Mr. Guasti."

Said Sutro, "Wait a minute." He reached for the telephone and called Morrow. "Give this kid twenty-six hundred dollars and send him back home," he ordered. To Block he said, "Never mind about Guasti. You stay right where you are."

That was before 1911. After the C.W.A. took over complete ownership of Lachman & Jacobi, a "government man" walked into Sydney Block's office and demanded all letters written to him and his father by Lachman & Jacobi. Troubled, he went with the "government man" to the district attorney's office, there to be asked, "Why is it that you had the same price as your competitors on such-and-such a day?" Block told them he didn't know, and telephoned Morrow as soon as he got back to his office.

"Well," recalled Block, "it wasn't long after that that the barrels were all marked 'Capital stock owned by California Wine Association,' Lachman & Jacobi Brand, C. Schilling & Company Brand, or Italian Swiss Colony Brand, and it was all clarified."

In the 1906 San Francisco earthquake and fire the C.W.A. lost some ten million gallons of wine but, being well insured, not much money. A number of its cellars and warehouses were ruined, but its Casa Calwa, then under construction in the southern part of the city, was little damaged and quickly completed. Later that same year construction was begun on Winehaven, the huge facility across the bay to the north just beyond Point Richmond, which became its central cellar.

Although Charles A. Wetmore alleged that such big, soulless corporate winemaking "kills the enthusiasm of the connoisseur and elevates only the cold-blooded views of the manufacturer on lines of labor-saving machinery and cheap labor" and that "the trust is the tomb of the artist," there was the other side of the coin. If great wines were not produced—and undoubtedly some were in small quantities—the general level of quality was said by all to be good, and this did much to give buyers confidence in all California wines.

Although the businessmen were in control of the business, they prudently left control of the winemaking to the wine men. Henry Lachman of S. Lachman & Company was the first to be put in charge of the cellars. He trained his successor, Almond R. Morrow. Lachman is said to have been the greatest of California's winetasters, and Morrow to have followed closely behind. Their ability to analyze and to blend was as important as all the bankers' money to the success of the C.W.A.

Before Prohibition put an end to winemaking, the C.W.A. was operating some fifty-two wineries, many carrying such famous names as Brun & Chaix, Natoma, De Turk, Eisen, Las Palmas, Greystone, and Madrone. It had even been sole sales agent for Leland Stanford's Vina brandy. All together it was in control of more than 80 percent of the state's wine in the second decade of this century. Meanwhile, however, small and medium-sized wineries flourished, on the whole aided by the stability the giant had created.

Well before the Eighteenth Amendment went into effect, the C.W.A. had stopped making wine. In the last six months of 1919, when it was legal to sell wine abroad but not in the United States, it shipped out nearly 4,000,000 gallons, but at the beginning of 1920 it still had 6,750,500 gallons on hand in California. Some was disposed of through legal channels in the Prohibition years, but not until Repeal, thirteen years later, was the last sold. A few bottles of it still remain, treasured in sequestered cellars.

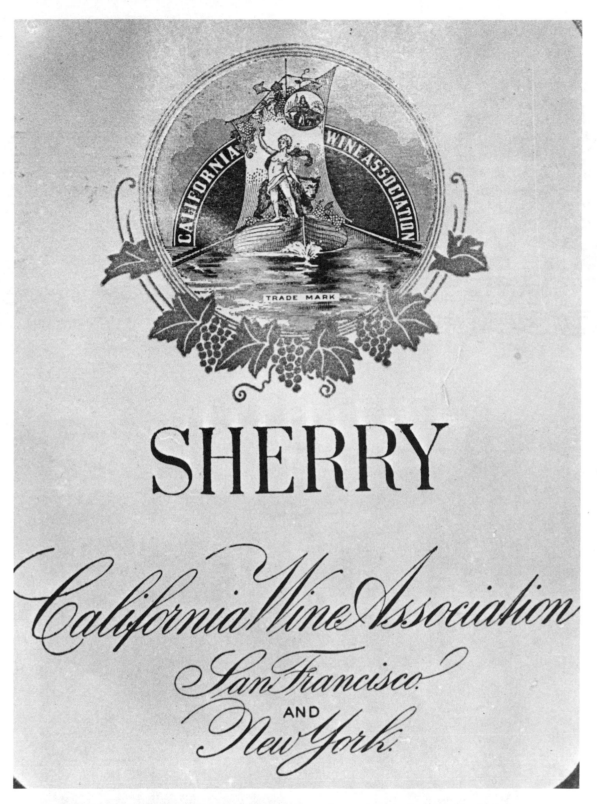

SHERRY

California Wine Association
San Francisco
AND
New York

The California Wine Association's trademark showed a young Bacchus standing in the prow of a ship presumably heading out through the Golden Gate, with the grizzly bear, symbol of the state, standing behind him, and the state seal on the sail above. Here it is used on one of its labels.

162

◄ George Hearst's Madrone Vineyard, near Glen Ellen in Sonoma County, was named after a great tree under which its earlier owner, General Charles P. Stone, used to sit and reminisce with his fellow Civil War veterans, William Tecumseh Sherman and Fighting Joe Hooker. After Hearst bought it in 1885, he built near Stone's small old wine cellar a big new cellar with a 340,000-gallon capacity, and a separate fermenting building. In the latter, according to an article in the Hearst-owned *Examiner,* "machinery is used everywhere. The boxes of grapes are carried up to the crushing-room by an endless chain moved by steam power. Then they are carefully sorted and picked over, the refuse going to the compost heap and the ripe and perfect grapes to the crusher, from whence the juice flows into the vats to be drawn off later into tanks, there to ferment until it is ripe enough to be placed in casks for the second fermentation." In the vineyard, because the soil was said to be similar to that of the Médoc, Hearst had Cabernet (whether Sauvignon or franc was not stated), Merlot, and Malbec, planted in place of Zinfandels that were there. There must have been other grapes as well, for in 1887 and 1888 Madrone made claret, hock, sauterne, and Riesling. After George Hearst's death in 1891 the estate, like many another, passed into the hands of the California Wine Association.

◄ Isaias W. Hellman, who had become acquainted with California viticulture and winemaking as a pioneer Los Angeles banker and then as part owner of a major winegrowing estate in the Cucamonga district, decided to back the California Wine Association with both money and influence, of which he had a great deal. Here he sat in his banking office in San Francisco, where he had moved his headquarters in 1890.

► This bucolic riverside view of the Uncle Sam cellar belied the size of the winery that C. Carpy & Co. brought into the California Wine Association. It was one of several large wineries in the city of Napa, along the Napa River. Their wines and brandies were loaded directly onto ships to be carried to San Francisco.

The great Greystone winery building just north of St. Helena, still a dominating structure today, was built in 1888 and 1889. This photograph was taken during construction of its entryway arch. William B. Bourn, a San Francisco industrialist and investor who owned vineyards in the Napa Valley and was familiar with the wine men's problems in those trying years, built it to carry out an idea. His plan was to create a facility where small vineyard owners could bring their grapes to be crushed and the wine aged, and where small winemakers could bring their wine to be cellared. He would advance money to them, to be repaid when the wine was sold. It was an arrangement similar to that proposed for cooperative cellars. For several reasons, chief among them a sudden shortage of grapes in the valley due to heavy phylloxera infestations, the plan was not carried out. The huge structure, the largest stone winery in the world at its completion, had a potential capacity of nearly two million gallons. However, although some grapes were crushed and wine made under the direction of Bourn's partner, Everett Wise, the structure was vastly underutilized. Then Charles Carpy bought it and took it into the California Wine Association when his C. Carpy & Company became one of the founding members. It was equipped with 1,349,000 gallons of cooperage, and the words "California Wine Association" were spelled out in whitewashed rocks across the embankment in front. Here the Association made one of its relatively few estate-bottled wines, Vine Cliff Riesling. Today Greystone is the Christian Brothers' showplace champagne cellar.

Winehaven, the California Wine Association's central winery, was a complex of buildings that took several years to complete after construction started late in 1906. Built on the edge of San Francisco Bay, it was "about an hour's steamer ride from the city," as Percy T. Morgan noted when he proudly described it. The cool, even climate was ideal for a wine cellar, and the Association's directors decided not to stint on size. For a time it held the title of the world's largest winery. The great steel and concrete main building faced with red brick looked more a fortress for a warring European city state than a haven for wine, but it apparently fulfilled its function well. It was designed to hold ten million gallons, but A. R. Morrow noted its actual cooperage totaled only six and a half million, of which more than five million was redwood. The facility was at first used for treating, blending, aging, bottling, and barreling wines brought here from other C.W.A. wineries, but about 1911 equipment was added to handle grapes brought from Lodi area vineyards. This was the C.W.A.'s main distribution point, too, where wine was loaded directly onto rail cars, and from the long Winehaven dock onto ships bound for American, European, and Asian ports. Here, during Prohibition, the Association's remaining wine was stored, and the structure's foreboding aspect combined with its forbidden contents made it an intriguing landmark. When Repeal came, there were plans to sell it to someone who would return it to its original use, but the Navy suddenly requisitioned it, and it remains today a naval storage depot.

18. The Pre-Prohibition Years

Shortly after 5:12 a.m. on April 18, 1906, people in San Francisco felt the earth quake beneath them. Animals felt it a few minutes earlier. Young Louis M. Martini, not yet but soon to be a winemaker, was delivering a wagonload of his father's fresh-dug clams to a downtown fish market.

"I had an old horse, an old mare, Julia, about twenty, twenty-five years old, and just before the earthquake she began throwing her head. I said, 'What's the matter, Julia?' Then for fifty-eight seconds it lasted. Nothing to do. Everything collapsed." Martini started home to the south shore, his wagon still full of clams. Some frantic people offered to buy his whole load if he would drive them to the Ferry Building so they could leave the city. He did, made a few trips more, then hurried back to the Bayview district along the Embarcadero as the city started to burn. If he had taken a route over Rincon Hill a few blocks west, he would have been assailed by the odor of mingled smoke and wine draining from big casks in San Francisco dealers' warehouses.

Wineries all along to the north and south of the city, in Napa, Sonoma, and Santa Clara counties and beyond, sustained serious losses. But San Francisco was California's center for aging, blending, trading, and shipping wine, and the losses from its vaults were tremendous.

The California Wine Association lost ten million gallons, and estimates of the city's total have until recently stood at fifteen million. Researcher William F. Heintz, however, re-examined all the records he could find and came up with a figure about double that. He included not only the wine in the commercial cellars but also that in the many casks in the basements of home winemakers, Italian San Franciscans especially, and also in the bottles in the more sedate wine cellars of the wealthy. However much there had been on April 17, some of course went to save buildings by being thrown on flames to quench them, especially on Telegraph Hill where many of the Italians lived. A certain amount was undoubtedly gulped down in the terror of the moment. But most of the city's wine simply sank into the ground beneath the buildings where it was quietly aging, making San Francisco soil surely the winiest in the world, unequalled even by that of Pompeii.

A secondary problem caused by the earthquake and fire was the loss of sulfur stored in burned buildings, so that most vineyardists were unable to follow the usual practice of dusting their vineyards that autumn. Charles Ash of the C.W.A. thought the lack of dusting might have been responsible for the spoilage of grapes caused by the micro-organism called *tourne,* which made gas form in the wines, and bottles explode on wine store shelves for the next few years.

There were some triumphs, however. A certain amount of C.W.A. wine was stored in cellars with cement floors and walls. Charles Ash was given the job of trying to salvage this wine that was mixed with charred wood from its burned casks. It was unpotable as wine, and brandy distilled from it experimentally tasted unpleasantly smoky.

"I was sent up to Stockton," he later recalled, "where a laboratory was available, and was told not to return until I could produce brandy good enough for fortification. I was lucky. I observed that when wine was made alkaline and then distilled, the smoky taste in the resulting distillate was accentuated. When made acid the reverse took place. It was also noted that oxidizing agents further improved the quality of the brandy." So the wine was treated with sulfuric acid and potassium permanganate, and distilled into good fortifying brandy. This was done mainly at the big West winery, El Pinal. It was young Louis S. Wetmore who became the wine industry hero of the disaster by getting it there.

Louis Wetmore, son of Charles, was at twenty-four the manager of the C.W.A.–affiliated West winery. As soon as news of the damage to the association's San Francisco wineries reached Stockton, he acted fast and ingeniously. Within three days of the disaster he had chartered three river steamers and several grain barges lying in the Stockton harbor, and got them to the wharf at the foot of Third Street in the city. He had brought men from El Pinal, and together they laid a pipe line along Third and by a circuitous route to the wineries' cellars, principally the Lachman & Jacobi vault.

Somehow—heaven knows how—he got San Francisco's critically overworked fire department to use fire engines to pump the wine out of the cellars into the pipe line, which delivered it into the holds of the grain barges.

They were towed by the steamers to landings in Napa, Sacramento, and chiefly Stockton, where the wine was pumped once again into tank cars and taken to C.W.A. wineries, while the young hero Wetmore went about the more prosaic task of rounding up office furniture to be shipped down to the association's hastily established headquarters in its unfinished but little damaged Casa Calwa.

Most San Franciscans took the earthquake and fire in good part, looking upon it as a remarkable adventure. Many of the homeless treated camping out in the parks as a lark. Wrote Charles K. Field, one of the city's light-hearted young literati,

If, as some say, God spanked the town
For being over frisky,
Why did he burn the churches down
And save Hotaling's whiskey?

Hotaling's warehouse was located in the relatively undamaged area between Telegraph Hill and the Bay, as was Italian Swiss Colony's building, the city's only major wine cellar to escape harm.

The years between the earthquake and the Panama-Pacific International Exposition of 1915 were years of reconstruction for San Francisco and optimism for all of California. The state's bounty and riches were looked upon as limitless. Its wonders were treasured by its residents and admired by its visitors and new arrivals. The 1915 exposition, ostensibly in celebration of the opening of the Panama Canal, was in fact a celebration of the city's rebuilding.

In July an international viticultural congress was held at the fair, and it brought together the nation's leading wine men as well as notable international authorities. Most fairs leave behind tangible benefits—park buildings, landscaping—and such intangibles as a heightened awareness of art and architecture. San Francisco's first two expositions left benefits to viticulture particularly in the form of heightened awareness of the value of establishing standards for wines and for judging them.

In 1894, in response to the California wine men's anxiety about a repetition of what was termed a "rather trying experience," the judging of wine at the Chicago fair the year before, Arpad Haraszthy was again called into service.

He was asked to prepare, and did, "Instructions for the Jury of Awards, Midwinter Fair."

They were presented in a carefully thought-out document that included classification of wines by types and subtypes, and instructions for how they should be presented to the jurors. The dry red wines should be brought to them at between sixty and sixty-five degrees Fahrenheit; the dry white wines at between fifty degrees and fifty-seven degrees; the sweet wines, both red and white, at sixty-five degrees to seventy degrees; and the sparkling wines at forty degrees to fifty degrees. The temperature of the room in which the tasting would be done should be about sixty degrees. All bottles should be wrapped uniformly for anonymity and, "the removal of corks and capsules should be done by an attendant, so that none of the jurors may notice or recognize any mark tending to indicate who the exhibitor is." No competitor should be present when his wines were being judged.

The factors on which the wines should be judged were specified:

1. Brightness of the wine
2. Beauty of color or shades of color
3. Perfection of bouquet
4. Purity and delicacy of taste
5. Quality of body
6. Quality of savor
7. Proper alcoholic strength
8. Harmonious perfection of the whole

For sparkling wines, there were two additional factors:

9. Vivacity of sparkle
10. Duration of sparkle

Ten points were allotted to each, giving a score of eighty for the hypothetically perfect still wine, one hundred for the sparkling. The jurors' scores for each wine were to be averaged for the final score.

This set of criteria was carried over to the Panama-Pacific International Exposition twenty-one years later. The International Congress of Viticulture judging was held in May 1915, the congress itself in July. The two events brought together a remarkable group of great California wine tasters, men famous then and long after for their ability to perceive and to remember—the two necessities for wine tasters. These were men who tasted to buy and to blend, men responsible for the improvement of both quality and consistency in the state's wines.

On the international jury were three Californians: Henry Lachman, generally considered the finest taster in the nation; Charles Carpy, whom some, including himself, considered at least Lachman's equal; and Kanaye Nagasawa, whose perception was perhaps as acute as his colleagues' but whose experience was narrower.

Nagasawa was officially the representative of Japan on the jury, although it was at Fountain Grove in California that he learned about wine. A remarkably intelligent man, of inquiring mind, he was highly esteemed as viticulturist, winemaker, and wine taster.

Henry Lachman was a son of Sam Lachman, who in his generation was considered as fine a taster as A. G. Chauché, Arpad Haraszthy, or Hamilton Walker Crabb. Henry joined his father's S. Lachman & Company, wine merchants, in 1876, and learned quickly and well. Two years after Sam's death in 1892, Henry and his brother Albert took the firm into the California Wine Association, and Henry was put in charge of all its wine.

A few years later Charles Ash, just at the beginning of a long career as a wine chemist, applied to short, stocky, humorous but sometimes irascible Henry Lachman for a job with the C.W.A.

"What can you do?" asked Lachman.

"I can test wine for alcohol, extract, total and volatile acids, and so forth," replied the confident young man.

"All right," asked Lachman, "after you have these results, can you tell me if a wine is good or bad? Can you tell its quality? Will it stand shipment?"

Ash confessed he could not.

"Well," declared Lachman triumphantly, "I can tell all of these things by just tasting the wine. What do I need a chemist for?"

In telling the story many years later, Ash conceded that Lachman had been right; he could. That was in 1952, and Ash, who had by then come to know more than half a century of California wine men, still considered Henry Lachman "the greatest wine man we have ever had in California." He could, recalled Ash, "go through a hundred samples like lightning and classify them with uncanny accuracy. He could go over the same wines several hours later and repeat well over ninety percent of the observations made before."

Lachman, in "A Monograph on the Manufacture of Wines in California," a fairly technical treatise he wrote for the Paris Exposition of 1900, included one concise explanation of tasting that can be understood out of context.

> In tasting there is the "first taste," the "second taste," and the "good-bye," after the wine has left the mouth. On the "first taste" the body or extract is detected; on the "second taste," the acids, free and acetic; and on the "good-bye" the tannin, flavor, and defects are caught.

Ash credited Lachman with being the first wine man "who really graded wines and gave the customers just what they paid for." This practice was, of course, a major strength of the California Wine Association, and was passed along to A. R. Morrow, who was Lachman's assistant and then successor. Morrow vouched for Lachman's legendary ability, verifying the story that he could indeed taste a wine and, calling up his recollections of wines he had tasted on buying trips throughout the state, often name the vineyard from which it had come. Horatio F. Stoll told of his tasting a Cabernet Sauvignon at the exposition judging, and proclaiming, "This is wonderful! It's a Santa Clara County wine, but to save my soul I can't tell whose it is!"

Tasting wine and drinking it were two different things, however. At least until his retirement, Henry Lachman never drank wine, fearing it would blunt his perception, and his disciple Morrow followed the practice until Prohibition, when he began to drink a little wine with meals and found to his surprise that it affected his tasting ability not at all.

Charles Carpy, born in France, came to California at eighteen and by twenty-one was working in the wine business. In 1886 he established C. Carpy & Co., successor to a firm in which he had been a partner, with two wineries in Napa and two subterranean cellars in San Francisco connected by a galvanized iron pipe running under the street that separated them. In 1894 he added the big Greystone cellar, and later that same year took them all into the newly formed California Wine Association, of which he became president.

A bon vivant who never thought of abstaining from wine at meals, he was so well known for his tasting ability that he was asked to speak at the 1915 viticultural congress banquet on "How Do I Know Good Wine?" He began by explaining that it "is something that is governed by no rules and can be answered only by experience." Behind that, however, he explained, lay the taster's instinct to "know the good once he has been shown the difference between good, indifferent and bad." Given that instinct, "the next is experience and the power to make comparisons and the ability to remember the quality of every good, bad, and indifferent wine which a man has ever examined."

Then he outlined the qualities of a good wine from the point of view not of the professional buyer and blender but of the wine drinker.

> First, it should be brilliant. Second, it should appeal to the sense of taste; it should be clean; its vinosity should be pronounced; after tasting, it should leave upon the palate the clear, definite impression of cleanliness. Third, it should appeal very strongly to the sense of smell; the bouquet should be unimpeachable. Fourth, it should be served and tasted under proper conditions.

There was also a fifth test.

> A wine may have passed every qualification I have referred to, and still leave the man who has drunk two or three glasses sated or cloyed. This is a fatal defect. Any wine that leaves the drinker in the condition of "Oh, I don't want any more," or leaves him heated up like a furnace, is not a fine wine, no matter how much it may appeal to the senses of sight, taste and smell.

He concluded on a personal note.

> And now I will give you the final test of drinking good wine. Look at me. I have reached the age when most men are content to retire. I drink good wine and I avoid the bad. . . . I have good friends, good health, good digestion, all the comforts of life; and all these and the satisfaction of living I attribute in a large measure to the habit I formed in my boyhood days of drinking good wine, keeping good wine, and preaching the doctrine of good wine.

One wonders what another of the great tasters, Claus Schilling, thought of Carpy's talk as he sat at his table at the banquet with his son-in-law William Leichter, and A. R. Morrow. Schilling was a delegate to the Congress, but he did not speak or give a paper, perhaps because he had been extremely distressed by the death of another son-in-law and partner earlier that year. We have recollections of him from a younger associate, Horace O. Lanza, who a few years later, as a partner of Sophus Federspiel and William Leichter in another wine company, came to know and greatly admire Claus Schilling.

He was born in Germany and got into the wine business by becoming a bookkeeper for Gottlieb Groezinger about 1870. He and a partner subsequently bought out Groezinger, and then Schilling bought out the partner, establishing C. Schilling & Company in 1886. Lanza admired him for both his business acumen and his wine-tasting ability. Most of the wine brought to his San Francisco cellars he bought himself year by year.

> I recall his telling me that he always waited till the market was opened by his competitors, like Mr. Rossi, Bundschu, Lachman & Jacobi, and so on, and then he would go out and offer two cents higher. But he never bought all the wines that the producer had on hand. He simply tasted and took the cream. Do you see why he was paying two cents higher? He said to me, "I would pay two cents higher, but when I would sell my wine I'd get ten cents higher than my competitor." And because he would pay that two cents higher, they always waited for him to come around before they would sell.

As to his tasting ability, Lanza continued, "I never saw a man that could taste and judge the quality of wine the way he did. He was fair but he could also be 'full of the Dickens.' " Recalled the younger man:

> He told me once that they had a display of wines in the city, and they had committees of wine men to judge these wines. He displayed some white wine and he got first prize. That is, it was accepted as the best. There was also in the display a wine made by a gentleman that lived down the Peninsula, some wealthy man who had just a small private winery of his own for his pleasure. And Mr. Schilling said, "I tasted that wine and it was better than mine. The judges had given the flag for the second prize to this gentleman. So I took the flag of first prize

from my wine and put it on this gentleman's, and took his flag of second prize and put it on mine."

"Why did you do that?" asked Lanza.

"Jesus Christ," replied Schilling, "didn't I show those judges I knew more about wines than they did?"

The July days of the International Congress of Viticulture were busy and lively, coinciding with Wine Day at the fair, which was celebrated with wine punch for all visitors. The delegates to the Congress who had come from other parts of the country were entertained vigorously, wined, dined, sung to, and versified at. Charles Bundschu composed new words to a popular song under the title "Our Eastern Delegates," which began:

> You've traveled far the Fair to see—Upidee, upida!
> You've brought with you much mirth and glee—Upidee, upida!

and which pronounced the Eastern delegates and their wives to be "the jolliest crowd we've met in our lives."

But, jolly as it all was, the fear of Prohibition hung over the gathering. There was discussion of how to promote what Andrea Sbarboro called "true temperance," the use of table wines as a home mealtime accompaniment, and, on the other hand, damning of the "holier-than-thou" prohibitionists. Wrote a minor local poet, Waldemar Young, in the poem "Wine Day at the Fair,"

> So herald now Prince Zinfandel,
> Nor may his shadow wane!
> And Burgundy, stout friend is he,
> And old Sauterne—could better be?
>   And king of all, Champagne!
> They make this world a better spot—
> They do not tell you: "Thou shalt not!"

Five years later, the "Thou shalt nots" won. In 1919, the national Prohibition law went into force. The wine men had fought hard to separate their industry from the distilled spirits industry. They failed. Wine was, as it had long been, considered one with the other "intoxicating liquors" and with them had been the subject of prohibitive legislation in California as well as elsewhere in the nation.

Prohibition had a long history in America, even in free-wheeling California. The year Maine went dry, 1846, California authorities passed an ordinance prohibiting the sale of "any liquor or wines of any kind" in the town of Monterey while a number of bored American soldiers and sailors remained stationed there. Gold-rush San Francisco had street preachers inveighing against the sin of inebriety, and by 1854 was the home of the Temperance Society, the Cadets of Temperance, the Daughters of Temperance, and the Sons of Temperance, soon to be joined by the Dashaway Society, which devoted itself to dashing away alcoholic beverages.

In 1855 the Temperance Party appeared on the California ballot; it emerged again in 1875 as the Prohibition Party and as such remained every year from 1879 on. It was notably unsuccessful, although Charles A. Wetmore had found legislators of other parties to be "prejudiced by temperance society appeals" against the 1880 bill to establish the Board of State Viticultural Commissioners.

In 1892 the Prohibition Party put up the old famous pioneer General John Bidwell for president of the United States. He had come to California in 1841 and eventually became a farmer and vineyardist in the Sacramento Valley; he had not been known to feel strongly one way or another about alcoholic beverages until he married a militant Prohibitionist.

Women were considered a large factor in the passage of the Eighteenth Amendment, and suffragists, full of their new voting power, were worst of all. Yet Mrs. Abigail Scott Duniway, the influential West Coast suffragist, denounced the idea of Prohibition in ringing terms to the applause of delegates at the 1915 viticultural congress, and the women of Lodi were credited with keeping local option from their vineyard-ringed town in 1914 when they cast their very first votes.

California's grape growers and winemakers formed organizations to fight Prohibition through lobbying and lawsuits. The new State Board of Viticultural Commissioners, established in 1913 under Clarence J. Wetmore's leadership, tried but failed to stem the tide. Andrea Sbarboro spoke at rallies and distributed copies of his pamphlets on "true temperance." The American Wine Growers' Association distributed copies of Professor Edmund H. Twight's essay "Wine—A Food," in which he explained the nutriments in wine and advised, "We should always use wine with food and in the same way as food, that is temperately." But it was all to no avail. There was nothing to be said in favor of wine that was as dramatic as the pictures the prohibitionists drew of broken homes, abandoned children, and paupers' graves.

San Francisco in flames after the earthquake of April 18, 1906, was portrayed dramatically by Theophilus Reichardt in this view from the bay off the Embarcadero.

SAN FRANCISCO, APRIL, 1906
CELLARS OF CALIFORNIA WINE ASSOCIATION A CHAOS OF HOOPS AND DEBRIS AFTER THE GREAT FIRE WHICH DESTROYED THE CITY

The earthquake shook down the brick walls that surrounded these wine casks and cracked the one on the left. The fire that followed burned the others.

The two-and-a-half-million-gallon cellar of Lachman & Jacobi on Rincon Hill, one of the finest in the state, was partly shaken down by the 1906 earthquake, then gutted by the fire in its wake.

Some of San Francisco's Italian Telegraph Hill dwellers who made their own wine used it to save their homes from destruction by the fires that followed the earthquake.

Paul Masson's champagne cellar under the Hotel Vendome in San Jose lost many of the bottles that had been in free-standing racks when the earthquake hit.

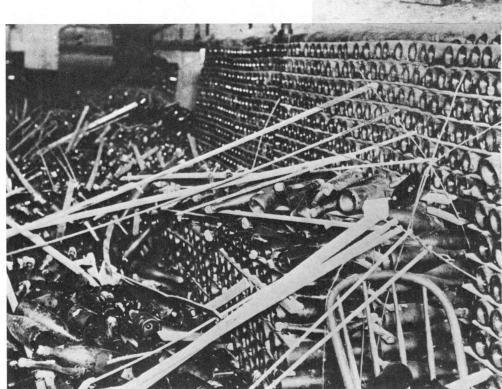

In this cartoon, European nations participating in the 1915 Panama-Pacific International Exposition salute the California bear who is making wine for the toast.

The jury judging more than a hundred California wines entered in competition at the Panama-Pacific International Exposition was highly prestigious. Shown here, Henry Lachman is seated at the right end, tasting. Next to him, standing with papers in his hand and examining a glass of wine, is Charles Carpy, who was chairman of the jury. Next left, looking down at his glass, is W. H. Mosby of Australia, and next to him making notes on the wines in their books are A. F. Gouvea of Portugal and Japanese-American Kanaye Nagasawa. Next to Nagasawa is J. E. Quiroga of Argentina, sniffing, and next to him U. Talocchini of Italy, examining the wine in his glass. At the end of that side of the table is J. A. LeClerc of New York; facing him on the other side of the table is Horatio F. Stoll, who was in charge of the Wine Temple where the tastings took place. The bottle opener is unidentified. Two jury members not present here were F. C. Cook of Washington, D.C., and Frederic T. Bioletti of the University of California.

On the day this photograph was taken, there was an interchange concerning the always arguable question of American wine nomenclature. Said the Portuguese representative, Mr. Gouvea, after he had tasted the seventeen samples of California port that were entered, "They are excellent. You don't have to go outside of California to get good wines. But they are not Oporto ports. They are port type and should be so branded."

One of the Californians objected. "But they are made from Portuguese varieties of grapes by the same process used in Portugal, and when we call them California ports we identify the type without intending to deceive the purchaser into thinking he is buying the foreign port."

"Nevertheless," responded Gouvea, "they should be branded 'port type.' "

Lachman interposed.

"See here, supposing you purchase a Percheron stallion in France and also a Percheron mare and bring them here to California and a colt is born. What would you call the colt—a Percheron?"

Responded Gouvea easily, "American type—yes."

California, The Wine Press of the World

THE RESULTS OF INTEMPERANCE

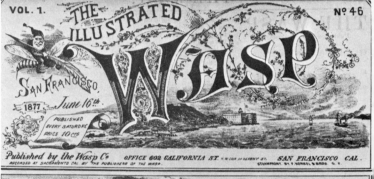

"THE RIGHT OF WAY"

Cartoons like "The Results of Intemperance" proved more influential with the nation's voters, who favored the Eighteenth Amendment, than those published by *The Wasp* in its long anti-Prohibition crusade. In "The Right of Way," the locomotive Common Sense, with Bacchus astride it, scatters the hypocritical Temperance Fanatics.

19. Prohibition

ROHIBITION lasted more than fourteen years. The Volstead Act, which implemented the Eighteenth Amendment's proscription of manufacturing, selling, or transporting intoxicating beverages, went into effect January 16, 1920. On July 1, 1919, however, the long delayed World War I law to prevent the manufacture of alcoholic beverages from foodstuffs finally became effective, actually beginning the long dry period. Julius Perelli and two partners who were operating a southern California winery asked for an injunction against enforcement of the wartime restriction on the ground that the war was over, but the government alleged that since the treaty was not yet signed the war was not actually over, and the court agreed. There was also a strong attempt to have the wine industry exempted from this law. Herbert Clark Hoover, then wartime food administrator, believed that it should be. President Woodrow Wilson, in Paris, advised Congress that he agreed, but when Congress did not go along, he dropped the idea, perhaps for political reasons in the face of obviously strong national prohibitionist sentiment.

That was probably the death blow to the wine industry's fight for a separate existence. Exemption from wartime Prohibition might well have set the precedent for exemption from the Volstead Act. Defeated again, the California wine men nevertheless went on fighting sporadically in the courts, the Congress, and the administrative agencies to be exempted from the "intoxicating beverages" category.

Winemaking did not cease, of course. Permits were given to commercial wineries for the legal production and sale of wine for sacramental and medicinal purposes and also for use in cooked foods (Campbell's Soup for instance) and as a flavoring in such things as tobacco products.

Statistics for the period are slippery, although statistical methods and recordkeeping had advanced markedly since the late nineteenth century when so much conjecture was needed to analyze the industry.

We do know with some certainty, however, that the California wineries' biggest pre-Prohibition year was 1912, when they made fifty million gallons of wine, and that their production then decreased annually until 1919, when they made only twenty-seven million gallons. During the Prohibition period the total fell drastically. Official figures of wine reported made by licensed commercial wineries during the first eight years of Prohibition give an average of less than five million gallons a year, then a rise to six and a quarter a year for 1928 to 1931. However, since there was an unknown amount of unreported winemaking in licensed wineries during the dry years, the relationship of the official figures to reality is only guessable.

If in the years just before Prohibition everybody in the United States had shared equally in the total amount of wine consumed, each man, woman and child would have downed a little more than half a gallon a year. During Prohibition, however, the figure rose. It averaged more than three quarters of a gallon— 0.8 gallons per person according to estimates, a tenth of a gallon more than the previous all-time high of 0.7 in 1911. Where did the extra wine come from? Partly perhaps from the clandestine commercial production, for these estimates are based upon grape tonnage and include illegal as well as legally produced wine. But more of the increase clearly came from home winemakers' cellars. There was a tremendous increase in home winemaking.

An amendment to the Volstead Act allowed continuation of the longstanding tradition of allowing each American head of household to make up to two hundred gallons a year of "non-intoxicating cider or fruit juice in the home" for use by family members. Wine was, in practice, allowed to fall into this definition so here, paradoxically, it was exempted from the intoxicating beverages category.

American home winemaking had been on the rise since 1915, judging by out-of-state shipments of California wine grapes. The rise was in response to the increase in "dry" states and communities. Nevertheless, when in June of 1919 strangers suddenly appeared in California vineyards offering $30 a ton for the coming autumn's wine grapes, growers who had been getting from $10 to $20 could hardly believe their ears. The would-be buyers were said to be agents for groups of eager home winemakers in other parts of the country, and even if they were not precisely that, they undoubtedly were buying for mainly such producers.

In any case, they formed a welcome market. California growers who agreed to sell for $30 in June must have kicked themselves in July when the bids went up to $35, and again in

August when they reached a high of $50. The season ended with some buyers paying $70 a ton. The next year Zinfandels and Missions brought as much as $125 a ton, according to journalist Bailey Millard, who recorded these remarkable events in 1920. Millard reported that James P. Allen, a southern California vineyardist who had been trying in vain to sell his vineyard, found himself in 1919 handed a check for $21,000 for his grapes, a sum larger than he had hoped to get for the whole property.

In 1925 twenty thousand carloads of grapes were shipped out of California, some to be eaten but most to be made into wine. California itself accounted for by far the largest number of home winemakers, however. By 1925, forty-five thousand heads of household had filed declarations that they intended to make up to two hundred gallons a year, and undoubtedly twice that many were making that much or more without benefit of official filing. If only the forty-five thousand had made only their limit that year, the total would have been nine million gallons, nearly twice the figure reported made by the state's commercial wineries in the early years of Prohibition.

Grape prices continued high and plantings increased, especially in the San Joaquin Valley. Carl F. Wente, the banker son of the founder of the family winery, gave a talk at a Wine Week dinner in Livermore in 1962 and reminisced about the Prohibition years. Vineyard land that had sold for $100 an acre before Prohibition went to $500 in 1921 and sold in 1923 not uncommonly for $1,000. "The purchaser," he recalled, "could go to an Eastern grape buyer and get an advance up to two hundred to two hundred fifty dollars per acre, secured by a contract on next year's crop, and use the money to make a down payment." The atmosphere for such speculation was created by the Eastern buyers who would "wander around the wine grape districts" in the autumns.

"Fresno and Modesto were the headquarters for these men. They were, may I say, an odd group." Most used hotel lobbies and street corners as their places of business. The purchase of a carload of grapes by one of them was just the beginning of the trading. "The car might have been billed to Pittsburgh, but the final buyer would have it rerouted to New York or some other destination." In 1923 the heat went out of the market and this group of buyers disappeared, to be largely supplanted by California growers going to the Midwest and East to sell their own grapes, often directly out of the rail cars in which they were shipped.

For a few years longer there were more new plantings and the market rocked along, although costs of all kinds increased more than grape prices. Then the ever-larger number of grapevines once again produced more grapes than buyers wanted, and once again in the history of the California viticultural industry the market broke. Many vineyardists who had mortgaged and overmortgaged their land lost it.

Continued Wente:

> You may wonder what the banks or insurance companies did who may have had loans on these properties. I know what the Bank of America did because I was in charge of some of those valley banks. And I also know what most of the so-called independent banks did because I had the job of cleaning up after they could no longer stand the strain and they asked us to take them over. A few of these banks were sold, but most of them were rescued by the Bank of America, converted to branches, upon our agreement to pay depositors in full. How do I know? I vas dere, Cholly.

Thus did a man who later became its president account for one chapter in the growth of the institution that in 1945 became the world's largest commercial bank, a position it held for more than three decades.

From the viticultural point of view, another problem was being created over these years. Most of the grapes that were being planted were not good wine varieties. The results of decades of searching for the finest wine grapes and experimenting to see which would do best where in California were being almost wiped out. What was wanted for shipping was hardy thick-skinned grapes with lots of red color. Many of the final users of them were foreign-born people accustomed to making farm wines, and color meant to them flavor and sturdiness. Others liked enough pigment to give wine that would not look pale when stretched by watering. In response, many California vineyards were either replanted or grafted

from good grape varieties to "shipping grapes." Brother Timothy recalled that when the Christian Brothers bought their Mont La Salle vineyard in 1930, they found twelve acres of a shipping grape called Alicante Ganzin, "probably the most intensely colored red grape that you can find. It was very dark. We used to sometimes laugh about it and we'd say, 'Well, you can crush that and take it and paint the barn with it.'" With an eye toward better varieties, the Brothers pulled it out.

Another grape with similar name and characteristics, Alicante Bouschet, was widely planted. A heavy bearer, thick of skin and full of color, it was the grape most highly prized in the Eastern United States. According to Maynard A. Amerine and Vernon L. Singleton in their authoritative book, *Wine,* it was reported that some Easterners could get six hundred or even seven hundred gallons of so-called wine from a ton of Alicante Bouschets by drawing off the juice, adding sugar and water to the solids left, and creating a second liquid that still looked reassuringly red.

Not all Prohibition period wine was made directly from grapes. Some was made from unfermented grape juice, shipped full strength or concentrated. A number of the California wineries operating under Prohibition Department licenses made grape juice, as did others set up to make only non-alcoholic grape products.

The Rossi twins, Robert and Edmund, and two associates bought back the original Italian Swiss property at Asti from the California Wine Association, grew grapes to sell, and made grape juices and concentrates. One of their products was named Moonmist after the nearby Valley of the Moon. It was advertised as "a pure natural grape juice concentrate; (no added sugar); both red and white syrups," which were "packed in full quart and pint bottles, and in No. 10 (8 lb.) lacquered cans."

Some of their grapes went onto rail cars, but some stayed in San Francisco. At their cellar there, the one that had escaped the 1906 fire, they would sell grapes to local home winemakers, then crush them, and put the juice in kegs that they would deliver. "We had French, German, Italians," Edmund Rossi said, "I used to call on them at their homes."

Thus the Rossis bridged the gap and were

able to start over in 1933, to make Italian Swiss again one of California's best known wineries.

Others bridged it with Prohibition Department licenses, making wine and wine by-products, operating on a reduced level. The Cella family, however, managed to expand its holdings during the dry years, adding in 1924 the Roma winery at Lodi to another it had bought five years earlier in Escalon, then another at St. Helena, and another at Manteca before Repeal. As the Roma Wine Company, it shipped fruit but also made sacramental wines, a 12 percent alcohol wine sauce for canners, a 6 percent wine sauce for cooks, and salted cooking sherry, as well as grape juice and concentrate. Back to ordinary winemaking in 1933, it became the state's leading wine company for the next decade.

On a smaller scale, two Catholic institutions, the Jesuit novitiate at Los Gatos, in the Santa Clara County hills, and the Christian Brothers novitiate at Martinez continued their established sacramental winemaking through the Prohibition years. In 1930, however, the Christian Brothers took the first step in an expansion that was to make them major wine producers by buying from Oakland vintner Theodore Gier his Sequoia estate in the hills northwest of Napa, which they renamed Mont La Salle.

Sacramental wines were the mainstay of a number of secular family wineries that continued on to post-Repeal prominence—those of the Concannons of the Livermore Valley, the Sebastianis of Sonoma, the Bianes of Cucamonga, and the Bisceglias of the San Joaquin and Santa Clara Valleys among them. Beaulieu Vineyard, started at the turn of the century by quintessential Frenchman Georges de Latour, laid the foundation for its later prestige with its wines made with the particular approbation of the Archbishop of San Francisco. The Wente family continued making wine with Beaulieu as its sole customer, operating for some years as Beaulieu Winery Number Two until Repeal, when it resumed its own bond.

Some wineries that were prominent both before and after Prohibition simply sat it out, like Simi of Healdsburg, and Petri of Escalon and San Francisco. But, surprisingly enough, a number of new wineries laid their foundations in the Prohibition period. These included the E & J Gallo winery. Although the Gallo winery was not established as a wine producing company until 1933, the Gallo brothers, Ernest and Julio, started working in their father's vineyards as boys, and beginning in 1927 were excused from school each autumn so that they could go to Chicago and New York to sell the grapes to home winemakers. From these home winemakers, from their father's experiences in selling wine before Prohibition, and from their own family's home winemaking, they learned enough to start a commercial winery at the ages of twenty-four and twenty-three when finally Repeal came.

Gruff, able Lee Jones, who had worked at West's El Pinal winery before being put in charge of a group of C.W.A. San Joaquin Valley wineries, organized the National Fruit Products Company at Lodi the first year of Prohibition, and oversaw construction and operation of its well-equipped winery, which produced sacramental wines, medicinal wines, wine tonics, cooking wines, and grape juice. Eight years later he presided over its million-dollar remodeling, left it for the newly formed Fruit Industries, then returned to it in time to take it, now renamed Shewan-Jones, into the post-Prohibition period as the finest winery in the United States.

It was during Prohibition that Louis M. Martini started his first independent establishment. An experienced winemaker by 1923, he and two silent partners established the L. M. Martini Grape Products Company that year in the winery at Kingsburg in the San Joaquin Valley that had been built by Italian Swiss. There he made, in his own words, "sweet wines, dry wines, brandy, concentrates, syrup, everything," and planned the winery that he would create in the Napa Valley as soon as Repeal came.

Did anyone ever try to buy your wines illegally? he was later asked.

"They tried, but I never sold to them. Someone offered me a hundred and seventy-five thousand dollars for a hundred thousand gallons of wine. Cash. I said no."

Other winemakers operating with legal permits said yes. Who, how many, how much wine they sold are unknown. Stories persist of fabricated hijackings to account for the loss of wine actually bootlegged, reports of broken hoses causing hundred-gallon spills, fires that mysteriously destroyed wine-laden casks, and barrels full of pale red water that sounded full when tapped by federal agents. For those wineries that braved it out through Prohibition were constantly inspected by government agents, and watched from afar as well by United States Assistant Attorney General Mabel Walker Willebrandt, who was in charge of prosecuting violators of the Volstead Act.

Most of California's pre-Prohibition wineries, however, simply went out of business in 1919, selling their buildings and equipment as they could, and their wine. At the Petri wine cellar in San Francisco, "just before Prohibition became effective, people with jugs were lined up for many blocks to buy the wine," recounted Louis Petri. "And the interesting thing is that my grandfather had about half a million gallons of wine when Prohibition was voted in, and right up to the last hour they sold the wine. They started maybe at twenty-five or thirty cents a gallon. The last of it was sold at a couple of dollars a gallon. He came out of it with a considerable amount of money."

Late in 1926 there emerged out of the dismal disorder of the grape market the first organization of California grape and wine men since the beginning of Prohibition. It was the California Vineyardists' Association, made up of grape growers and some winemakers. Two years later there emerged from it an allied organization of winemakers themselves, Fruit Industries, Ltd.

The key man in both was Donald D. Conn, a man who remained forty-odd years later an enigma to his California associates. They agreed, however, that he was a highly effective promoter, recalling that he had become interested in the California grape industry when he was assigned by a national railroad organization to unsnarl a tie-up of refrigerated cars that was adding to grape market problems. They did not recall it exactly the way he did, however, during a Fruit Industries crisis in 1932. As he told the San Francisco *Examiner:*

> While I was with the railroad association, I observed that cars of perishable grapes were piling up in marketing terminals due to gangster control. The shawled woman who came with a baby carriage to the sidings, to buy a few lugs of grapes to make her family some wine, was halted on the way home by the racketeer who demanded ten cents a lug for protection. She and others like her were frightened out of the market, and the racketeers paid the price they wanted to pay for grapes, to the detriment of the grower. It occurred to me that the only effective way to combat this vicious situation was to organize the grape growers and market their product direct to the homes.

The way Conn rallied support from the two organizations for the home marketing idea was, according to those who worked with him, by implying that he had the confidence of Secretary of Commerce Herbert Clark Hoover, and his promise of aid. Since Hoover had given earlier indications of sympathy toward the California grape industry and had family interests in vineyard land in the San Joaquin Valley, the implication did not seem unlikely. It was perhaps true, and it was especially helpful in the formation of Fruit Industries in 1929 when Conn could hold out the hope of financial aid from the newly created Federal Farm Board.

Conn's idea, and the Farm Board's as well, was to create an orderly and symbiotic market for fresh grapes, raisins, and grape products. Not enough growers signed up for his proposed plan, but both the raisin industry and the wine men (i.e., the grape products men) did, and received sizable government loans. They were to be used to create new grape products and especially to promote both the new and the existing ones, thus reviving the ailing viticultural industry.

In return for the Farm Board's largesse, Conn pledged allegiance to the Eighteenth Amendment.

The Fruit Industries product he developed was Vine-Glo. It was grape juice. Fruit Industries carried the Rossis' service of crushing grapes and delivering the juice in barrels a few steps further. It promoted the product heavily and established a nationwide sales and service system. In San Francisco several independent operators would follow the Rossis' barrels at a couple months' distance and rack off the wine into bottles for the buyers. But Fruit Industries offered racking off and removal or preferably replacement of the barrels at no extra cost. It also provided a clear instruction pamphlet explaining how to get Vine-Glo and make it into wine. You placed your order, specified either a five- or ten-gallon barrel ($16.50 or $29.50), received it upon delivery, put it in "any garage, pantry or closet," and left it strictly alone for sixty days until the service man showed up to bottle it. Satisfaction was guaranteed by Fruit Industries, which, it asserted, represented over 85 percent of California's grape industry, twenty thousand growers.

The buyer was assured that it was perfectly legal, under the National Prohibition Act, to make Vine-Glo in the home but not to sell or transport it. In fact a letter from the federal authorities, officially "Circular Letter No. 488," had been issued "To Prohibition Agents, Special Agents and Others Concerned" instructing them not to interfere with shipments of grapes, concentrates, or grape juices for home production of "non-intoxicating cider and fruit juices," and also not to interfere with such home production. It was issued at Conn's request, to implement the Vine-Glo plan which, he later said, had been worked out by him with Mabel Walker Willebrandt. That was in the autumn of 1929, shortly before she resigned as the federal government's chief prosecutor of Prohibition law violators, returned to private practice in Los Angeles, and was hired by Fruit Industries as its general counsel.

With the aid of the Federal Farm Board loan, the Vine-Glo plan was so profitable for a couple of years that the wine men who made up Fruit Industries went along with Conn's supporting Prohibition.

Not until the autumn of 1931 did any real problems appear. The first was the wine brick. This potential rival to Vine-Glo had the advantage of being easier for the shawled woman to get home than the lug-box-laden baby carriage, and cheaper than Vine-Glo. The bricks were made of solidified grape pomace and concentrate and pomace. They were about the size of two boxes of kitchen matches. Each cost two dollars, and made a gallon of wine. The wrappers carried instructions for dissolving the brick in water and the warning, "This beverage should be consumed within five days; otherwise in summer temperature it might ferment and become alcoholic."

The government agents clamped down on the wine brick sale briefly, which must have been a surprise to the manufacturer, the Vino Sano Company of San Francisco, for its inventor, Karl Offer, had the year before been cleared of charges of illegality in the northern California federal district court. Sales did continue, and several other bricks appeared on the market, but none was very successful. Vine-Glo would have been victorious had not the government followed a federal court decision and clamped down that same November on home delivery and bottling service, and then the next spring banned its sale.

Conn blew up, charging that the government had double-crossed him, that Fruit Industries had been formed only after he had conferred with officials, including Hoover, and been given their blessing on the product. He then declared his opposition to the Eighteenth Amendment and his determination to fight for its repeal.

This was in April of 1932, at the end of Conn's five-year contract as managing director of the California Vineyardists' Association. The organization relieved him of that duty but kept him on for another year, nominally to lead its fight for Repeal, but he gradually faded from the battle scene.

By then it was clear that Prohibition was on its way out. The old-line wine men who made up Fruit Industries began preparing for the future. So did others.

Prohibition ended when, on December 5, 1933, Utah became the thirty-sixth state to ratify the Twenty-first Amendment, repealing the Eighteenth. In the spring, 3.2 percent beer and wine had been legalized, and in the summer restrictions on medicinal alcohol were relaxed so much that if you went into a drug store and asked for Formula Number Six, you got vitaminized, mineralized sherry guaranteed to contain not over 22 percent alcohol that tasted much as most people thought sherry should taste.

Before Prohibition there had been more than 700 wineries in California. The number holding bonds during the dry period had declined year by year. In mid-1933 there were 130 legal wineries, and they held 23,438,000 gallons of wine, some dating back to before 1920 but most made in recent years. Many more permits were issued in the second half of 1933, so that on December 5 there were 380 wineries, and that autumn's crush added

35,817,000 gallons—not so far below the 1912 all-time high of 50,000,000.

It was a quick return, but the illusion of smooth sailing as quickly faded. With most wineries ill equipped, most winemakers inexperienced, and many wine drinkers lost, the California wine industry limped out of the chaos of Prohibition into the chaos of the Depression-ridden 1930s.

WINE LIST

FEDERSPIEL WINE CO.
RED

	½ Bot.	Bot.
Zinfandel	.30	.60
Burgundy	.40	.75
Beclan	.50	1.00

WHITE

Riesling	.30	.60
Sauterne	.40	.75
La Perla	.50	1.00

ITALIAN-SWISS COLONY
RED

Tipo	Split .30	.50	1.00
Zinfandel		.30	.60
Burgundy		.35	.70
Cabernet		.35	.70
Barbera		.40	.80
Asticolony	Nip .15		....

WHITE

Tipo	Split .30	.50	1.00
Riesling		.30	.60
Sauterne		.35	.70
Asticolony	Nip .15		....

SPARKLING

Asti Rouge (Sparkling Burgundy)	1.40	2.75
Asti Special Sec	1.40	2.75

CHAMPAGNE

Golden State, Extra Dry	2.00	3.75

"CALWA" WINES
RED

Hillcrest (Old Cabernet)	.50	1.00

WHITE

Vine Cliff (Finest Riesling)	.50	1.00

SPARKLING

Ruby Cliff (Spklg. Burgundy)	1.15	2.25
Gold Cliff (Spklg. Moselle)	1.15	2.25

CALIFORNIA WINE ASSOCIATION
RED

Zinfandel	.30	.60
Burgundy	.35	.70
Cabernet	.35	.70

WHITE

Riesling	.30	.60
Sauterne	.35	.70

MONT ROUGE

Zinfandel	.30	.60
Burgundy type	.75	1.30
Riesling	.30	.60
Sauterne type	.50	1.00
Sparkling Burgundy type	1.15	2.25
Sparkling Sauterne type	1.15	2.25

MONTEBELLO

Cabernet	.35	.70
Zinfandel	.30	.60
Burgundy	.35	.70
Riesling	.35	.70
Sauterne	.35	.70
Splits, Red or White, .15		

I. DE TURK

Medoc type	.35	.70
Zinfandel	.35	.70
Burgundy type	.50	1.00
Riesling	.40	.80
Sparkling Burgundy type	1.15	2.25
Sparkling Sauterne type	1.15	2.25

E. H. LANCEL CO.

Zinfandel	.30	.60
Burgundy type	.35	.70
Cabernet	.35	.70
Nectarubi	.50	1.00
Topazor	.50	1.00
Splits, Red or White, .15		

OUR OWN BOTTLING
Claret or White Wine, per glass, .10

	½ Bot.	Bot.
White Wine	.20	.40
Table Claret	.15	.30
Zinfandel	.25	.50
Cachet Rouge	.25	.50
Fly-Trap Private Cabernet	.30	.60
California Grignolino	.40	.80

SUTTER HOME WINE CO.

Zinfandel	.30	.60
Burgundy type	.35	.70
Cabernet	.35	.70
Riesling	.35	.60
Sauterne type	.35	.70
Red or White Splits, .15		

ITALIAN CHAMPAGNE

Passeretta Spumante	1.65	3.25
Bosca	1.65	3.25

IMPORTED CHIANTI

Chianti, Italian	.65	1.25

IMPORTED FRENCH WINE

Medoc	.75	1.50

PIEMONT WINERY

Zinfandel	.30	.60
Burgundy type	.35	.70
Sauterne	.35	.70
Riesling	.35	.60
Muscat California, Sparkling	1.15	2.25
Splits, .15		

CALWA
Calwa, Non-Alcoholic, Red or White, Pint, .30

A. FINKE'S WIDOW

Zinfandel	.30	.60
Burgundy type	.35	.70
Cabernet	.35	.70
Riesling	.30	.60
Dry Sauterne type	.35	.70

NAPA AND SONOMA WINE CO.

Zinfandel	.30	.60
Burgundy type	.35	.70
Riesling	.30	.60
Sauterne type	.35	.70

CRESTA BLANCA

Table d'Hote Souvenir	.50	1.00
Souvenir Riesling	.45	.90
Souvenir Sauterne type	.50	1.00
Sparkling Burgundy type	1.15	2.25
Sparkling Sauterne type	1.15	2.25
Paul Masson	1.75	3.50

MT. HAMILTON VINEYARD

Cabernet	.50	1.00
Riesling	.50	1.00

CHAMPAGNES

Golden State, extra dry	2.00	3.75
Veuve Clicquot	3.00	6.00

BEER, ALE, AND PORTER

Bass' Ale	Splits, .20	.30	....
Guinness' Stout	Splits, .20	.30	....
Schlitz		.25	.50
Budweiser		.25	.50
Gilt Edge Ruhstaller		.15	....

MINERAL WATERS

French Perrier	Splits, .15	.30	....
White Rock		.25	....
Jackson's Napa Soda		.15	....
Siphon Seltzer			.10

LIQUORS AND CORDIALS

Straight and Mixed Drinks	.15

Corkage, Still Wines, .25; Sparkling, .50

Before Prohibition, San Francisco, which has long boasted fine restaurants, had a firm tradition of wining while dining. Wine lists like this of the famous Fly Trap were long and catholic. The dry years killed many of these dining places, but they did not disappear quietly. NO WINE, NO POODLE DOG read a headline, noting the closing of one. TECHAU TAVERN CLOSES ITS DOORS read another, and TAIT'S, DOWN TOWN, PASSES IN DRY WAVE still another. CHARLEY'S FLY TRAP RESTAURANT FAILS announced one more demise, and the article below carried Charley Besozzi's pronouncement, ''A restaurant can't survive unless it bootlegs.'' While some of the famous names were later revived, old-timers assured young-timers that they were never again the same.

Laws did not necessarily prevent the drinking of alcoholic beverages in restaurants. This card, printed for distribution at a convention at the Whitcomb Hotel in San Francisco in 1924, implies that guests often brought their own bootleg stuff, and calls up unpleasant images of waiters sniffing glasses. More civilized were the waiters at small Italian restaurants who served the proprietors' homemade wine, discreetly and without fuss, in coffee cups.

SPECIAL NOTICE

Our guests are asked to kindly refrain from having any intoxicants on or about tables. No service will be given for only Empty Glasses. Furthermore, the management has instructed all waiters to IMMEDIATELY take up any and all glasses having the odor of intoxicants therein.

KINDLY CO-OPERATE.

COMMITTEE IN CHARGE

The demand for California grapes in the East and Midwest kept viticulture alive during Prohibition. Mr. and Mrs. Ernest Gallo were about to leave for Chicago on a combined honeymoon and business trip in August 1931 when they paused for a snapshot in front of a grape-laden railroad car. The Gallo family had by then successfully launched its enterprise of growing grapes and selling them across the country. Some of Ernest Gallo's earliest selling experience was on trips with an older vineyardist, Giuseppe Franzia, whose daughter Amelia became Mrs. Gallo shortly before this picture was taken.

This winery, built in 1903 by Theodore Gier and sold to the Christian Brothers in 1930, operated during most of Prohibition. Theodore Gier, a German-born Oakland vintner, is second from right, wearing a dark suit and black hat appropriate to the successful business leader that he was until the first World War, when he was accused of being sympathetic to Germany, and the Prohibition years, when he could not manage to modify his multi-unit winery operations to keep them within legal bounds. (He once even served a three-month jail sentence.) Nevertheless, his own wines and those of others he marketed were well respected, and he was looked upon as a victim of his times. The stone winery building he built at what is now called Mont La Salle is still in use, although the open fermenting tanks and the presses partly visible in the background, shown here as they looked just before Prohibition, have been replaced by modern equipment.

Mabel Walker Willebrandt, a brilliant lawyer who, as Assistant United States Attorney General, was given the job of prosecuting Volstead Act infractors, was for some years the object of much mirthful ridicule, the symbol of the holier-than-thou Prohibitionist. Educated in southern California, she had been a Los Angeles public defender of women before going to Washington to handle, besides Prohibition cases, cases involving tax laws and the Bureau of Federal Prisons. When she returned to private practice in Los Angeles in 1929 and Fruit Industries became one of her principal clients, she was labeled by the public press as either a hypocrite or a turncoat. This photograph shows her emerging from the White House in the autumn of 1929 after a conference with President Hoover, looking a little as if she had swallowed the canary. Neither she nor the president's office would reveal the object of the conference, but the newspapers labeled the visit a "mysterious mission." It occurred eight days after the date of the Prohibition Department's letter that in effect authorized Fruit Industries' ambitious plan for production and sale of grape juice for home winemaking.

In Los Angeles, thirty-five thousand gallons of confiscated wine were poured into a gutter early in 1920, in compliance with the law that all seized alcoholic beverages had to be destroyed. Late that same year San Francisco followed suit, officers spending seven hours breaking bottles and casks of wine taken in two hundred raids made in the previous four months. Women screamed, strong men broke into tears, and the Collector of Customs decreed that never again would the public be exposed to the sight of such carnage. Nevertheless, this federal agent in the northern city took sledgehammer to cask some years later, and the by then Prohibition-wise spectators reacted with only interested concern.

When wine bricks were launched on the New York market, they were immediately credited to Mabel Walker Willebrandt, although in fact they were made by rivals of her client, Fruit Industries. The first, called Vino Sano, was greeted with the headline, WINE BRICK WITH KICK; THANK MABEL. "The 'wine brick' is Mabel Walker Willebrandt's latest gift to Prohibition," read the article. And— "the biggest joke of all is that your Uncle Sam, benefactor of Europe's debtor nations and dispenser of millions in the cause of Prohibition, is unwittingly the backer of this latest dodge to cheat the dry law. It was President Hoover's Farm Board which loaned the California grape growers $10,000,000," etc. Mabel came into it because, said the article, it was she who "passed on the legality of all steps being taken by the 'wine brick' promoters." The legality, challenged but upheld, was not enough to make the bricks popular. If they got damp en route to the home winery, they dissolved into a gooey mess.

"After December 6, when Prohibition ends, we will all be smiling," the smiling woman on the cover of the November 1933 *California Grape Grower* is saying.

TO HEALTH OF U. S. CHIEF

Once again California sent wine to a head of state, this time to President Franklin D. Roosevelt, in gratitude for his support of Repeal. Cases of champagne and sparkling burgundy bound for the White House left San Francisco on May 1, 1933, ten minutes after the first revenue stamps for 3.2 percent beverages were issued there. They were sped on their way by one Miss Jane Barrett, drinking a toast to the president.

20. Building a New Foundation

IF you had come to San Francisco early in December 1933 to celebrate the first day of Repeal, as many did, you could have stayed at the Palace Hotel, one of the West's finest, for anywhere from $3.00 to $6.00 if you were alone, $6.00 to $10.00 if there were two of you. In its excellent Palm Court dining room, the table d'hôte lunch cost eighty-five cents, the table d'hôte dinner $1.25 or $1.75. For a bottle of California wine to accompany the meal, you would have paid $1.25 to $1.75. For the same bottle at a store you would have paid well under a dollar.

This was the brave new world into which California's winemakers emerged so optimistically. Just a little over three years had passed since the Wall Street crash. Herbert Hoover's administration had tried hard but failed to stem the ever-worsening Depression. The voters did not believe the Republicans could do it. In addition, some were swayed by the fact that Hoover was against Repeal, Franklin Delano Roosevelt for it. In 1933 the Democrats took over. As the final battles in the war for Repeal were fought, the Roosevelt administration began taking its bold steps to repair the nation's economy. It was the worst year of the Depression, and although things began to improve in 1934, they were still grave.

The problem common to almost all Americans, too little money, affected grape growers and winemakers. Many vineyards had deteriorated for lack of finances to maintain them. In addition, grafting and replanting to "shipping grapes" during Prohibition left California with a shortage of good wine varieties and a shortage of knowledge of them. All the work of the nineteenth century on grape varieties was available to few and forgotten by most. There was also an immediate lack of viticulturists who knew how to manage good wine grape vineyards.

Nevertheless, new wineries were started, bringing the total of new and old to 804 in 1934. Six years later there were only 538.

In 1958 Ernest Gallo, one of the survivors, looking back twenty-five years after Repeal, recalled the situation of the winemakers, himself and his brother Julio included. Speaking to his fellow members of the Wine Institute, of which he was board chairman, he said:

> We remember starting our wine business in the fall of 1933—during the very

depths of the Depression. What a time to be born! Grapes sold for eight to ten dollars per ton to wineries that were broke. My brother and I started that year with nothing but courage and a prayer. Most of the wineries that had survived [the fifteen] years of Prohibition were neglected, ramshackle affairs, and some had old, moldy cooperage and bad wines. You remember warehouses and barns were quickly converted to wineries by installing new redwood tanks based mostly upon credit extended by cooperage firms.

Five years later, speaking to the American Society of Enologists, which was soon to confer upon him its Merit Award, Gallo added a description of the wine men of the mid-1930s.

A few had been winery owners before Prohibition; another few had been in winery management. . . . They had for years been clinging to the hope that Repeal would some day come. But when it came, it found them an impoverished lot. By and large, however, the people who rushed into the wine business at Repeal were people who were attracted to it mainly because they saw a new industry coming into being. They jumped in with no experience, training, or capital, hoping to find a quick way to make money. Both categories of people had to think first of survival and only then of the consumer. Because of ignorance and/or necessity, they bought grapes as cheaply as possible, produced wine as cheaply as possible, and sold it as cheaply as possible and couldn't pay their debts.

Comparing their wines with the vastly better wines of 1964, Gallo noted, "Then, table wines were heavy, very dry, high in tannin, usually oxidized, coarse, harsh and often sour." One of the reasons was the dearth of experienced winemakers and technical information.

On the repeal of Prohibition, the little winemaking knowhow available to the industry was limited to a handful of older men who were entering the wine business as proprietors, and to a few pamphlets published around 1914 and earlier by Professor Bioletti of the University of California. For example, all my brother and I knew about winemaking at the time of Repeal was how my father used to make wine in the basement for our own use. Some of you may remember what homemade wine was— something like grape juice in December and something like vinegar in June."

The Gallos looked for an experienced winemaker but found none. They were more successful in locating printed material.

"A search of the local library unearthed two of Professor Bioletti's pamphlets," continued Ernest Gallo. (It was a search hindered by the librarian's hesitancy, for the cloud of Prohibition still hung over winemaking. Finally, however, she found them in the basement where they had long been stored away.) "These pamphlets were probably the difference between going out of business the first year because of an unsalable product, and what was to become the Gallo winery of today."

Information soon began to flow once more, however, from the university to the winegrowers. The enologists, viticulturists, and agricultural economists at Berkeley and Davis turned out a prodigious number of practical articles, mainly for *The Wine Review,* and the *California Grape Grower* and its successor *Wines & Vines,* defining wine types, explaining fermentation processes, giving warnings of market fluctuations, and much more. Professor Bioletti himself contributed some. He had been hired by Professor Hilgard in 1889, taught courses in enology and viticulture before Prohibition, and had frequently bicycled from Berkeley to Napa County to meet with winegrowers. Now he took to a flivver to visit vineyards and advise vineyardists until his retirement in 1935.

It was William Vere Cruess, however, who "mobilized his staff and immediately set about helping the California wine industry re-establish itself on a sound basis," as his younger colleague Dr. Emil Mrak later recalled. The work was difficult, and it "required the rediscovery of efficient methods of growing and processing grapes and the re-education of those who managed the industry. Among the problems that demanded solutions were those of what grapes to use and when to harvest them, which chemicals to add to the must, how to prevent bacterial spoilage, and what metals to use or avoid in processing the wine. Professor Cruess's labors in these areas were herculean."

A California farm boy who proved to be a very good student, Cruess had worked with Bioletti and gained practical winemaking experience before Prohibition. During the dry years he turned his patience, attention, and inventiveness to food processing, developing such successful products as canned fruit cocktail and such transitory ones as raisin-chili chutney. As soon as Repeal seemed assured he turned much of his energy back to wine. He wrote papers, at first drawing upon his and his colleagues' pre-Prohibition studies and later on research they again undertook at the university. One paper, based on work done between 1911 and 1916, was on the value and methods of using pure yeast cultures and sulfur dioxide—the same substances Edmund Rossi had used covertly at Italian/Swiss Colony in those years. It saved many a gallon of wine made by tyros. He wrote dozens of papers on wine, most completely practical, but some abstrusely scientific.

Cruess also wrote the first authoritative book on winemaking to be published in the United States in the twentieth century, *The Principles and Practices of Wine Making*. With all these, he had time for research and, more important to the revival of California winemaking, for teaching short courses to people who could not go to college for more than a few days at a time but were eager and quick learners. He conferred with winemakers who came to visit the university. (After the young Gallo brothers had been there, he remarked to a graduate student assistant that he had never answered so many questions in one day in all his life.) And he took his younger university colleagues to visit wineries and conferred with winemakers throughout the state.

On one trip Cruess and Maynard A. Joslyn discovered the secret of a wonderfully touted device for preventing grape juice or wine from spoiling. It was a secret gadget in a little black box. An entire plant had been equipped around it. They found, not to their great astonishment, that someone had reinvented pasteurization.

Joslyn was a brilliant creative scientist in a community of brilliant scientists on the university's Berkeley campus. A native of Russia, he became a student of Cruess when he was working on his Ph.D. in chemistry, and they collaborated on many papers and research projects dealing with food and wine.

In the mid-1930s the university assigned to Josyln and Maynard Amerine of the Davis campus the task of preparing a series of publications to guide the still-struggling wine industry in making sound enological decisions and following them. This resulted in three classic bulletins on the commercial production of table wines, dessert wines, and brandies. The first two were later revised and expanded into two books, which remain the authoritative American works on table and dessert wines, known throughout the world. That the authors should have happened to have the same first name was a coincidence that leaves some Europeans with the impression that they were written by one man with a hyphenated last name.

Maynard A. Amerine, who was to become the voice of the university on wines—their scientific, historical, cultural, and even literary interpreter—studied at both the Berkeley and Davis campuses; in 1936, the year he was awarded his Ph.D., he became an enologist on the Davis staff. His department chose him carefully and saw to it that he was trained for the position of leadership that he later assumed.

To bring him knowledge of the years before Prohibition, Edmund H. Twight, the Frenchman who had taught at the university from 1901 to 1906, then gone on to many jobs in private enterprises, was brought back. Educated in viticulture and enology at Montpellier, Twight had first learned about American wines at the California Wine Association, where he worked under Henry Lachman, that peerless taster, and Charles Ash, both of whom strongly influenced him. Twight became Amerine's mentor and tasted wines with him and other staff members, drawing upon his long knowledge and memory.

"We had five or six hundred samples of wine coming in every year," Amerine later recalled, samples made experimentally at Davis from different vineyard areas, "and neither Winkler nor I had any great amount of experience in critically evaluating wines. So he immediately helped us to establish some norms." Twight also conversed with Amerine in French, which was useful when the university sent the younger man to Europe to broaden his knowledge of enology, and incidentally to set him off on a future as a cosmopolite.

Professor Albert J. Winkler reminisced about all the wine tasting. "You had to have a good memory. And you had to keep at it. I never did develop a very sharp palate because of my age at the time, but Amerine and I tasted twenty wines in the forenoon and twenty wines in the afternoon from the time we started in 'thirty-six until World War II. I became fairly good, but I never equaled Amerine."

Winkler spent his entire professional career at the university, where he had received his doctorate in plant physiology in 1921. Throughout the dry years he had done both basic and practical research on *Vitis vinifera*, re-examining many long-held ideas and conceiving new practices of grape culture and training. These he later brought together in his *General Viticulture,* the classic work on that subject.

In 1935 he began his studies of factors affecting wine quality—thus the importance of learning to perceive quality by tasting. He concluded in due time that the main factor was climate and the most important aspect of climate was temperature. With Amerine, who had found him "a student's ideal professor" and was now a Davis colleague, he gathered climatological data and compiled "heat summation" tables. From these came the mapping of the state's vineyard areas into five regions, Region I being the coldest, Region V being the hottest. On the basis of this research they published recommendations indicating which region is best for each of California's main wine grape varieties. Thus in little more than a decade of concentrated scientific study, they formulated the full span of knowledge sought by Californians for a century—what grapes grow best where.

It was a formidable achievement. It has kept California's winegrowers from many a blunder and directed them to many a success. While not all follow precisely the results of the Winkler and Amerine studies, those who defy them proceed with caution. Both Winkler and Amerine are today convinced that with better measurement of climate and temperature variables, a total of at least fifteen viticultural regions may in time be identified in California.

While the wine men could turn to the university for help on matters of viticulture and enology, they were on their own when it came to protecting and advancing their interests in the legislatures and the marketplace. In October of 1934 a couple dozen representatives of California wineries met and signed articles of incorporation for an organization they named the Wine Institute. In time it became the strong arm and voice of the industry.

It did not spring into being at full force, however. It was a voluntary trade association, and a certain amount of money was needed to join, at a time when money was short. It got off to a slow start. Three months after its organization meeting, only forty-two had signed up. That was December 1934. Miraculously, however, in three months' time the number tripled. What happened? A. P. Giannini stepped in.

Some months earlier Congressman Emanuel Cellar, who had a major hand in post-Prohibition federal wine legislation, had written Giannini, head of what was still an organization dominated by one man, the Bank of America, suggesting that "the wine group ought to get together and organize as closely as possible," and that Giannini himself should be "the Moses that will lead the grape and wine industry out of the wilderness." It was not in Giannini's character to take such an overt role, but his bank was the industry's major financer, he himself was a friend of many of the winemakers, his fellow Italian-Americans, and he was not unused to performing miracles in his own way. He made a direct appeal by telegram to Paul Garrett of New York, whose New York-based Garrett & Company had important California interests, to join the Institute and be an example for others to follow. He probably made many more appeals less formally, as he held his famous sidewalk conferences or as winegrowers called on him to discuss loans. He also assigned Burke Critchfield, an agricultural economist who was a bank vice president, to work through the California State Chamber of Commerce on sign-ups. Others of course— its staff and its core members—contributed to the speedy growth of the Wine Institute that spring, but there is no doubt that Giannini made his contribution. Somehow the waters parted and 110 members came in. By the end of the year Critchfield was off lobbying across the country for state laws favorable to California wine, and the Wine Institute represented three quarters of the state's industry.

Like the groups that the wine men had been forming ever since they met together at the State Agricultural Society conventions, the Wine Institute offered a forum for the exchange of ideas and practical information. Its first president was A. R. Morrow, still vigorous at seventy-one. He had continued supervising the remnants of the California Wine Association before they were brought into Fruit Industries in 1929, when he became Fruit Industries' general manager. Harry Caddow became the Wine Institute's full-time manager. He had been an assistant to Donald Conn but was as far from being a high-pressure promoter as a man could be. Mild, conciliatory, knowledgeable, he would be for the next twenty years a balance wheel for the Institute's second in command, Leon D. Adams, who had had a persuasive hand in its formation. Adams became the chief sparkplug and sometimes controversial idea-and-action man of the organization.

Adams was in 1934, as he would be forever after, a complete wine enthusiast, full of missionary zeal. As a young journalist he had traveled to Europe and observed what he considered the civilized use of wine, which was in some contrast to Prohibition-period America's guzzling. On his return he covered the San Francisco Bay Area Prohibition beat for California newspapers, became acquainted with the writings of Andrea Sbarboro on wine as the beverage of temperance, and came to know and admire the Rossi brothers. After Repeal he tasted with Morrow, interested himself in everything about wine, and fought hard for the recognition of wine as an agricultural rather than a manufactured product. He worked effectively at replacing the Prohibition image of winemakers as lawbreakers by bringing to the public the civilized aspects of the history of California winemaking and equating it with the cultured men who were continuing it. He also, on another level, found a young attorney and legislator, Jefferson Peyser, who was willing to take on the fledgling organization as a client and for forty-odd years fought what he called the "tangled thicket" of laws and regulations impeding the making and selling of California wine.

Ten days before the end of Prohibition, Italian Swiss Colony staged a big sendoff at Asti for its first new-era rail shipment to the East. The celebration was complete with local maidens in Swiss peasant costumes that Leon Adams had rushed in from a San Francisco theatrical costumer. The picture, picked up by the newspaper wire services, crossed the nation almost immediately. The New York–bound wine arrived at the Jersey City railroad yards on the eve of Repeal.

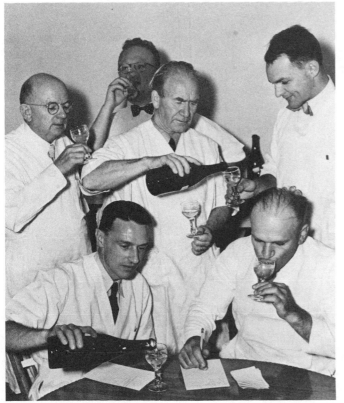

By 1938 the State Fair wine competitions had become important events. Judging was well organized, and juries were made up of both University of California and industry men. This group, tasting what had by that year become a large and widely representative number of wines, posed for a picture showing all the principal activities involved in wine tasting except spitting. The man at the upper left examining the wine visually is Louis Wetmore, hero of the 1906 fire. The others are university men who were working hard to make the winegrowers aware of quality. In the center William V. Cruess is pouring wine into Maynard A. Amerine's glass. Behind Professor Cruess, tasting, is Maynard A. Joslyn. Seated, pouring, is George L. Marsh, and about to taste is Albert J. Winkler.

Professor Frederic T. Bioletti of the University of California, whose career in viticulture and enology had begun long before Prohibition, tasted wines (out of tumblers!) at California's first post-Prohibition State Fair competition. In 1934 Bioletti became the mentor of Harold P. Olmo, initiating the interest in grape varieties that carried the younger scientist to fame as a developer of important new grapes. Bioletti hired him as a research assistant on a grape improvement project on the Davis campus in 1932, while he was still a graduate student. Although Bioletti's office remained at Berkeley, he spent part of his time at Davis and for the next half dozen years would often wake up his assistant before dawn to set out for vineyard visits. "He was a very short man, frail looking, with large glasses, but boiling over with energy," recalled Olmo. "Little by little I got to take over the driving, because it used to make me very uneasy, and other people more uneasy, because he got to be quite erratic in his driving." He also became careless about leaving his hats, to which he was deeply devoted, at one place and another, so that Olmo frequently had to double back to retrieve them. But these were unimportant traits, for he remained mentally as well as physically energetic, and transmitted a great deal of knowledge of and experience with grape varieties to the younger man. He also worked on vineyard practices. In Olmo's words, "Professor Bioletti's early work was in many of the same fields that Professor Winkler later perfected and got into a more scientific vein."

Harold P. Olmo, who got practical training in plant genetics by working on tobacco plants, later transferred this experience to grapes. He explained the work on Bioletti's plant improvement project, in which he participated: "We had to emasculate the flowers with very fine forceps. You have to be very steady, and you have to take this little cap off the flower. It's just a couple of millimeters wide. You use jewelers' forceps and operate on one flower at a time; there are often a thousand or more in a cluster. So it takes a long time to make these crosses, and it's tedious work." It was not too tedious for Olmo to continue, however, for by just this technique he created new grapes for the table, and new wine varieties that have quickly become useful in the production of better table wines. He also became a formidable "plant hunter," and on one particularly perilous trek collected from some rocky ledges near the Afghanistan-Persia border specimens of the wild ancestor of *Vitis vinifera*. Their descendants are still propagated at Davis.

In the center Professor Olmo watches a visiting Spanish viticulturist consider the scent of a wine made experimentally from one of his newly developed grapes, Carmine. The occasion was a University Coast Counties Grape Day.

Edmund Henri Twight, who became an important member of the University of California's staff for two post-Prohibition years, inherited from his father, a professor at the Sorbonne, a love of linguistics and botany. Through his mother's relatives in the Midi, he became acquainted with winemaking and then went on to study it at the national school of agriculture at Montpellier. He left France to avoid mandatory military duty and began the first of many wanderings. Reaching California in the late 1890s after stays in Canada and Australia, he worked at the California Wine Association under Lachman and Morrow, and in 1901 was named Assistant Professor of Viticulture at the University of California's Berkeley campus. Having done laboratory research, published papers on both viticulture and enology, and done field work in the state's vineyards with notable success, he for some reason suddenly resigned in 1906. Maynard A. Amerine, the biographer of this man whom he knew well but found always a "complex and many-sided character," could not explain why. During the next thirty years he worked for a distiller, a number of wineries, and for a few years during Prohibition at the Sunkist raisin cooperative where he developed a grape candy that, to his long-term regret, was never marketed. In 1936 he returned to the university for another highly productive period, during which Amerine worked with him. There, before again moving on, he exerted important influence upon many in regard to upholding the quality of wines on the one hand and industrializing its production on the other.

This photograph shows him in the laboratory at Cresta Blanca, where during the 1940s he was briefly winemaker.

The enology building on the Davis campus of the University, with its pilot-size winery, distillery, and cellars, was built in 1939, and from it have come a steady outpouring of winemaking studies and advances. Bioletti had drawn up plans for a commercial-size winery. Winkler and Amerine, however, who had made some three thousand fermentations over the past five years, knew the advantage of smallness. They geared it to five-gallon lots, which proved to be large enough for conclusive results and yet small enough for practicality. Here a student poured grapes into one of its presses.

The Golden Gate International Exposition, held at Treasure Island in San Francisco Bay in 1939 and 1940, gave California winegrowers a chance to show the world how far they had come since the end of Prohibition. There was a Temple of Wine, as there had been at the 1915 Panama-Pacific International Exposition, and to dedicate it Carl Bundschu, whose father had been the main propellant of the 1915 Temple, and who had himself been promoting this one since 1934, served Maywine punch to all comers.

There was a general exhibit, which this crowd is entering on its 1940 opening day, and there were special exhibits created by individual wineries. That of Italian Swiss included a wine garden serving sandwiches and wines. Most famous of all was Roma's display, which was the center for its nationwide broadcast of Art Linkletter's interviews with fairgoers. At the 1939 fair, a five-member jury tasted 402 California wines in general commercial distribution and gave the highest prizes to Beaulieu burgundy and Wente Bros. Sauvignon blanc.

Symbolizing the difference between the pre-Prohibition and post-Prohibition periods are these two photographs of loading grapes to be hauled to the vineyard. Horse-drawn wagons like this in the San Joaquin Valley had been in general use. Now motor trucks, often somewhat improvised like this one in the Napa Valley, came to supersede them.

21. Getting Through the 'Thirties

Had California winemakers anticipated at the beginning of 1934 that the next seven years would be a roller coaster ride rather than a smooth train trip to success, fewer of them would have leaped aboard. Nearly a third of them were hurled off. There were 804 wineries in the state in the first post-Prohibition year, only 526 in 1941.

A few prospered. More made it through with difficulty. A remarkable number somehow managed to grow. The agricultural cooperative movement, backed by the Roosevelt government and implemented for California wineries by the quasi-governmental Berkeley Bank for Cooperatives, gave impetus to a number of wineries owned and operated by grape growers. Many of them had grown "shipping grapes" during Prohibition and were now encouraged by the university specialists to replant to better wine varieties.

The state's largest winery organization of the years immediately following Repeal was a super-cooperative made up of a number of wineries, some of which were in themselves cooperatives. It was the corporation with the prosaic name Fruit Industries, Ltd., reborn in July 1934 as a cooperative. Two of its most prominent members were, however, family-owned.

The Italian Vineyard Company, under the management of able, convivial James Barlotti since the death of Secondo Guasti, Jr., still cultivated the state's largest vineyard and made its wine at the Guasti winery, which Secondo, Sr., had had constructed. Its winemaker now was Marius Biane, who as a young French immigrant had begun his career in 1893 under Emile Vaché, then continued it as a partner with Emile's brother Adolphe and in time married his daughter Marceline. The Vaché family, from the Cognac district of France and prominent in southern California, traced its beginnings in California wine heritage back to the 1830s, thereby giving the subsequent members of the Biane family a long genealogy. Philo Biane, one of the sons of Marius and Marceline, had gone to work for Fruit Industries in 1930 and had been sent to France to learn the Charmat method of sparkling wine production, which upon his return he introduced for making California champagne. He went to Guasti to assist his father, then succeed him as winemaker. In 1941, still only thirty-two but well experienced, Philo became assistant to A. R. Morrow and subsequently succeeded him as production manager of Fruit Industries. Many years later Philo Biane would return to Guasti as owner, with his sons, of Secondo Guasti's big stone winery.

Another family-owned winery member of Fruit Industries was headed by Antonio Perelli-Minetti, one of its original incorporators. He built the A. Perelli-Minetti & Sons winery at the southern end of the San Joaquin Valley in 1934. Intelligent, eager to experiment and move ahead, Antonio Perelli-Minetti had been growing grapes and making wine up and down the state for nearly three decades before being drawn to this area by the legendary Joseph Di Giorgio during Prohibition. In the early 1930s he started buying acreage south of Delano, a free-and-easy agricultural community where it is said you could get a drink then anywhere in town but the post office and the bank. He acquired small parcels that had earlier been bought by people who had hoped oil might lie under them. The soil was alkali, "awful to look at," Perelli-Minetti recalled years later as he glanced out of his office window over his flourishing vineyards. (As he had said, referring to Secondo Guasti and the Cucamonga Desert, "The Italians, all they see is wine, any place they go.") On the land he slowly reclaimed he built a million-gallon winery that became an important Fruit Industries producer. One of Antonio's sons, Mario, became for a time manager of Fruit Industries, and two others, Fred and Bill, were at Delano.

Members of the super-cooperative varied in number as they went in and out. There were usually from eight to a dozen. At one time, after the name had been changed to the California Wine Association, the pre-Prohibition organization which it had absorbed and had hoped to emulate, there were eleven members and a well publicized label, Eleven Cellars. But most of the wine was sold in bulk, and over the years the number of members dwindled until finally, in 1970, only A. Perelli-Minetti & Sons was left. Even after the heirs of Antonio, who lived an active ninety-five years, sold the company in 1981, they retained the rights to the old California Wine Association labels—Greystone, A. R. Morrow (for brandy), Guasti, L & J (for Lachman & Jacobi), Calwa, and nearly two hundred more.

Bisceglia Brothers, another family-owned company that also sold its wine mainly in bulk, was for a short time the state's second largest wineseller. The first Bisceglia brothers in America were Joseph and Pasquale, who found their way to southern Santa Clara County in the late 1880s, planted vines of course, and of course made wine. They sold it locally by the barrel, and since that was a small enterprise for two energetic young men, they also cleared land and sold wood, and they established a cannery. Prospering, they sent for two more brothers, Bruno and Alphonse, and the four of them built up what was the largest privately owned cannery in the state when they sold it in 1938. Meanwhile they had built up the wine business too, choosing to remain in it rather than in canning with its more complex array of products and processes. They had operated during Prohibition and stored up a big enough inventory to get off to a running start at the end of 1934. They had several large wineries in the Fresno area and at one time owned Greystone in the Napa Valley. After the second generation succeeded the first, it consolidated operations in one well-equipped winery near Madera, which in 1974 became a part of the Canandaigua Wine Company of New York and continued making wine and brandy under Pasquale's able son Bruno.

While the large proportion of California's wine was sold in bulk in those years to be bottled by others—much of it to Eastern and Midwestern bottlers who marketed it under various labels—a few followed the advice of Isaac De Turk and other nineteenth-century wine men and bottled their own under their own labels. It was a more difficult way to sell wine, demanding more equipment, more time, more planning, and more promotion—in short more capital. Those wineries that were more successful bottlers of their own wines became the best known: Italian Swiss and Cresta Blanca, for instance, and especially Roma.

Just before the end of the nineteenth century, John Battista Cella (born Giovanni but known as Battista) came to the United States, and a few years later was joined by his brother Lorenzo. They were an effective team, Battista the entrepreneur, Lorenzo the expansive salesman, both ambitious to achieve the American dream of success. In New York they established a wholesale wine business, buying both imported and California wines. Among the latter were those of the Petri family, and when in 1915 Battista Cella made his first visit to California to see the Panama-Pacific Exposition, he met the Petris and invested in their Petri Cigar Company, which made both Italian-style stogies and wine.

Nine years later he bought a winery near Lodi. It had been named Roma by Martin Scatena, who had established it in 1890, and although the Cellas came from the Piacenza region in northern Italy, they let the name of the Italian capital stand. In 1924 Battista, leaving Lorenzo in the East to handle sales, moved to Lodi to manage the Roma winery. The next year when he applied for a Prohibition Department winemaking permit, he listed his age as forty-five, his status as a naturalized citizen of the United States, and his assets as four hundred thousand dollars. Until Repeal Roma made wines for sacramental, medicinal, and cooking uses, grape concentrate and grape juice, and also shipped fresh fruit. Then early in 1933, eager to jump into the post-Prohibition market, it broke ground for a big addition to the Lodi winery. California's secretary of state turned the first spadeful of earth and Miss Flori Cella broke a bottle of champagne over his spade. There were speeches, music, a gala luncheon party, and good press coverage. It was the first of many events, all marked by fanfare and celebration, that would keep Roma's name before the public.

The new addition, completed in time for the 1933 crush, made the Lodi Roma plant the largest in the nation, as the Cellas were quick to announce. It was modern and in many ways innovative, and they showed it proudly to all comers, pointing out the new brandy distillery, the recently installed French sparkling wine equipment, the high-capacity crushers, the big fermentation tanks of coated cement, the temperature controls, the seven million gallons of cooperage.

Then in 1935 they bought the two-year-old Santa Lucia winery at Fresno, enlarging its storage capacity over the next few years to nineteen-and-a-half million gallons, and its production capacity to fit. Now the Lodi winery became the nation's second largest and the Cellas proclaimed the Santa Lucia, renamed Roma, to be not only the nation's but the world's largest.

Along the way they acquired other interests, including a Sonoma winery so that they could follow the longstanding practice of blending north coast counties table wines with those of the San Joaquin Valley. At Fresno they created a yeast laboratory, the first in any United States winery, and an experimental laboratory where they developed new types of wine including one they called Sautel. They installed a battery of high-capacity filters and commercial laundry equipment to clean and sterilize the filter cloths. No wonder Schenley Distillers saw Roma as a good investment and in 1942 persuaded the family to sell the company.

The Cellas did not cease being California winegrowers, however. After a few years as Schenley executives, they continued growing grapes and making wine on their own under the name Cella Vineyard, John B. Cella II taking charge after the deaths of his uncle, Battista, and his father, Lorenzo, in 1959 and 1960. He later took it into the cooperative Allied Grape Growers. The subsequent moves that propelled it into Heublein, Inc. are part of the remarkable story of Louis Petri. In 1981 John B. Cella II himself joined Guild Wineries, which had acquired the Roma label and the big Fresno Roma winery, completing the circle.

Wineries of different kinds of fame also entered the field and created their impression upon the 1930s, some trailing their Prohibition permits behind them, others—like the Gallo brothers of Modesto, the Pedroncellis of Geyserville, the Berteros of Gilroy, the Ferraras of Escondido, and the Accomazzos of Cucamonga—adding wineries to their vineyards.

It was in this period that the Lodi district came into its own as a wine region. Since the latter decades of the nineteenth century, grapes had been grown in its flat, fertile fields, cooled by breezes blowing from the ocean through the Carquinez Straits. From its vineyards the beautiful Flame Tokay, a pride of California, went to tables in San Francisco and the East. Not until after 1900, however, was there much winemaking. The Roma winery that Martin Scatena built was one of the earliest.

When Battista Cella arrived in Lodi in 1924, he found few rivals for the area's grapes beyond the winery at nearby Woodbridge that

Samuele Sebastiani had bought from a pre-Prohibition cooperative, and the National Fruit Products Company, nucleus of the later Shewan-Jones winery. By 1935, however, when Cella shifted his base of operations to Fresno, there were ten more big wineries, most of them new or radically modernized, most of them cooperatives formed by the district's hard-working German settlers who had earlier been happy to sell him their grapes. Community Grape Corporation was the first of the cooperative wineries to be backed by the Berkeley Bank for Cooperatives and allied New Deal agencies. East-Side Winery, however, found its own financing among its growers and remains today proudly independent, with many of its members descendants of its founders. By 1938 there were eighteen wineries, two of which were to become initial members of the big Guild wine group. The Lodi district reported that it was the source of nearly a quarter of the nation's wines that year. Later, as other areas developed, it dropped to a tenth, but it has maintained that position for three decades.

In the Napa Valley, Beaulieu Vineyard, which had kept its prestige high, heightened it further when Georges de Latour brought Russian-born Andre Tchelistcheff from France to make his wine. Nearby, Louis M. Martini brought his newly built winery slowly into production, and created a fair-sized sensation when he released his first Napa Valley wines in 1940. In the Livermore Valley the Wente family started bottling under its Valle de Oro label, the Concannons slowly broadened their market beyond the churchmen who had been their loyal customers, and Cresta Blanca forged ahead in spite of a fire in 1933 that destroyed its pasteurizer and many gallons of aged sherry. In Sonoma County, Fred Haigh, son-in-law of one of the founders, took the Simi winery at Healdsburg out of hibernation and put its well-aged wines on the tables of the still famous Hotel del Monte, where Josiah Stanford's bottles once had reigned.

In Santa Clara County, B. Cribari & Sons, winemakers since early in the century, after operating in a holding pattern through Prohibition, bought an old C.W.A. winery at Madrone and expanded it to around half-a-million-gallon capacity. Paul Masson, whose sparkling pink Oeil de Perdrix and champagnes made history in the pre-Prohibition days, continued winemaking briefly before selling his winery to an impassioned young stockbroker, Martin Ray. Nearby, Almadén (no longer New Almaden) added 165 acres of vineyard and renovated its winery.

In the San Joaquin Valley there was much activity among the big pre-Prohibition wineries. St. George was reactivated. Lucius Powers, Jr., once more opened the old Lac-Jac winery of Lachman & Jacobi near Parlier, renaming it Mt. Tivey, and hiring as winemaker Carlo Cetti, an old Italian Swiss wine man whose experiments in making dry wines in the valley might have come to something had not the winery changed hands in 1937.

Twenty-nine miles east of Fresno, the old C.W.A. Wahtoke winery was sold in 1933 to a trio of grape growers headed by one of the most dynamic men ever to appear among the state's winemakers. He was Arpaxat Setrakian, known as "Sox." Poised in his sentiments between the valley's raisin growers, of whom he had long been a leader, and the state's winegrowers, Setrakian was never out of the eye of the storm. An emotional orator whose Armenian-tinged English and tears-on-demand could move almost any crowd, he remained controversial so far as the wine men were concerned until his dying day in 1974. Yet he was respected by most, and loved by the raisin growers, whom he represented on federal boards and on the international commission that allocated most of the world's raisins. With a kind of characteristically consistent contradictoriness, he was for many years chairman of the commission, although the United States was not a party to the convention.

In 1936 Setrakian and his same associates took their winery into a San Joaquin cooperative they organized under the name California Growers Winery, which became a major factor in the state's bulk wine business. Like Fruit Industries, however, it gradually lost members, and in 1972 it was reorganized as a corporation by Robert Setrakian, one of California's remarkably large group of second-generation wine men who have contributed to the progress of the industry in recent decades.

Another immigrant who, like Setrakian, became an attorney before devoting himself to grape and wine interests, was small, vigorous

Horace O. Lanza. He had been brought to New York state as a child from Sicily, proved remarkably bright, and entered the wine business more or less by happenstance as World War I and the anticipated shortage of European wines approached. Not always successful at first, but astute, he managed to come out ahead buying and selling wine in 1919, and soon after formed a California corporation with Sophus Federspiel, a highly respected industry leader who had begun his career with Italian Swiss, and William Leichter, through whom he met the much admired Claus Schilling.

They called their corporation Colonial Grape Products, and through the Prohibition years they made a variety of permitted wine products. Early in the 1920s Lanza was offered the remnants of the California Wine Association, its remaining vineyards and wineries included in the price of the wine on hand, three million dollars. Federspiel talked him out of it. Later Lanza took Colonial into Fruit Industries but withdrew because he felt powerless against the dominant Guasti and Garrett interests. On the eve of Repeal he and a partner bought California Grape Products Company, which had been established in 1920 by Antonio Perelli-Minetti and several associates in the winery of the more interestingly named French-American Wine Company. During World War II Lanza bought the by then dispirited Guasti holding and built it back up before selling it less than two years later to Garrett & Company.

Meanwhile he continued leading California Grape Products, of which he had bought major interest in the early 1930s, and its successor Calgrape Wineries, with its large plant and vineyards near Delano, and it remained until the mid-1970s an important source of California bulk wines. During most of these years Lanza had as an associate another unusual man, Harry Baccigaluppi, a national authority on the wine trade and, more important for California, a man of remarkably equable mind who served the entire wine industry as a conciliator of dissidents and a creator of esprit de corps.

If ever a group needed cool-headed leaders, it was the California wine men of the latter 1930s. Their general situation was chaotic due to various mainly unrelated factors. The old patterns of wine selling had almost disappeared. Free trade among the states was denied by law for this product. The Depression continued, abating almost imperceptibly to many. Wine consumption increased less than anticipated as some consumers switched to stronger beverages now available. Of those who continued loyal to wine, many also continued loyal to their Prohibition home-winemaking bootleggers, who it was said peddled millions of gallons yearly, cheap and of course tax free, formidable competition for legitimate winemakers.

Prices were extremely unstable. Price cutting kept profits low. Since many wineries were underfinanced, they suffered the chronic winemakers' problem of not being able to afford to store their wine long enough to age it properly. The young wine they sold gave headaches to the buyers and the wine industry as a whole. Together with that made by tyros, it drove some customers back to the bootleggers whose products were familiar and tolerable, others to beer and spirits.

And then there was the weather, which, varying from year to year more than usual, dispensed larger and smaller crops impartially and without advance notice. If the wine men had listened carefully to warnings by Giannini Foundation agricultural economist Sherwood W. Shear and such market authorities as Harry Baccigaluppi, they might have averted problems, but most went instead from hope to crisis to hope to crisis. Having increased facilities and production with more optimism than assurance (and in the face of low returns), they created a debacle in 1936. There was so much more wine than people were able or willing to buy that prices plummetted. Then the weather intervened, giving a short crop that year and less wine the next, so that 1937 was so much better that they again went full speed ahead. In 1938 sales and prices dropped once more.

Finally to the rescue came a combination of forces: the Bank of America, the Wine Institute, the State Department of Agriculture, and the winegrowers themselves. There were two actions. One was the establishment of the so-called prorate program, which sent almost half of the state's 1938 grape crop to be distilled into brandy and high-proof spirits rather than being made into wine. Another communication went from A. P. Giannini to Paul Garrett in New York, introducing Burke Critchfield, who had again been pressed into service and wished to discuss a program for "substantial wine industry advertising and market stabilization," the prorate plan. It was financed by the Reconstruction Finance Corporation and five banks. Four contributed 20 percent of the banks' share, the Bank of America 80 percent.

The next year, according to Carl Wente, it again looked as if another bumper crop would befall the vineyardists, and some of the wineries that were afraid of more unaged wine being dumped onto the market by their weak neighbors asked the Bank of America to help finance a cooperative venture to pay an equable price to the growers and allow the winemakers to age their wine. It was similar to the cooperative warehousing plan that had been proposed in the *Examiner*'s 1889 series of articles on the problems of the winemakers of that day. The bank was willing, and Central California Wineries was established, buying two cellars, Louis Martini's at Kingsburg, and Greystone at St. Helena, which the bank itself had recently taken over from Bisceglia Brothers. The Martini sale included two million gallons of sweet wine, but not the highly prized sherry that Martini took to the Napa Valley with him as the nucleus of that winery's famous sherry solera.

The plan worked, at least for a time. Grape prices rose, and to cover the increase the bank advanced more money to the cooperative. Then, as Wente recalled, "some of the nonmembers, jealous of the vintners and growers in the co-op, complained of price fixing." The Department of Justice was about to start antitrust proceedings when "Schenley Distillers bought a couple of the C.C.W. wineries and the government case fell on its face." That was the end of Central California Wineries, but two years of financial support helped tide the winegrowers over.

The other plan, which matured into a more lasting organization, followed in a sense an undoubtedly long-forgotten idea advanced by Charles A. Wetmore in 1883. He had proposed that part of the federal taxes paid by the wine men be returned to the state to use for the promotion of viticulture. Now in 1938 the pro-gram for "substantial wine industry advertising" that Giannini had mentioned to Garrett was implemented under the California State Department of Agriculture. A marketing order for wine, similar to the marketing orders for tomatoes and other established agricultural products, was voted in by the winemakers, who agreed to tax each gallon of their product to pay not only for promotion but also for quality control and a variety of research programs. It created the Wine Advisory Board. Working with the Wine Institute over the next thirty-seven years, it did indeed contribute to a steady increase in the market for California wines, while backing research in viniculture. In its final years the board underwrote a project of the Regional Oral History Office of the University of California at Berkeley, which, in interviews with twenty-five wine men, preserves much of the history of the state's winemaking through the first three-quarters of the twentieth century.

As for the prorate, its effects lasted longer than the plan itself. The brandy and high-proof "mellowed into exceedingly smooth collateral," remarked Jesse Jones of the Reconstruction Finance Corporation.

Meanwhile, Otto Meyer, an affable, experienced third-generation wine and brandy maker, had come to the United States from Germany in 1938 and, as he recalled in one of the Regional Oral History Office interviews, "made a very careful study of the brandy situation in California because I saw that a very good brandy could be made from the grapes available here, but nobody really believed it." He talked with A. R. Morrow, who was considered the state's leading authority and was convinced that nobody in the United States would buy anything but unblended 100-proof bonded brandy. Meyer believed that to make a palatable brandy you had to blend it and bottle it at a lower alcoholic content. Then he learned about the prorate brandy. There was a large supply of it in bond, stored in various warehouses throughout the state. Soon it would have to be withdrawn and taxes paid on it. Meyer set to work. "I tasted each lot of those millions of gallons of prorate brandy to get acquainted with the inventory and classify it by quality and type. It took me about four or five months to do that." He then went to the producers of those lots that met his standards to discuss buying their options. One was so glad for the opportunity to get out from under the tax threat that he at first thought Meyer was asking him to pay to relieve him of his tax obligation. Then Otto Meyer, with his brother-in-law Alfred Fromm, who was working with the Christian Brothers, went to Giannini's bank to see about help in financing the buying of the options and going into the brandy business. Meyer later recalled:

> This was one of the most impressive business experiences of my life, one which couldn't happen anywhere else. We were told, "You fellows come up with ten cents and we will loan you ninety cents on each dollar at two-and-three-quarters-percent interest, and you go to work." This was the answer which Alfred Fromm and I got from the Bank of America in spite of the fact that our English wasn't very good at the time! Much is talked about the opportunities in this country, and so many generalities are offered, but this is a concrete, specific case of what it really means.

So the Christian Brothers began their highly successful brandy making, and later the Paul Masson winery under Otto Meyer's direction—primary steps in the post-World War II revitalization of California brandy making.

Philo Biane, whose career began during Prohibition and continued into the 1980s, was interviewed by the University of California's Regional Oral History Office, which recorded his recollections of his winemaking forebears, his more than two decades with Fruit Industries, and many details of California winegrowing that might never have been preserved had not the Wine Advisory Board underwritten the oral history project.

Antonio Perelli-Minetti, the son of an important Italian winemaker, as a boy helped tread out grapes in his father's Barletta winery, later studied at the Royal College of Viticulture and Enology at Conegliano, and upon graduation in 1901 decided to pursue his career in California. Always adventuresome and in search of new enterprises, he was involved in many. During Prohibition he planted vineyards in Mexico, became a friend of Pancho Villa, and was for a time an informal emissary between Villa and the United States. Returning to California, he became a founding member of Fruit Industries and, as it turned out, its longest-lasting participant. His family firm was in the end its sole remaining member.

The winery of A. Perelli-Minetti & Sons, located at the southern end of the San Joaquin Valley, was surrounded by what appeared to be desert before Antonio Perelli-Minetti reclaimed it and planted vineyards.

Beniamino Cribari was one of the many Italians who emigrated to California in the early years of the twentieth century and became vineyardists. The winery he established was carried on successfully by his sons through the Depression years and later became a member of the big Guild cooperative, for which his grandson, Albert, became winemaster. The sturdy Beniamino was photographed in the vineyard one Sunday in 1940 just after he had returned from church with his family. His son Angelo, who made the photograph, had asked him to put on his working clothes, but he went only so far as to take off his tie, unbutton his vest, put on his boots, and grab a hoe. The resulting picture shows a proud, independent California Italian vineyardist, typical of a group that made up a sizable part of the state's winegrowing community.

Battista Cella, looking the serious, ambitious businessman that he was, and Lorenso, looking the expansive salesman that he was, shook hands in front of a row of bottled samples of their wine, marking some happy but now forgotten milestone in the dramatic success of the Roma Wine Company.

After the Cella brothers bought the Santa Lucia winery in Fresno and renamed it Roma, they expanded its capacity from one and a quarter million gallons to six million, making it the largest single winery in the world of its time. In 1971, four years after this photograph was taken, Schenley, which had bought it in 1942, sold the largest part of it to Guild Wineries, which renamed it the B. Cribari & Sons winery.

To promote the biggest winery in the world, Roma hired the biggest man in the world, Jack Earle. Here at a dinner in New York in 1941 Earle stood between Lorenzo Cella and his son John Battista II, who was in the Army for the duration.

With a rather incongruously elegant engraved invitation, Roma launched one of the California wine industry's early attempts to package wine in cans. A few others had preceded it, and still others have followed. Perhaps the next will be successful.

Brother Timothy began his years with the Christian Brothers as a novice in Martinez, where they had established their first winery. Not until they had moved their headquarters to Mont La Salle, in the Napa Valley hills, did he begin his career in winemaking. In 1935 he ended several years of teaching in the Brothers' schools to join the winery staff. As cellarmaster for four decades, he has seen the Christian Brothers' winemaking grow and its label achieve national importance. As a public figure, he himself is symbolic of the long involvement of the Catholic church in winemaking in California.

22. World War II and the Distillers

WHEN World War II began its sweep across Europe, American winemakers looked upon it with even more mixed emotions than they had looked upon the sweep of the phylloxera across the European vineyards seven decades earlier. No one wanted another war, but of course the supply of imports would be curtailed and American wine might be expected to fill the gap, at least at home.

But war then came to the United States too, even if it did not invade its land as the phylloxera had. It brought restrictions on the use of grapes, many of which were mandatorily made into raisins for food. It brought shortages—of rail cars, of cartons, of metal bottle caps, of labor. It also took away the services of young and middle-aged industry leaders as they joined the armed forces. All these and more disrupted California winemaking just as it was achieving its first stable post-Prohibition prosperity.

Seven months before Pearl Harbor, *Fortune* magazine carried a long article titled "The Great Wine Boom," pointing out the anticipated shortage of imported wines and the consequent opportunity for "the upper bracket" of the American wine industry to make and market fine wines. It called up the name of Frank Schoonmaker, the author and wine merchant, who was preaching this gospel in his mild but persuasive way. The year before, he had turned up at Louis M. Martini's in the Napa Valley looking for wine to buy. Recalled Martini later, "He came down to my cellar and saw all my vats were marked with the varieties. (I was one of the first after Prohibition to make all my wine with the name of the grape and season.) So he began to get interested." He bought some Sylvaner and Folle blanche. "I like him," Martini added (this was several years before Schoonmaker's death in 1976). "Very intelligent man. And he knows wine. He has a good palate. He is a good writer, and he is a good promoter. He is idealistic, and very honest." It was in 1941 that Schoonmaker and Tom Marvel published their book *American Wines,* which dignified California wines. Not only Martini but all others were grateful except those who were offended by the characterization of California's own traditional angelica. ("It is said that Angelica takes its name from Los Angeles. Better products have taken their names from smaller towns.")

Schoonmaker, as *Fortune* pointed out, was calling for the use of such varietal names as Folle blanche and Sylvaner, rather than borrowed generic ones like burgundy and chablis, and "California sauterne," which was used frequently for almost any slightly sweet white wine. He was also by then selling Martini and Wente wines, and was soon to add those of Korbel and of Almadén, which he helped guide through its Louis Benoist years. To him is due much credit for encouraging the making of quality wines and bringing them to the attention of the American public.

But it was not in the area of fine wines that the big action of the 1940s lay. When Lewis Rosenstiel bought Roma for Schenley Distillers, Inc., he declared that it was to supply "the wine of the people," lining up with the old California Wine Association and the new purveyors of standard American wines.

Wartime diversion of distilled spirits to use in munitions rather than beverages brought four big distilled liquor companies into the California wine business. It was the first major infusion of capital since 1901 when I. W. Hellman and his fellow-bankers had put the then staggering sum of "something over" a million dollars into the California Wine Association. In another longer article, "The Big Wine Deal," *Fortune* examined this action at about its peak in 1944. The whiskey companies had come, *Fortune* pointed out, because they wanted to have something to sell so as to keep open their lines of distribution, and because they had money with which to buy wineries, and because wine presented a favorable temperance image. (The last showed how well the Sbarboro message had been carried over by crusader Leon Adams and his associates.)

The movement had a precursor in 1938 and 1939 when Schenley bought a small fruit distillery in Manteca from Roma, and National Distillers acquired Shewan-Jones in Lodi, both mainly through interest in distillates. But it really began in 1941 with the first takeover of a winery that owned no still.

Artie Samish, the California state legislature lobbyist who was labeled the Secret Boss of California, represented many large interests, Schenley among them. According to the 1944 *Fortune* article, when he asked Lewis Rosenstiel if he wanted to buy the Cresta Blanca winery and the eight gold medals its wines had won, Rosenstiel replied, "What the hell are you talking about?" Samish explained, and Rosenstiel

bought it for Schenley from Lucien Johnson, who had bought it from Clarence Wetmore.

Early the next November Rosenstiel bought the Roma wineries from the Cella family. A few days later he closed the deal for Greystone cellars and the former Martini Grape Products winery at Kingsburg, buying them from a subsidiary of Central California Wineries and thereby, as Carl Wente noted, letting both C.C.W. and the Bank of America off the antitrust hook. By 1944 Schenley had expanded its plants and had more than thirty-five million gallons of storage capacity in California. It was by far the state's largest wine organization.

The year 1942 saw the second of the major incursions. To its modest holding of Shewan-Jones, National Distillers added the Italian Swiss Colony organization, with its original winery at Asti, and La Paloma near Fresno, which had been built about 1919 by the Tarpey family and purchased by Italian Swiss in 1941. The sellers were the Rossi brothers and their longtime associate, winemaker Enrico Prati, and another rather surprising partner, Joseph Di Giorgio, the big Kern County fruit grower and shipper. It was in 1932 that Di Giorgio had put his camel's nose into the Rossis' tent door.

"One day in midsummer of 1932 I was driving past the Italian Swiss Colony winery at Asti," he recalled at an event honoring him in 1937,

> and I was thinking about what I could do with thirty thousand tons of grapes on the vines and no market for them. I stopped and asked them if their winemaking facilities were intact and was given an affirmative reply. As a result of the conversation we diverted a large portion of the tonnage to their winery, where the grapes were made into wine on a gallonage partnership basis. The following year national Prohibition was repealed and the deal proved very profitable to both of us. This was the forerunner to our entering the wine business and our association with the Italian Swiss Colony.

Although Di Giorgio had by 1937 a winery of his own, and was to buy, sell and build others, the arrangement with Italian Swiss continued for many years, and after Italian Swiss bought La Paloma he delivered quantities of his grapes there. He sold his share of the gallonage back to Italian Swiss but not for money. Instead he took stock in the company. By the time National Distillers bought Italian Swiss in 1942, Di Giorgio owned more than a third of its stock. He profited too by Schenley's purchases, for he held more than a quarter interest in Central California Wineries. He took in about two million dollars that year from the outlanders.

National Distillers became the third largest wine company in California, with around seventeen million gallons' storage capacity. Fruit Industries remained, as it had been since Roma nudged it out of first place, the state's second largest, with twenty-two million gallons of cooperage, continuing California-owned. Sturdy old A. R. Morrow declared it would never sell out to these newcomers.

Others did, but they were small potatoes compared to those who did sell out to Schenley and National Distillers. In 1942 Seagrams bought control of Paul Masson. Only Masson and Cresta Blanca among the old, small prestige wineries were sold to the distillers. In 1970, his forty-fifth year as president of the Canadian firm, Distillers Corporation-Seagrams Limited, Samuel Bronfman recalled the background of his association with the Paul Masson property. In 1932, visiting Germany, he met and became a friend of Franz Sichel, a member of a family that had been in the wine business in Germany and France for generations. "Imagine my surprise," recalled Bronfman, "when Franz landed unannounced in Montreal in 1942, a refugee from the Nazi holocaust." Bronfman suggested that he go to California to look into forming a wine business there. He went, and in San Francisco found Alfred Fromm, whose family had owned a winery next to the Sichels' in Mainz. Together they started working with the Christian Brothers, and then, in partnership with Seagrams, formed the wine sales firm of Fromm & Sichel. Through them Bronfman learned of the Masson winery, and somehow persuaded Martin Ray to sell it. Ownership has varied, being sorted out among Seagrams, Fromm, Sichel, and Otto Meyer, who became its president, but guidance has remained consistent, growth steady. Joseph E. Seagram & Sons, now sole owner, is the only one of the four big distillers that came into the California wine industry in the 1940s and stayed continuously.

Hiram Walker was the fourth. In 1943 it bought a winery and vineyard in the Cienega district of San Benito County that Ed Valliant and his family began operating in 1934. The history of winegrowing on the property has been traced back to Philo Biane's ancestor, Théophile Vaché, who started a vineyard here in 1854 and twenty-five years later was on record as making ten to fifteen thousand gallons of wine a year from his mainly French varieties of grapes. Before opening his own "wine depot" in Hollister, he was said to have taken most of his wine to the farther-off mission town of San Juan Bautista in an ox-drawn puncheon on wooden wheels. Others operated the Cienega vineyard from the 1880s until Prohibition. After Hiram Walker bought a New York wine firm, W. A. Taylor & Company, it put Valliant under the Taylor name, along with two other California companies it bought the same year. They were both in Santa Rosa, one the old De Turk winery, the other the vineyard and winery that had been owned since 1902 by the Rafaelo Martini family, including the third-generation Elmo Martini. In 1951, when Hiram Walker began withdrawing from California, it sold the Martini property back to the Elmo Martini family and two members of the Prati family of Italian Swiss, whereupon it assumed the name under which it has continued, Martini & Prati. Then in 1955 Almadén Vineyards took over the Cienega property under lease, and eight years later bought it, thereby closing that Hiram Walker chapter. The corporation would return, however, in 1981 to buy the Callaway Vineyards and Winery at Temecula in Southern California.

In 1953 National Distillers too withdrew from California winemaking, although it would return later to buy Almadén. It had closed down Shewan-Jones in 1949. Now it sold Italian Swiss to Louis Petri's creation, Allied Grape Growers.

In 1950 Schenley had sold Greystone cellars to Christian Brothers, and its California winemaking activities began gradually winding down. By 1968 they had all but stopped. Its share of the state's wine production had dropped to a bare 5 percent. Three years later it sold the Roma label and part of the winery to the Guild Wineries, a cooperative, keeping the rest of the big Fresno plant for making brandy and aperitifs. It sold the Cresta Blanca label to Guild too, although it kept the Cresta Blanca Livermore Valley winery and vineyard until 1981, when it sold them to Wente Bros.

What happened? Why did the three companies that held nearly a quarter of California's total cooperage in 1944 and close to a half of its stocks of aging wine the next year drop out of the nation's leading wine state? Well, of course, conditions changed after the war so that they could go back to their primary interest, distilled spirits. That is to put the best face on it. In fact they found that whiskey making does not necessarily a winemaker make. What they apparently failed to understand at that time was that winemaking and even brandy making are too closely based upon agriculture to be as controllable as the distillation of spirits. However much the winemaker tries, he does not always succeed in winning from the vineyard exactly what he wants. Moreover, as one old-line Californian who worked with the distillers said, "You don't run the wine business like you do the whiskey business, because the profits are not there. In the wine business you work with pennies, and in the whiskey business you work with dollars." And, as another who was in the thick of it in the 1940s remarked, you can't have Wall Street controlling everyday decisions. "For example," he explained, "when the grape and wine market was high, they were buying wine and grapes; when the market was low, they were out of the market. They were just doing it backward because they were trying to run it from New York, and they were not successful in doing this. I remember there was a tremendous drop in the price of wine during the year following the end of the war." He paused. "They lost their shirts. It was after that they wanted out."

What he was referring to was the circus of 1946 and the debacle of 1947.

The war in Europe ended in May 1945, the war with Japan in August. After a big crush got underway that autumn, panic sales put the wholesale price of dessert wines at around 50 cents a gallon. By February of 1946, however, it was approaching $1.00. In April it was pushing $1.40 and in short supply, as wholesalers and retailers alike started loading up. Early that month Sox Setrakian publicly sounded the tocsin. He told the San Francisco *Examiner* that the distillers were "invading California vineyards" and offering as high as $80.00 a ton, while the wine and raisin men were geared to $50.00 a ton.

Before the circus was over and the dust was laid, prices went to over $100.00 a ton—$110.00 and more in some cases. Some options changed hands half a dozen times before the harvest, and there was the incredible autumn spectacle of winery agents stopping grape-laden trucks along the roads, asking what price they were delivering for, and offering to up the ante if they would divert their loads to their wineries.

There were several reasons why this happened. Wartime price controls went off that summer. There was pent-up demand that was, however, over-estimated by wholesalers and retailers alike. And there was an apparent attempt by one of the distillers to make and buy the lion's share of California wine that autumn. It made agreements with independent wineries to make wine for it on a cost-plus basis, putting no ceiling on the price they were to pay for grapes. So they went into the vineyards competing, since the cost would not come out of their pockets. They drove the price up and up for everyone, the other distillers as well as the rest of the California winemakers who crushed that year. And, ironically as usual, nature turned especially bountiful and dealt out a big crop of grapes so that the crush was the biggest on record. Almost everyone was rewarded with more wine than was wanted, especially in the face of the wholesalers' still-well-stocked warehouses and the retailers' still-well-stocked shelves. By 1947 the marketplace was a shambles. Estimates of losses by the two largest distillers ranged from fifteen to twenty million dollars. No one dared guess how much the others lost. Many wineries went out of business. Still others formed new alliances.

The Napa Valley Cooperative sold all its wine in 1946 to Schenley's Roma for 85 cents to $1.05 a gallon—this was dry wine, not the higher-priced dessert wine—and returned $135.00 a ton to its grower members. So buoyed up were they that they decided to hold at least part of their wine off the market in 1947 and sell on speculation. The price fell so low that even those buyers who had contracted for the rest of their vintage said, "Never mind. Keep the down payment and the wine too." In the end they disposed of it for 25 cents a gallon. The next year they started selling all their wine to the Gallo winery and have continued ever since. They credit the Gallos with being instrumental in stabilizing the market in their valley and beyond.

The Fountain Grove vineyards and winery were photographed by Russell Lee, one of the Farm Security Administration's finest portrayers of rural America, in January 1942, the month after Pearl Harbor. The dormant vines and buildings appeared serene, unaffected by world events, but in fact the winery was under the immediate management of winemakers trained in Germany who had recently fled the Nazi regime. After the death of Kanaye Nagasawa, the property had been bought by a wealthy mining engineer, Errol MacBoyle, and was at this time producing table and sparkling wines that were highly regarded. Two of the German winemakers continued in the California wine industry for many years. Kurt Opper, a skilled taster and blender, became winemaster at Paul Masson, and Hanns J. Kornell, a champagne expert, established his own champagne cellars in the Napa Valley.

"Wine delivery truck raised on blocks because no tires were available" was the explanatory caption given this picture by the photographer. It was one of Fountain Grove's, inactivated by the wartime shortage of rubber.

There were still many Japanese working at Fountain Grove, drawn there by Nagasawa, who had died eight years earlier. The two men bottling and corking wine here may have anticipated the order then under discussion that the next month, February 1942, would uproot them and send them to "relocation camps" for the duration of the war in the Pacific.

Upon the completion of the Friant-Kern Canal in the early 1940s, Kern County had water enough for planting vineyards that in effect extended southward the great San Joaquin Valley grape-growing area.

In Kern County wild grapevines covered whole trees and demonstrated "the wonderful richness of the soil and its adaptability to the vine," according to the land developer who commissioned Carleton E. Watkins to make this and other photographs about 1889. The vigor of the vines must have impressed a number of landholders in the same period, for the 1891 state directory of grape growers lists many small one- and two-year-old Muscat vineyards. Later, Joseph Di Giorgio may well have been impressed too, for in 1920, the year after he bought twenty-four thousand acres in Kern County, he started planting his huge vineyards, which were irrigated by pumped ground water.

The small family-owned California companies that remained independent through the 1940s carried on with spirit. Here, under the gaze of a bevy of peasant girls, Miss Bertha Beringer crashed a bottle of champagne against a San Francisco cable car to inaugurate a Wine Week celebration.

23. *Native Sons*

I n the wake of the receding distillers, two California firms emerged.
They were led by three native sons, Louis Petri, Ernest Gallo,
and Julio Gallo, all still in their thirties when World War II ended,
but all experienced wine men by then.

Louis Petri was born in 1912 in San Francisco's North Beach district,
where the various members of his industrious, well-to-do family had their
homes, their cigar factory, and their wine warehouse. By then dapper old
Raffaello, who had started them on their way, had made his son Angelo,
Louis' father, president of the Petri Cigar Company and its subsidiary,
the Petri Wine Company. Angelo was laying the foundation for the stable
business career that would carry the family through Prohibition comfortably
with their Marca Petri cigars and allow him to re-establish its wine business
in time for Repeal.

Young Louis was very bright and destined for a career as a doctor
when in the summer of 1934 he fell in love with Flori Cella, the daughter
of Battista Cella, the young woman who had ceremoniously broken the
bottle of champagne over the lieutenant governor's spade the year before
to signal the beginning of construction at the Cellas' Lodi winery. He went
on to medical school in St. Louis, stuck it out until Christmas vacation
and even returned after, but, in his own words, "the glamor of both families
getting into the wine business and my strong desire to marry Flori made
me decide to quite med school and come home."

He began as a barrel washer, but his father arranged for him to take
special instruction in the evenings with University of California viticulturists
and enologists—A. J. Winkler and William V. Cruess among them. He
had been a chemistry major at the University of California and he set up
a small laboratory in his family's laundry room to learn, with the help of
his older cousin Bob Bianchini, wine analysis. They even conducted a few
research experiments. He soon moved on from barrel washing but not
into any sinecure. Always vigorous, eager to learn and to progress, he
was ready in 1938 to take on the responsibility of general manager.

In advance of Repeal, Angelo Petri had, reasonably enough, assumed
that table wines would again, as they had before Prohibition, make up
the major part of the market. Not so. American palates turned to sweet
wines. The three small north coast wineries that Angelo had taken over

had to be augmented by another in a warmer area, so they bought the Alba Grape and Fruit Company in Escalon, renaming it Petri. There they could make both dry and sweet wines, but until their production of dessert wines got underway they bought them from Louis M. Martini at Kingsburg. Eventually they bottled under the Petri and Albano labels, but in the beginning they sold their wines locally in fifty-gallon barrels and shipped the rest east in tank cars. By the end of the decade they had bought two of the bottling companies to which they shipped wine; that way they knew they would not have to fight over prices or worry about losing them as customers. It was the kind of thinking that would illuminate Louis Petri's career.

In 1949, five years after succeeding his father as president of the family company, Louis led it into the first of a series of fairly sensational moves. He bought the big Mission Bell winery and distillery near Madera from Krikor Arakelian. With its 8,300,000 gallons of storage capacity, the deal brought the Petris' total up to 19,300,000 gallons, third largest in storage capacity among the state's wine organizations, putting National Distillers in fourth place. Four years later Louis Petri bought Italian Swiss from National Distillers, and his organization jumped to first place.

It was not as Petri Wine Company, however, that it achieved this peak, for Louis Petri's inventive mind and remarkable ability to follow up ideas with action had supplanted that with a *rara avis,* a bird such as the wine industry had never before seen. If it had aspects in common with the old California Wine Association, they were incidental. It was basically a new kind of creation.

After buying Mission Bell, Petri had put it and the other holdings into a new family corporation, United Vintners, Inc. In 1951 he organized Allied Grape Growers, a cooperative, then turned United Vintners into a cooperative as well and sold it to Allied Grape Growers. This is, in his own words, how it happened:

> When we bought the Arakelians out we began to be a pretty good sized operation. Naturally, our sales grew with each acquisition. And this was when we began to run out of money. It wasn't so much what we paid for the plants, but every ton of grapes that we bought had to be paid for, and then we had to age the wine. The turnover of our money was slow. It was because of this that we got the bright idea of forming Allied Grape Growers. But that had a very peculiar start. It started very bad, but ended up the greatest deal we ever made.
>
> It started out when I got a group of large Thompson Seedless growers in the Madera area together. There had always been a problem of getting enough Thompson Seedless grapes at the beginning of the season, and getting them in fast enough so that you could make a stockpile of high-proof alcohol to have available to fortify wine grapes that came in later in the season.

He succeeded in getting the Thompson Seedless growers to supply him with grapes on a contract that called for paying them a fourth of the price that they would have received had they made them into raisins. Then "the raisin market turned extremely hot," raisin prices went up, and Petri found he was paying much more than he had anticipated. He called the Thompson Seedless group together and suggested they form a cooperative, Allied Grape Growers, which would work with United Vintners on a profit-sharing basis. United would pay Allied for its grapes over an eighteen-month period instead of all at once, and the two organizations would share the profits of the sale of the wine. United would go on making and selling the wine under its labels, and Allied would in turn buy the Escalon and Madera wineries at "a very low price—book value" out of their profits on the wine. It was extremely complicated, but as Petri said, "It worked out great. They received enough money over market to buy the plants for free."

The original Thompson Seedless group represented about twenty thousand tons of grapes. When they formed Allied Grape Growers, with Louis Petri working out the principles and helping them set up the cooperative, they took in members who added over a third more. Then "right after the first crush, growers were knocking at the door to become members of Allied. It grew fast and by the end of the third year the sign-up was about sixty or seventy thousand tons of the hundred-and-twenty-to-thirty-thousand-ton total we were crushing, about half our requirements. It was about then that I bought Italian Swiss Colony, which was about the same size as ourselves."

Naturally, requirements again increased, so Petri "worked like hell to enlarge the co-op because we needed more grapes." When in 1959 Allied completed purchasing United, lock, stock, and barrel, the number of grower members had increased from the original 210 to more than 1,000 and was continuing to increase. In 1961 John B. Cella II took his family holdings into the Allied-United combination to augment it still further, and three years later John Daniel sold Inglenook to the organization. All this occurred under the continuing leadership of the vigorous Louis Petri, who had contracted to remain with the organization he had created and did so until 1967. Two years later Heublein, Inc., the big national food and beverages organization, startled even Petri by offering to buy most of the stock of United Vintners from Allied Grape Growers. He was called back in to help negotiate that and, later, Heublein's purchase of the outstanding shares. It was almost as unusual a deal as those he had put together, for it was the first time on record that a corporation had bought a cooperative, which was what United was.

Over the years since he had begun as a barrel washer, Louis Petri had made not only business innovations. In the 1930s, when the can companies were making a big push to promote their containers in place of bottles, he got a glass company to make a light-weight bottle that was competitive in cost with a can; it was a twelve-ounce bottle that he named the "Little John," and it was a big supermarket hit. He paid a great deal of attention to packaging Petri wines, and was probably the first California winemaker to hire fine designers to work out bottle shapes and labels. In the field, practices were developed that have since become common. Rather than trucking grapes long distances, field crushing stations were established and the must taken to the wineries in filled containers. Gondola trucks, not unlike those carts drawn along on tracks at the Italian Vineyard Company, were devised by Bob Bianchini to dump grapes directly into the crushers. Topping all the innovations, however, was the S.S. *Angelo Petri*.

The idea of transporting wine in a tanker ship had been conceived many years earlier by Louis Wetmore, he who had filled barges with wine after the 1906 San Francisco earthquake. He had even had a New Jersey shipyard make drawings for a vessel to carry California wine throughout the world, but World War I had stopped the project, and it was long forgotten by the 1950s when Louis Petri dreamed up the same idea. The impetus was the continuing rise in rail rates.

"I knew most of the railroad people," said Petri. "We threatened them that unless they gave us some rate reductions we would build the ship, but they never thought we would or could do it." Petri could and he did.

He found half a tanker that had split in two during a World War II voyage. The front end of it had twirled around and smashed into the back, so that, as Petri liked to point out, it was the only ship in history whose bow hit its stern. The front sank, and the stern half was towed to Alaska and used as a power plant during the war. Petri found it in Seattle where it was about to be junked and had it towed to the Bethlehem shipyard in San Francisco, where he had it made into a whole ship again and fitted with big stainless steel tanks for carrying wine to Eastern bottling plants. Two weeks before it made its maiden voyage in 1959, rail rates were lowered. Ten years later Louis Petri could point out that they were less than half what they had been before.

The S.S. *Angelo Petri* saved winemakers and wine drinkers many a dollar. Similarly beneficial was a bold move made during the same period by the Gallo brothers. Confronted by rising bottle prices, they built a bottle-making plant at their Modesto headquarters. The day it opened in 1958, bottle prices dropped.

Bottle-making equipment had been tightly held. It was difficult to learn about, to find, to purchase. The Gallos decided to crack this long-standing glassmakers' tradition, and they succeeded. They learned the technology, they secured the equipment, and they went further, devising new techniques that increased their glass plant's efficiency. Research on the effect of light upon wine and the effect of glass color upon light brought them also to another innovation, the use of green glass that protects the wine by screening out ultraviolet rays. The research was done in the Gallo laboratories.

In 1956 a formal research program had been established under Charles M. Crawford, a

Berkeley and Cornell University graduate in enology who had since 1942 held various increasingly responsible positions in production and quality control with the growing Gallo organization. For this program new laboratories were added to its existing facilities. Julio Gallo noted at the time the value of practical research in the wineries to supplement the basic scientific research of the university, and gave the aims of the new program:

> By practical research, viticultural practices and grape and wine quality can be improved, thereby broadening the outlets for California grapes and increasing financial returns to growers. Our company has already been able to assist other wineries whose wines we market under long-term mechandising agreements together with our own, by providing technological assistance in helping solve their vineyard and cellar problems.

Still other wineries would benefit as Gallo's scientists, who in 1958 moved into a new quality control and research center equipped with highly advanced instrumentation, published papers on their findings. They not only developed improved winemaking and blending techniques, they also developed new analytical instruments of remarkable complexity—among them a huge gas chromatograph that analyzes, basically by color, what the human nose can perceive only crudely—the volatile components of grapes, wine, and brandy. The laboratory has continued to maintain its position in the forefront of American grape and wine research facilities as the Gallo winery has continued to maintain its position as America's leading producer of wines, which it achieved in the mid-1960s.

As recounted earlier, the Gallo brothers began making wine in 1933 with only the simplest knowledge of the complexities of production and merchandising. They learned steadily, put their profits back into their company, grew not by acquisition but by internal expansion. When they bought the Las Palmas winery at Fresno in 1954, for instance, they were not buying a business or a label, but land and in effect a hollow building, for they completely re-equipped and expanded the winery. Wine made here and in the winery they built at Livingston in 1970 goes to the big Modesto headquarters, which serves as the main aging, blending, bottling, and distribution center.

The grapes and the wine they make come from many parts of California. One of Gallo's major innovations was its establishment of a grower relations department, an outgrowth, like the laboratories, of longstanding practices. From it goes the kind of help to the growers that Julio Gallo—always a demanding buyer of grapes—mentioned in connection with the beginning of the research program. In 1967 came the initiation of ten-to-fifteen-year contracts to selected growers who would plant premium wine grapes, another step in California's pursuit of better grape varieties that began in the 1850s. The result: a steady supply of the kinds of grapes the Gallo winery wants for the kinds of wines it makes.

Contracts with winemakers bring it more wine tailored to its specifications from wineries like the Napa Valley Cooperative and others in the coastal valleys. Recently it has added a Sonoma County winery of its own, one established in the 1880s and operated for many years by the Frei Brothers, who started sending their wines to the Gallos a quarter century ago.

The system seems complex and is. What is most remarkable about it is that the Gallo brothers run so tight a ship that all wines that go out under their labels conform precisely to their standards, consistently, year after year. They are wines that appeal to Americans, and they have not been unchanging. The Gallos are credited with foresight almost amounting to prescience about what American wine drinkers like. Although not all their test-marketed wines have appealed to consumers, most have. Among these are low-alcohol fruit-flavored wines, which appealed to people not used to drinking wine but which introduced them to it so that they subsequently moved on to more conventional kinds. And the Gallos contributed to the education of American palates to table wines and varietal wines, and they then moved along with the increasingly sophisticated tastes into producing increasingly sophisticated wines.

In a small wine town in Italy not far from the Piedmont area where the Gallos' ancestors lived, an export manager who had been selling wines in the United States remarked that the Gallo brothers had created a market which all winemakers have shared in. He added a joke, a suggestion that everyone who sells wine in the United States should pay the Gallos five cents a bottle in gratitude.

The Petri winery at Escalon drew upon the grapes of its area, at the northern, cooler end of the San Joaquin Valley. Just after Prohibition it was presided over by Raffaello Petri's younger Italian-American partner, Dante Foresti, who predicted Louis Petri's rise: "When the wine came back, I told Louis (he was studying to be doctor) 'Let's get in the wine! Some day you'll be the biggest man in it!' My God, it happened!"

Angelo Petri here stood before portraits of his uncle, white-mustachioed Amadeo who started the Petri Cigar Company, and his father, Raffaello, who got the family into the wine business by first buying and selling wine at the San Francisco hotel he operated and then a few years before Prohibition buying a winery of his own. He had come to the United States before 1890 from Tuscany, where he had worked in a winery. In America he became what his grandson, Louis Petri, called "a Diamond Jim Brady" who "always wanted the best, whether he could afford it or not." More practical was Angelo, who sold wine for him until Prohibition, then at Repeal took the family back into winemaking by buying, among other properties, a winery at Escalon, and giving his son Louis a chance to make his imprint upon the California wine industry.

The Mission Bell winery at Madera was rebuilt and modernized in the late 1940s by its owner since 1920, Krikor Arakelian, and sold to Louis Petri in 1949. It was originally constructed by Italian Swiss Colony in its California Wine Association years, and was joined again with it in 1953 when Louis Petri bought Italian Swiss for United Vintners. The 120-foot column still was and remains its outstanding feature. In the cupola next to it is the huge bell that gave the winery its name. It weighs more than five tons, and its hourly tolls could once be heard for miles around. The winery, further expanded, is today the largest of the United Vintners properties, since 1969 under Heublein ownership.

Louis Petri was photographed as he signed the contract to turn over his family-owned United Vintners to the grower-owned cooperative he had created, Allied Grape Growers. He was surrounded by Allied officers Tilden Ginzol, Walter Vincent, Buddy Iwata, and Robert McInturf, who was president of the cooperative. Petri, as outgoing as he appeared in this picture, was, for all his business acuity, a spontaneous and unusually humane man.

The S.S. *Angelo Petri,* shown here passing under the Golden Gate Bridge on its way to its home port of Stockton, could carry in its twenty-six stainless-steel tanks nearly two-and-a-half million gallons of wine. Its cargoes were taken to bottling plants in Newark, New Jersey, and in Chicago, those for the latter carried from Houston up the inland waterways in glass-lined tanks on barges. Louis Petri, whose inventiveness knew no bounds, even found return cargoes that would not contaminate the tanks: soda ash, commonly used for cleaning wine tanks, and liquefied corn sugar. The ship's most dramatic moment came when, making its way fully laden through the Golden Gate one stormy day in 1960, it hit a "green wave" that poured in through an air vent and shorted its electric motors, then tossed the vessel onto a sand bar. Towed back to the Bethlehem shipyard where the ship had been rebuilt, it was fitted with a new anchor, rudder, and propeller and put back into operation within a month. "The day she went back into service," said Louis Petri, "was the day I went into the hospital with a heart attack."

The Gallo brothers, Ernest and Julio, share all major decisions, and both taste their wines every day they are in Modesto. They have parallel responsibilities, however, Ernest for marketing, Julio for production and field operations. It is said that they long ago established an open-ended formula for growth when Ernest told his brother, "I'll sell all the wine you can make," and Julio replied, "I'll make all you can sell."

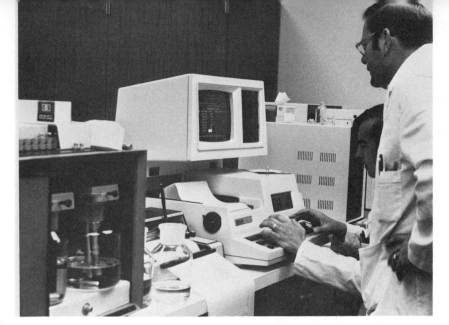

Flavor-profile graphs of wines can be created in the Gallo research laboratory by the highly complex instrument at the right, a gas chromatograph, that is controlled by and feeds into the computer terminal. Such flavor graphs can be stored for later retrieval so that flavors of different or similar wines can be compared. The instrument on the left is a liquid chromatograph that analyzes such nonvolatile materials as grape proteins and sugars.

The Gallo headquarters, its buildings set on landscaped ground along Dry Creek in Modesto, is a successful exercise in architectural civility.

At the Gallos' Fresno winery, white tanks accounting for about a third of the organization's 265 million gallons of storage capacity make an impressive array.

24. The Wine Explosion

IN 1950 California winemakers sold nearly 132 million gallons of wine, a healthy 22 million more than they had sold ten years earlier. The quantity had been rising steadily and continued to rise most years at the rate of three or four million gallons until 1968, when sales suddenly started taking off. The next year they jumped ahead by more than 7.5 million. The next topped that by 15 million. The next topped that by 23.5 million, and 1971 topped its preceding year by 32 million gallons. In the twenty-one years since 1950, the wine men had better than doubled the amount of wine they sold.

This was, in statistical terms, the beginning of what Leon Adams has called the wine revolution. If you consider it an evolution, however, you can trace its beginning to the years just after Prohibition when the University of California was crusading for better wines and better grapes, when the winemakers were developing or re-perfecting their techniques, when Adams himself was beginning his crusade to bring civilized wine drinking to the American people. Civilized wine drinking in his mind and in the minds of many other wine men meant drinking wine with meals—dry wines, the kind that had made up the largest part of California's pre-Prohibition production. It was no coincidence that the years that saw the dramatic rise in California wines were the same years that saw the balance tip from a predominance of sweet wines to a predominance of dry table wines.

California had, in fact, been producing decreasing amounts of dessert wines for more than a decade, while the increase in table wines had been accellerating. In 1967, the year before wine sales started leaping, the state made for the first time since Prohibition more table wines—wines under 14 percent alcohol—than dessert wines. And for the first time since Prohibition, Americans across the country bought more dry wine than sweet. How did this change in taste come about? Many factors no doubt contributed to it. For one, more Americans were traveling to Europe and experiencing regular drinking of table wines with meals. For another, fashion—perhaps based upon these Europeanized American tastes. For still another, the well-established tendency for new wine drinkers to like sweet wines and, as they become more familiar with the beverage, to prefer drier kinds. And, very important, the increasing quality of American table wines.

They were indeed better, for the wine industry had seen a tremendous improvement in wine grapes, the technology of winemaking, the equipment available, and the winemakers' will to supply the public's ever-more-demanding taste, whatever its source.

Improvements in the vineyard were many. Refinements of the region system, for determining which grapes grow best where, brought the word "microclimate" into the viticulturists' vocabulary. Professor H. P. Olmo and his colleagues at Davis developed a program for getting reliably disease-free vines to growers who were planting or replanting vineyards. Olmo himself developed remarkable new wine grape varieties, and he advanced the principle of improvement within grape varieties by selection of superior clones and made it practical by selecting and helping distribute them, to the vast improvement of vineyards planted to them.

More vineyards of grapes that make noble wines in France—Cabernet Sauvignon, Pinot noir, and Chardonnay—were planted in the coastal valleys especially, while new varieties for table wines took up increasing acreage. Two now widely planted were developed by Olmo both to withstand heat and to give good wine. They are Ruby Cabernet, a cross of Cabernet Sauvignon and Carignane that combines the flavor of the former and higher yield of the latter, and Emerald Riesling, which is a cross of White Riesling and Muscadelle and in warm regions gives must with enough acid and fruitiness to be used with advantage for blending in both still and sparkling wines.

Better pruning and vine-training techniques were developed by Winkler, Olmo, and others at Davis, and by Professor Vincent Petrucci, who in 1947 established viticultural studies at Fresno State College (now a State University) with a fifty-thousand-dollar grant from the Roma Wine Company.

Improvements in the winery were parallel. For example, better methods for making wines clear and brilliant began with the introduction of two substances that absorb particles, bentonite, a clay, and diatomaceous earth. Cellulose filter pads were introduced, and later thin membrane filters with pores so fine that wine that passes through them is sterilized. Centrifuges, too, came into common use for removing particles. Gradually iron and brass in the winery were replaced by stainless steel in everything from pipes and pumps to conveyors and presses. Variable-pressure presses were introduced from Europe, to give the winemaker better control over the end product. Refrigeration equipment that allows temperature control during fermentation and storage and the chilling of wines, especially white wines, for final clarification, became practical to install in wineries. Vastly improved laboratory techniques and equipment have allowed enologists to analyze samples at each step of the winemaking process.

All of these innovations gave California winemakers the ability to make better wines of all kinds and especially to improve their white wines, which had been poor for the most part when compared even to the standard white wines of the world's best winemaking regions. In 1976 for the first time more California white wine was sold than red, and by 1980 people were buying more than twice the amount of white as red wine. That year white wine accounted for 56 percent of California's production, rosé 23 percent, and red only 20 percent. It was speculated that, since white wines are customarily consumed chilled, this shift may have been partly accounted for by people who were used to drinking chilled soft drinks, partly by people who had been drinking chilled pop wines, the rather sweet fruit-flavored low-alcohol wines that were sold widely during the early 1970s. In any case, the improvement in California's white wines, based upon better grape varieties as well as improved technology, gave the public a palatable beverage to choose.

Although most of the years after the hard times following the market break of 1947 were prosperous, there were two dips. In the early 1960s an anticipated oversupply brought apprehension and a plan for taking grapes off the market similar to the prorate of 1938, but in the end no lasting problem. In the mid-1970s there was a more serious drop in grape prices brought about by many factors including over-optimism—perhaps so strong as to be called euphoria—caused in part by two California banks' forecasts for great growth and profits from winemaking in the next decades. The first was issued in 1970 and contributed to a big jump in the establishment of new vineyards which matured four and five years later and caused a market glut—a pattern familiar ever since the southern California wine mania of the 1850s.

At the same time, America's increased interest in wines caused importers to anticipate that more people would buy more Italian and French wines than they did at least immediately—the Bordeaux scandals damaged the standing of the latter—which added to the general market malaise.

By 1978, however, grape prices were back up and optimism blossomed again.

The high level of prosperity during most of the 1970s and the decline of the dollar against foreign currencies brought European and Canadian investments in existing California wineries and vineyards, and in one case construction of a new winery in the Napa Valley by the important French firm Société Moët-Hennessey. American corporations, notably the Coca-Cola Company, also bought wineries, anticipating growth in consumption.

Across the United States interest in wines became almost a cultural movement. When Americans come to be interested they tend to become enthusiasts; they want to know all about the object of their affections. Magazines devoted to telling consumers all about the world's wines began to be published in the late 1960s. Columns began to appear in newspapers and in magazines as diverse as *Vogue* and the *Journal of the American Bar Association*. Courses in wines on all levels from the simplest to university extension classes drew large attendance. Wine tastings—analytical, social, and in between—became fashionable. Winemakers, whose reputations had been about on a level with bootleggers' in the mid-1930s, became highly respected, even revered—cult heroes, some of them. Winegrowing became idealized and romanticized. It caught the imag-

ination of all kinds of people from Walden-eyed young hippies to successful business and professional men, as it had caught the imagination in the century before of such men as Julius Paul Smith, who had made a pile in mining, and sea captain turned businessman Gustave Niebaum. In the slump years of the latter 1970s a few of the novice winegrowers, underinformed, underfinanced, or both, washed out, but there were not enough of them to stem the tide of the ever-increasing number of bonded wineries in California.

The number of wineries had increased the year after Prohibition, then started declining steadily year by year until the end of the decade of the 1960s, when it started up again. In 1966 there were 231 wineries, in 1970 there were 240, in 1975 there were 321, and in 1982 more than 550. Many were small and dedicated to producing wine as idealized as their visions of the happy life of the winegrower. A surprising number have come very close to their goal, making extremely fine wines.

They also made another contribution. They gave young enologists, who might have waited a generation to be given a free hand, a chance to follow their own ideas. Louis P. Martini pointed out in a paper at a 1980 American Chemical Society symposium that many "people in other professions" who started small wineries hired recent university graduates in enology:

The young graduates immediately found themselves in the position of being cellarman, winemaker, vineyard manager, and enologist. With their newly acquired technical knowledge, a head full of ideas, and a free hand, they set about creating new wine types, changing old wine styles, introducing new production techniques, planting grapes where there were none before, and turning out good, clean, sound wines that have caught the fancy of the consumer.

Maynard A. Amerine, here examining experimental wines in the cellar of the University of California Department of Viticulture and Enology, which he headed for many years, has an overview of California winemaking based upon nearly half a century of direct observation. Today, in his view, the state produces the best everyday wines in the world and some of its finest as well. Among the advances that he has witnessed (and he himself has participated in many of them), he considers these the most significant: selection of the proper grape variety and clone for each climatic region; prevention of overcropping of vineyards, which has now happily been eliminated by the better growers on their own initiative and in response to the strict demands of the more enlightened winemakers; better timing of the harvest; temperature control during fermentation, especially for white wines; and a notable increase in technical knowledge in the industry as trained men and women have gone into the wineries, and as advanced scientific books on viticulture and enology have become available.

Sprinklers have replaced smudge pots and piles of burning rubber tires for frost protection in many of the state's vineyards. They are used for irrigating as well. Here they are in operation in an Almadén vineyard in San Benito County. In other vineyards, tower-mounted wind machines and surface blowers drive frost away.

Drip irrigation, pioneered in Israel, is being installed in many new vineyards and in many old ones as well. Here it is in use in a several-decades-old vineyard planted on the site of the Buena Vista vineyard of Agoston Haraszthy, who condemned irrigating vines.

233

Mechanical harvesting has become common throughout California, and field crushing is becoming increasingly so. In this photograph taken at Wente's Arroyo Seco vineyard in Monterey County, Pinot blanc grapes are being harvested and delivered directly to the crusher, which is pulled along by a tractor in front of it to keep abreast of the harvester. As the grapes are dropped into the hopper the stems are removed, and then they are crushed directly into the stainless steel tank. When each tank is filled, sulphur dioxide is added to prevent oxidation and the development of spoilage micro-organisms, as it would be if the grapes were stemmed and crushed at the winery. (Some pump in air as well.) Then the closed tank is put on a flatbed truck to be taken to the winery in the Livermore Valley. Some wine men believe that this type of field crushing will become the rule even where vineyards are close to home base, for the must arrives at the winery retaining the freshness of the quickly crushed grapes. In recent years it has given winemakers access to vineyards far beyond their areas, allowing them flexibility undreamed of in the past. In the 1930s the Petri family, which pioneered a simpler kind of decentralized crushing, had to add to their north coast wineries another one in Escalon in order to make dessert wines; it would not be necessary today.

A program of state inspection of grapes as they arrive at the winery has contributed to the higher quality of California wines. Here an inspector takes a sample of grapes from the center of a load being delivered to Guild's Cribari winery at Fresno. It will be analyzed for sugar and acid content.

Deborah Anne Cutter, winemaker at Field Stone Winery, is one of the growing number of women enologists. They began graduating from the University of California at Davis in the 1960s and started work in state wineries. A number have, like Mrs. Cutter, moved up to top positions. Mary Ann Graf became winemaker at Simi in 1973, and when she left in 1979 was succeeded by Zelma Long, who had been winemaker at the Robert Mondavi winery. Dawnine Sample moved up to the position of resident winemaker at Domaine Chandon the same year. Other women are standing in the wings. Meanwhile, in 1974 the U.C. Davis Department of Viticulture and Enology named its first woman faculty member, Dr. Ann C. Noble, and in 1980 named its second, Dr. Carole Meredith.

Almadén Vineyards' four-acre Cienega Cellar houses 37,299 oak barrels for aging its wines. Each holds fifty gallons and must have wine added every three or four weeks to prevent oxidation. The man on the traveling platform doing the topping is wearing a miner's lamp because the cellar is unlighted. Fortunately it is situated a little distant from the Cienega winery, which is astride one of California's major earthquake faults and, in addition to making wine, maintains instruments which help government seismologists keep track of the fault's frequent movements.

Small family wineries in which wives worked along with their husbands were common before Prohibition and have had a resurgence since the mid-1960s. Joan and Frank Cadenasso of Fairfield carry on a tradition started by Frank's father, Giovanni, when he established his first winery nearby in 1906. While the family ceased winemaking during Prohibition, Frank planted his first vineyard in 1926, and in 1934 the present Cadenasso winery started crushing. Standing before bottles and award ribbons in the salesroom, the Cadenassos sell wine and dispense samples and lots of good conversation.

Susan and Robert Enz did not lay eyes upon their vineyard until 1967, and then it was to buy the property as a home for themselves and their young children. When Robert first looked at the property with its decades-old vines, he asked, "What are those bushy-looking things?" Six years later he stopped working as an engineer to spend full time working alongside his wife in the vineyard and start making wine as well.

When Robert Mondavi and Baron Philippe de Rothschild shook hands in a Napa Valley vineyard one winter day in 1980, they symbolized not only their own joint venture but also the French interest in California vineyards that had begun in the early 1970s. The Mondavi-Rothschild venture was for making a French-style Cabernet tentatively called "Napamedoc" after the Napa Valley where it is being produced and the Médoc region of France, where the famous Chateau Mouton-Rothschild is located. From the first vintage, presided over in 1979 by winemakers from both houses, came the initial sale in 1981 of a case—still in the cask—for twenty-four thousand dollars at a charity auction.

In 1972 the French house of Moët-Hennessy bought land in the Napa Valley and started building its large winery for both sparkling and still table wines. Other smaller French investments followed, and in 1981 Piper-Heidsieck and Sonoma Vineyards made the first crush in the new winery they built for another Franco-American sparkling wine.

The process of blending to make a wine finer than any of the individual wines that go into it is both an art and a science, dependent upon the blender's sensory acuity, his knowledge, and his experience. Although there are winemakers who prefer that wines be 100 percent one variety, one vintage, and even one vineyard, more follow the concept voiced by Agoston Haraszthy when he compared one-grape wine to vegetable soup made only of carrots, and of Hilgard who believed "judicious blending" to be "the height of the art of winemaking." Here Louis P. Martini, who has for many years experimented with blends, following both his own judgment and that of panels of tasters, considers the blending of four wines in the winery laboratory.

25. A State of Vines

In the Napa Valley, where California's most expensive wine grapes grow, the best available vineyard land was selling for more than thirty-thousand dollars an acre in 1980. Keith Bowers, Napa County's veteran farm advisor, attributed the high price to well-financed "new people" who wanted to become grape growers and winemakers, and the lack of "new land" suitable for vineyards. It had been several years, he reported, since anyone had bought Napa County land with the realistic hope of making a living growing grapes.

The situation in the Napa Valley was worse than but not unlike the situation that had been developing in most other established grape-growing areas of the state for the past quarter century, creating fear that California might run out of vineyard land. Concurrent with the wine explosion was a population explosion, and also, so to speak, an affluence explosion. Grapes and people tend to favor the same geographical locations, so urbanization was taking its toll just as it had since the mid-nineteenth century when Los Angeles lost its sobriquet "City of Vineyards." Now homes, factories, businesses, and roads were taking over land at an accelerated pace.

There are several ways for Californians to tackle the problem of urbanization of farm land. One is to take refuge in the provisions of the 1965 Williamson Act, a state law that allows growers to put their lands into agricultural preserves and pay taxes based upon their current use rather than potential real estate value. Some vineyardists, especially in the Napa and Livermore valleys, have done so, relieving in some measure the economic pressure that has forced others to sell to developers. Another approach is through zoning laws to keep buildings from replacing vineyards. Notable was the action by the Napa County board of supervisors in 1981 that protected land in the fine wine grape area known as the Carneros from being invaded by a residential community.

Another way is to expand plantings in still uncrowded areas where, before the wine explosion, economics discouraged the development of new vineyards. Lake County, which had numerous small plantings before Prohibition, has seen a modest revival, and Mendocino, the northernmost coast country to grow grapes in significant quantity, has increased its acreage in the past decade. In the foothills of the Sierra Nevada old vineyards have been revived, new ones planted, and new wineries built.

Yet another way is for grape growers to find whole new vineyard areas, or at least areas new to viticulturists of the past half century, and this has been done. Clearly it has not relieved the situation in the tightly held Napa Valley. It has, however, allowed the growers of the Santa Clara Valley, which started losing its agricultural lands to subdivisions and aerospace industries in the 1950s, to turn to their neighbor to the south, Monterey County, for vineyard land.

In 1959, the Wine Institute, well aware of the growing problem, asked the University of California's Department of Viticulture and Enology to look for new land where quality wine grapes could be grown. Professor Albert J. Winkler, climatic regions well in mind, toured most of the state in the department's Ford, and concluded that there were ten thousand to twenty-five thousand acres not immediately threatened by urbanization that could produce premium wine grapes. Of these, he said, "probably the largest single potential growing district for fine wine grapes is in the Salinas Valley."

The Salinas River runs through the central valley of Monterey County unobtrusively, sometimes underground, leaving the earth on each side dry as desert except when it rages over its banks or man intervenes by drawing water for irrigation. Such intervention has made the valley the lettuce bowl of the nation, but few had seen its arid foothill lands, blown by daily winds, as vineyard land. Vines had been grown at Mission Soledad, near its center, and Mission San Antonio de Padua to the south, but they left no tradition of viticulture. A Frenchman named Tamm grew grapes up high above the dusty town of Soledad near the towering Pinnacles before World War I, and there had been scattered small vineyards during Prohibition, but in 1959 there were not enough grapes growing in the county to be recorded it its annual crop report. Winkler found only a few vines in home gardens and one neglected nine-acre vineyard, but they were enough to convince him of the area's potential. Water was indeed available if not evident, and those afternoon winds came from Monterey Bay and cooled the valley to a level desirable for grapes.

Immediately two wineries that were being squeezed out of the Santa Clara Valley bought land. They were Paul Masson and Mirassou, and they joined together to establish a nursery to propagate their best vines. In 1962 they started planting, and in 1966 they crushed their first grapes. By then Wente Bros., crowded for space near its Livermore Valley winery, had joined them. In 1970 Almadén, which had large vineyards in San Benito County just to the east across the Gavilan mountains, began planting toward the southern end of the Salinas Valley. Small wineries were beginning to spring up, and large and small vineyardists were coming in to supply not only the valley wineries but also others to the north, and south, and east. In 1974 The Monterey Vineyard made its first crush, and in 1977, having been bought by the Coca-Cola Company of Atlanta, it was starting a period of steady growth. Two decades after Winkler's survey, there were more than thirty thousand acres of premium wine grapes growing between the city of Salinas and the southern border of the county, most of them characterized by strong varietal flavor that sometimes needs taming. Moreover, the new grape region extended on through the coastal valleys of San Luis Obispo and Santa Barbara counties. This continuous strip from Salinas to the city of Santa Barbara, known as the Central Coast viticultural area, has contributed significantly to the increase in California's premium wine grapes.

Mission San Luis Obispo, in the center of what is now the lively little city of the same name, was San Luis Obispo County's earliest winegrowing establishment. Among those who carried its tradition forward was the Frenchman Pierre Hypolite Dallidet, who in 1853 settled down on acreage next to the mission's vineyard and by the 1860s was growing grapes and making wine. He became the area's first and for some years only commercial winemaker, and he also sold cuttings of Charbono, Black Malaga, Muscat of Alexandria, and others of his vines to nearby vineyardists. Russ Taylor, one of today's impassioned part-time winemakers, has delved into the story of Dallidet. He believes the Frenchman supplied cuttings for the first commercial plantings in the now highly productive Santa Maria vineyard area that spans the San Luis Obispo–Santa Barbara county line.

The St. Rémy Winery at the now forgotten

community of Musick, southeast of San Luis Obespo—not far from another of today's newly developing wine areas, the Edna Valley—was another famous winery that in the last years of the nineteenth century and the decades just before Prohibition was a pleasant place where the area's folk visited and sampled the wine and took home a cask or so.

Paso Robles has a shorter history of wine-grape growing, the first famous practitioner having been Ignace Paderewski, who went there for the hot mineral waters in the pre-Prohibition years, bought land, and planted a vineyard adjacent to what would later become one of the area's best-known vineyards, Hoffman Mountain Ranch. Today in Paso Robles legends of all sorts about the great pianist abound, among them that he was the first person to bring the Zinfandel grape to California.

Neither legend nor records tell us just when the first Zinfandel vine was planted in the Templeton area, which runs westward into the hills between Paso Robles and San Luis Obispo, but Templeton's old vineyards and its wineries became and remain noted for their Zinfandels. The area was as famous a place of pilgrimage during Prohibition as St. Rémy had been earlier, and old-timers recall driving from miles around to buy kegs of its famed Zinfandel grape juice.

These and other smaller vineyard areas in San Luis Obispo County had some six hundred acres of wine grapes in 1970. In the wine explosion they increased nearly eight-fold and are still increasing.

Santa Barbara County has seen an even greater growth. Its wine grape acreage was, like that of Monterey County, so insignificant that it was not reported in 1970. A decade later it stood at over seven thousand acres, with more being planted and still more planned. Mission Santa Barbara, which had supplied the huffy Sir George Simpson with the only California wine he found palatable, had been succeeded in winemaking by a number of small grape growers and winemakers in and around the city of Santa Barbara, the most famous grower of course being Doña Marcelina, and the next most famous Justinian Caire, who grew grapes and made wine on the offshore Santa Cruz Island, one of California's romantic places.

The Santa Ynez Valley, just across the range of stark mountains that form a backdrop to the city of Santa Barbara, is the Napa Valley of the Central Coast. Fine wine grapes grow very well there although, curiously, Mission Santa Inés, today spelled Santa Ynez, to which California's first American winegrower made his way in 1818 after jumping ship, had no great luck with its vineyard. In the 1970s half a dozen wineries were started and a great many acres of grapes planted. By the early years of the next decade, the area seemed well on its way to achieving the kind of prestige for its wines that the northern valleys had taken decades to achieve.

Quite different is the other remaining upstart viticultural area, the only one in southern California proper. It is in southeastern Riverside County, centered on Rancho Temecula, once held by the famed early Los Angeles winegrower Jean Louis Vignes. When Vignes claimed it in the early 1840s it had an existing vineyard, small, amid plantings of corn and wheat, which his overseer cultivated along with taking care of the cattle that grazed on the surrounding hills. There is no indication, however, that Vignes sought to enlarge the vineyard or have its grapes hauled the eighty-odd miles to Los Angeles, and only scattered vineyards of little more importance than Vignes' succeeded it. For years the dusty cowboy town of Temecula was known mainly for its saloon keeper, Joe Winkel, who achieved fame by being frequently mentioned by name in the comic strip *Krazy Kat*.

Then in the 1960s two of the group of companies founded by industrialist Henry J. Kaiser, together with an Eastern associate, decided to develop some eighty-seven thousand acres of Rancho Temecula and three adjacent ranchos. It was not to be another residential development but a community of cattle ranches, orchards, vineyards, industrial plants, and homes, with a restrained community and tourist center. Water was a key, and a water district was formed. Now known as Rancho California, it spreads over the hills across from old Temecula, which has spruced itself up considerably.

Philo Biane, who was then president of Brookside Vineyard Company at Guasti and well aware that the vineyards of that area were being crowded out by urban development and sickened by smog, undertook experimental plantings at Rancho California and, being successful, led the way to major vineyard plantings. By the early 1980s some three thousand acres of wine grapes had been planted. Vineyards ran ahead of wineries, so that their grapes or field-crushed must were supplying other areas, but by 1982 there were more than half a dozen wineries in the area. It is unlikely that any of them crushes grapes from that long-forgotten vineyard tended by Vignes' overseer, for they would have been lowly Missions, and the Temecula area is now devoted to premium vine varieties.

In the late 1850s, every section of California except the high mountain and desert areas along its eastern edge was growing grapes, even the counties at the far north. In 1858 Agoston Haraszthy asserted that "almost any locality will do" for grapes and that there were five million acres in the state suitable for vineyards.

In 1880 Charles A. Wetmore, that influential intellectual combination of practical viticulturist and dreamer, wrote that, if the demand existed, thirty million acres of California land could be planted to grapes and could produce a billion gallons of wine each year. This was bold prognosticating indeed, for all of California covers only a little more than a hundred million acres, and at the beginning of the decade of the 1980s only thirty-four-and-a-half million acres of it were given over to all of its many kinds of agriculture.

Such demand has not appeared; if it does, undoubtedly more areas can be developed. Vincent Petrucci has studied viticultural practices used in frost-bound Russian vineyards. Many California enologists have carefully observed techniques used wherever wine is made around the globe, in countries with as wide a range of conditions as exist in this state of valleys, deserts, and mountain lands. So who is to say that after two centuries of what may in the long run seem merely conservative exploration of the potentialities for wine in California, another two centuries may not see the realization of Wetmore's dream of a tenth of the state's land given over to vineyards and a sixth of its families happy vineyardists?

A Pinot noir vineyard stood here the day before this photograph was made in 1980. Then came a bulldozer uprooting the vines, and a huge truck to carry away the remains. Only a few venerable trunks were left behind, and they too would soon be gone as the site was prepared for construction of a road in this fast urbanizing part of Solano County.

Peter Mirassou came to this spot in the Salinas Valley in 1961 and the next year began planting vines to supply his family's Santa Clara County winery. Working with other growers, winemakers, university specialists, and Monterey County farm advisor Rudy Neja, he pioneered development of what has become California's largest premium wine grape area. He and his family worked also with equipment builders to develop a mechanical harvester that would pick the grapes without harming them (the results were tested with tasting panels, who preferred the wine from grapes mechanically harvested) and a field crusher so that the must rather than the whole grapes could be trucked to the winery. In the winter-bound vineyard behind him in this photograph are aluminum pipes for sprinkling to prevent frost damage and to irrigate the vines.

243

The Paul Masson Pinnacles vineyards and winery east of the town of Soledad are the source of most of its table wines today. The first crush at the winery in 1966 was marked with a gala luncheon in honor of the University of California men who had done research on the Salinas Valley as a viticultural area, suggested grape varieties, and helped find disease-free vine stock from which to plant the vineyards. They have continued to advise the area's growers and wine-makers.

The Chalone vineyard, two thousand feet above the Salinas River, near the towering Pinnacles in the Gavilan range, is planted in sparse soil on limestone. In the early years of this century a Frenchman named Tamm came upon this tract and, seeing the similarity of the soil to that of the French Champagne region, planted traditional champagne grapes here. It is said that Paul Masson bought some and found they made good champagne.

World War I called the mysterious Frenchman back to his homeland, but others carried on the vineyard, and winemakers recognized the quality of the grapes and bought them. In 1960 a small winery was built, and a few years later Dick Graff, who was intending to be a banker, became mesmerized by the idea of making wine here. He studied at Davis to learn how, formed a small corporation to buy the land and modernize the winery, and now effectively presides over one of the world's picturesque small wine estates. In this photograph Pinot noir grapes are being harvested.

The Monterey Vineyard winery, in the Salinas Valley, built in 1974 and since expanded, receives some two thousand tons of grapes each year to make wine for its own label, and ten times that for the wine it produces separately for Taylor California Cellars. Here grapes, and the juice that has separated from them following machine harvesting, are delivered into one of the winery's stainless-steel crushers. Dr. Richard Peterson, president of The Monterey Vineyard since its first crush, believes the full potentialities of the relatively new Salinas Valley viticultural area will not have been fully explored until the end of this century.

Six miles west of Paso Robles and fourteen miles east of the Pacific Ocean lies the Hoffman Mountain Ranch, on hilly land adjacent to that once owned by Ignace Paderewski. It was planted in walnut and almond groves when Beverly Hills cardiologist Stanley H. Hoffman bought it, but after he became an amateur winemaker and made an informal wine tour of France he looked at the chalky soil with the same wine-mindedness as Paderewski and came to the same conclusion: It was good for growing grapes. In 1973 he and his wife moved there, he continuing his practice and watching over the vineyards with the expert help of Andre Tchelistcheff, who as consultant has guided the development of the vineyards and the winery. The two Hoffman sons, David and Michael, at first winemaker and vineyard superintendent respectively, have since switched places, so that the wines bottled under the HMR label are now made by Michael. The winery, built in California barn style, presents a weathered exterior; in contrast is the shiny stainless-steel equipment inside.

Santa Cruz Island, twenty-three miles off the coast south of Santa Barbara, was perhaps the most unusual winegrowing site in California. Here Justinian Caire, a San Francisco merchant, born in France, bought land, established a pleasant summer home for his family, and in the 1880s planted Cabernet Sauvignon, Petite Sirah, Pinot noir, Barbera, Malbec, and Cantal, later adding Zinfandel. In two large structures built of red brick fabricated on the island, he made and aged wine that he shipped to market in casks from this island dock on his schooner, the *Santa Cruz.*

246

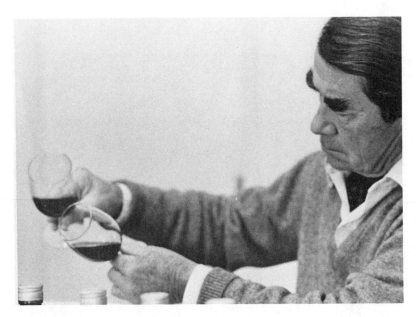

Andre Tchelistcheff, born in Russia before the revolution, became an officer in the White Russian army fighting in the Crimea, then a student of agronomy in Czechoslovakia, then a student of enology in Paris, and finally a viticulturist and enologist in California. From 1938 until 1973 he worked with Beaulieu Vineyard, turning out some of the finest wines of the era. Then he began a new career as consultant and has been an important factor in the success of a number of California's new and re-established wineries, guiding them through their difficult early years.

The Firestone Winery, the largest in the Santa Ynez Valley, was established by A. Brooks Firestone, who foresook rubber tires in order to plant a vineyard here in 1973, in a joint venture with Suntory, Ltd., of Japan. Andre Tchelistcheff advised on the plantings of Cabernet Sauvignon, Pinot noir, Johannisberg Riesling, and Chardonnay. The hilltop winery sits snugly among its vineyards, which stretch out over three-hundred-odd acres of hilly land.

This flourishing Temecula vineyard was planted in 1969 on what many considered unpromising sandy soil. It is the Callaway Vineyard, established by Ely Callaway, who had formerly devoted himself to textiles as president of Burlington Industries. He built a well-planned and well-equipped winery and brought it into successful operation before selling it and its 170 acres of surrounding vineyards to Hiram Walker in 1981.

Afterword

The sources upon which this book is based are almost as diverse as the people who have created the California wine industry over the past two centuries. They include major written works on California history and minor ones as well, for wine has been part of much of California's past. We have of course drawn upon the basic works on the state's wine history up to the late nineteenth century mentioned by Leon D. Adams in his Foreword, and upon many that have followed. Since the publication in 1951 of Vincent P. Carosso's *The California Wine Industry, 1830–1895* (until now the most comprehensive book on the subject) more material on the early period has become available, some of it used by recent historians, some used for the first time in this book, and some undoubtedly yet to be explored.

We have also used published material by recent writers. Much has come from Maynard A. Amerine, who has also read portions of this book and given us the benefit of his knowledge and judgment; from Ernest Peninou and William F. Heintz, both of whom have also been generous in giving us additional material from their files; from Leon D. Adams, who has also encouraged and aided us; from Roy Brady, who has opened a new window on the beginning of California viticulture; and from Charles L. Sullivan, the author of a number of articles on California wine history.

Special mention should be made of the reminiscences of the men who participated in the interview series conducted by the Regional Oral History Office of the Bancroft Library, Amerine and Adams among them, which gives a broad view of the first three-quarters of this century.

We have also drawn upon a great deal of ephemeral material—manuscripts, minute books, records, statistical tables, labels, bills, pamphlets, unpublished reports—some in our own files, much more in libraries throughout the state. We wish to thank the staffs of the Wine Institute and of the many other organizations that have been kind enough to give us information and access to their collections. The following is a list of the major libraries and historical repositories, and the staff members who have worked most closely with us:

The Bancroft Library, Lawrence Dinnean, William Roberts, and James R. K. Kantor; the California State Library, Kenneth Pettit, Gary Kurutz, and Grace Imoto; the Huntington Library; Alan H. Jutzi and Virginia Rust;

249

the California Historical Society, Maude K. Swingle; the Special Collections Department of the Shields Library, University of California, Davis, Donald Kunitz; the Special Collections of the Madden Library, Fresno State University, Ronald J. Mahoney; the Wine Museum of San Francisco, Ernest G. Mittelberger; the Los Angeles Museum of Natural History, Bill Mason; the San Diego Historical Society, Sylvia Arden and Larry and Jane Booth; the San Francisco Public Library, Gladys Hansen; the Chancery Archives of the Archdiocese of San Francisco, James deT. Abajian; the Santa Barbara Mission Archives, Bogdan Deresiewics and Richard S. Whitehead; the California State Archives; the Society of California Pioneers; and the Santa Barbara Historical Society.

James deT. Abajian gave us data from his own files. He also read the manuscript and made valuable suggestions, as did Friench Simpson. Joan Ingalls of the Wine Institute from the beginning cheerfully provided material and helped us search out many an obscure fact, and read the manuscript as well.

Members of the California wine industry were generous in giving us information we requested and access to photographs: Brother Timothy, Ernest Gallo, Charles M. Crawford, Virgil Galleron, Harry Baccigaluppi, Philo Biane, John B. Cella II, Andre Tchelistcheff, the Stanley Hoffman family, Peter Mirassou, Richard G. Peterson, Ely Callaway, James Concannon, the Wente family, and members of many winery staffs who have replied to our inquiries. We have also to thank retrospectively the winery men and women who, over the years, have given us information for articles that has added to our store of knowledge.

Philip Hiaring, publisher of *Wines & Vines,* allowed us to scan many photographs. Marjorie Lumm of the Monterey Winegrowers Council gave us up-to-date information on that fast-changing region. Others who have shared with us specific knowledge and photographs include Rimo Bacigalupi of Berkeley; D. Steven Corey, Helen Caire, Victor C. Faure, Albert Shumate, and Warren R. Howell of San Francisco; Margaret Coyner of San Luis Obispo; Russell W. Taylor of Atascadero; Charles J. deMateis of Laguna Beach; William and Mary Hood of Twenty-Nine Palms; Harold P. Olmo and Vernon L. Singleton of the University of California, Davis; and Vincent Petrucci of Fresno State University.

We alone, however, are responsible for any errors and for interpretation of events. We have been necessarily selective rather than inclusive. The choices of men and wineries of two centuries which, viewed through the long lens of historical perspective, we have considered to be the most significant, are solely ours.

Two points of interest to some readers should be noted. We have not in most cases attempted to reconcile anomalies or differences in grape variety nomenclature, since it has varied over the years and even now is not always agreed upon. And we have departed from traditional dates where research has indicated others.

San Francisco
May 28, 1982

Ruth Teiser
Catherine Harroun

Sources of Illustrations
Numbers refer to pages

James de T. Abajian, 185 lower • Almadén Vineyards, 54 lower, 233 center, 235 lower • Harry Baccigaluppi, 175 upper, 187 lower • Bancroft Library, University of California, Berkeley, 5 upper, lower, 7 center, 13, 14 center, 15 upper, 23, 24 upper, 24–25 lower, 26, 31 lower, 33 upper, 42–43 lower, 43 upper, 44 upper, 44–45 lower, 45 upper, 47, 53, 61, 62 lower, 69 upper, 71 upper, 79 lower, 87, 112 upper left, 133 lower, 134 lower, 143 lower left, 152 upper, 187 upper center, 199 upper, 210 center right • Frank H. Bartholomew (photographic print courtesy John Howell—Books), 42 upper • Beringer Vineyards, 90 upper • Esther Born, photographer, 198 • Helen Caire, 246 lower • California Historical Society, 63 lower, 92, 137 upper, 173 upper, 195 upper • California State Archives, 41 lower, 138 lower • California State Library, 14 lower, 25 upper, 33 lower right, 46 lower, 56 lower, 71 lower, 78 lower, 88 upper, 109 upper, 123 upper, 133 upper right, 134 upper, 145 lower right, 173 lower, 174 center • Callaway Vineyards and Winery, 248 • J. B. Cella II, 209 upper, 210 upper • Christian Brothers Collection, Wine Museum of San Francisco, 14 upper, 176 right, 210 lower left • Concannon Vineyard, 126 upper • Charles J. Demateis, 144–145 lower • Fresno City and County Historical Society, 136 upper • Fresno State University Library, Special Collections, 110 upper, lower, 111, 119 center, 185 upper • E. & J. Gallo Winery, 186 upper, 228 upper, center • Guild Wineries and Distilleries, 208 lower, 209 lower, 234 lower • Huntington Library, 63 upper, 70, 80, 143 upper, lower right • F. Korbel & Bros., 81 • Library of Congress, 93, 217, 218, 219 • Los Angeles County Museum of Natural History, 151 lower, 153 lower, 154 • Louis M. Martini winery, 237 lower • Paul Masson Vineyards, 55, 57 upper, 174 lower, 244–245 upper • Mirassou Vineyards, 54 upper • Robert Mondavi Winery, 237 upper • Ernest Peninou, 175 lower • Regional Oral History Office, Bancroft Library, 152 lower (from the late Edmund A. Rossi), 186 lower (from The Christian Brothers), 207 upper (by Catherine Harroun), lower (from the late Antonio Perelli-Minetti), 225 upper right and 226 upper (from the late Louis Petri), 195 lower (from University of California, Davis) • San Francisco Public Library, 77 upper, 137 lower, 146 lower, 162 upper, 188 lower right • Schramsberg Vineyards (photographic print courtesy Silverado Museum), 89 • Society of California Pioneers, 31 upper • Stanford University Museum of Art, 146 upper • Ruth Teiser and Catherine Harroun, photographers, 6 center, lower, 7 upper left, upper right, 88 lower, 196 lower, 208 upper, 227 upper, 228 lower, 233 lower, 234 upper, 235 upper, 236, 243, 244 lower, 245 lower, 246 upper, 247 lower • United Vintners, 91, 225 center left, lower left, 226 lower • University of California Archives, Bancroft Library, 112 center, lower • University of California Library, Berkeley, 5 center • University of California Library, Davis, Special Collections, 33 lower left, 72 lower, 135, 197 right • University of California Press, 101 upper • Wells Fargo Bank History Department, 162 lower • Wente Bros., 121 • Wine Institute, 6 upper, 32, 41 upper, 46 upper, 57 lower, 72 upper, 77 lower, 78 upper, 79 upper, 90 lower, 99, 100 upper, 100–101 lower, 110 center left, 119 upper, lower, 120, 122, 123 lower, 124, 125, 126 lower, 133 upper left, 136 lower, 138 upper, 144 upper right, 151 upper, 153 upper, 163, 164, 220, 233 upper • *Wines & Vines*, 15 lower, 144 center left, 174 upper, 196 upper, 197 upper, 227 lower (photograph by Philip Hiaring), 247 upper [*Illustrations not listed are from the authors' collection.*]

Index

DATE DUE

JAN 1 1 1983		
APR 1 8 1985		
SEP 1 8 1985		
OCT 2 1 1985		
SEP 2 2 1986		
OCT 1 3 1986		
DEC 8 1986		
MAR 1 0 1987		
GAYLORD		PRINTED IN U.S.A.